Existential-Integrative Approaches to Treating Adolescents

David Shumaker

Existential-Integrative Approaches to Treating Adolescents

palgrave
macmillan

David Shumaker
Mental Health Counseling Program
Suffolk University
Boston, Massachusetts, USA

ISBN 978-1-349-95210-6 ISBN 978-1-349-95211-3 (eBook)
DOI 10.1057/978-1-349-95211-3

Library of Congress Control Number: 2017940632

Cover illustration: Chronicle / Alamy Stock Photo

Printed on acid-free paper

This Palgrave Macmillan imprint is published by Springer Nature
The registered company is Nature America Inc.
The registered company address is: 1 New York Plaza, New York, NY 10004, U.S.A.

For Jonah, Mason, and Tricia
The loves of my life

Preface

This book is borne out of my strong belief in the power of existential therapy to help adolescents navigate the perils of a frequently challenging period of development in human lifespans. Kirk Schneider's (2008) Existential-Integrative Therapy approach seems particularly well suited to provide therapists a solid grounding from which to embark on the wonderful pursuit of trying to meet their adolescent clients on a much deeper level. Dr. Schneider, Dr. Shawn Rubin, and many other members of APA Division 32 Society for Humanistic Psychology have been most gracious in their support of my specific interest in working with adolescents from an EI perspective and this book is a logical outgrowth of their guidance and encouragement. By no means, however, is this book intended to be the final say on how clinicians can most effectively work with clients from this framework. The hope is that it serves as a catalyst for clinicians and researchers to more deeply consider the potential for EI applications to be utilized with this age group. Further, any misinterpretations, oversimplifications, or omissions in the depiction of EI and existential theory are solely mine and hopefully will not obscure the power that the approach has in helping adolescents.

As footnoted in the chapters where EI case examples are shared, while based on the lives of real people, the cases depicted in the book are composite representations of multiple client experiences where names, gender, and other potentially identifiable aspects of the case experience have been changed to protect client confidentiality. The dialogue that has been cited represent actual conversations that author has had with clients but aspects have also been altered to protect confidentiality.

Acknowledgments

I would first like to thank his graduate research assistant, Ms. Julia Grimm, for her tireless assistance in editing this book. If not for her incredible efforts I would still be working on this book. Her star will shine brightly in the mental health field in years to come.

I would also like to thank the incredibly supportive staff at Palgrave-MacMillan, including but surely not limited to Rachel Krause, Elaine Fan, and Kyra Saniewski. If it were not for Rachel, especially, who encouraged me to write this book, I would still be toiling in the darkness.

I would like to thank Suffolk University and the Psychology Department for supporting my research efforts. My wonderful colleagues and students have been a great source of inspiration.

I would also like to thank his past, present, and future clients for the privilege of working with them and their trust. While it has been said on multiple occasions by others much more distinguished, a therapist learns a lot more from his or her clients than what they teach.

Finally, I would like to thank my wife, Tricia, and two sons, Mason and Jonah, for their unconditional love, patience, and support in this book writing process. You are the hearts that keep my pulse running. This book is dedicated to them.

Contents

List of Figures

CHAPTER 1

An Introduction to EI Therapy with Adolescents

It should come as no surprise that existential-integrative (EI) therapy (EI) (Schneider, 2008) may be particularly suited for adolescents. EI endeavors to "set people free" (May, 1981) by creating conditions in the therapy hour that allows young clients to reoccupy aspects of themselves that may be denied. A therapeutic approach whose chief aim is to help clients achieve "experiential liberation" – an awakening that results in an enhanced ability to appreciate oneself and life at a deeper level (Bugental, 1978; Tillich, 1967) – would seem ideally suited for those progressing through a developmental stage frequently characterized by an intense search for self-identity and a love/hate relationship with the prospect of greater freedom and autonomy looming on the near horizon (Erikson, 1968; Marcia & Josselson, 2013). But, as has been noted before (Fitzgerald, 2005; Shumaker, 2012), relatively little has been written on how existential concepts and therapeutic approaches might be utilized with this age group. This lack of research attention reflects a broader trend where many graduate training programs have been slow to embrace EI and other humanistic approaches (Bassett-Short & Hammel, 2008).

Why might this be the case?

Throughout much of the 1990s into the present day empirically supported treatments (ESTs) have been considered the gold standard of practice (Chambless & Hollon, 1998). This well-intentioned emphasis on promoting scientifically grounded therapies with demonstrated efficacy has had a

D. Shumaker, *Existential-Integrative Approaches to Treating Adolescents*, DOI 10.1057/978-1-349-95211-3_1

paradoxical effect on the field, limiting the variety of evidence deemed acceptable when contemplating the usefulness of a therapeutic approach or technique (Laska et al., 2014). Existential therapies, in particular, have been historically reluctant to embrace the existing treatment outcome research methodology, arguing that it fails to effectively capture many of the treatment gains made with their approach (Lantz, 2004; Norcross, 1987). ESTs and the prioritization of randomized control trials (as well as a disorder-specific approach to treatment) have become synonymous for many with evidence-based practice (EBP) when, in fact, they are not one and the same (Evidence Based Practice in Psychology, 2006). EST starts with treatment method and applies it to a particular disorder or population while EBP starts with the client and then looks to see what research evidence might best work with that particular individual (Evidence Based Practice in Psychology, 2006). It would seem that treatment outcomes could be improved by integrating these approaches (Laska et al., 2014), but there remains considerable resistance by many to doing so.

Examples of this resistance are numerous. The consideration of therapeutic factors other than treatment method has been regarded by advocates of the EST approach as "unscientific" (Chambless et al., 2006). Common factors research (i.e., helpful relationship factors in therapy that are common to all therapeutic schools of thought) has gained some acceptance, but is viewed by some as having low potential to contribute to a scientifically grounded approach to therapy. All therapeutic modalities save cognitive-behavioral therapy (CBT) are dismissed by these staunch adherents to the EST model despite considerable evidence for the efficacy of a variety of approaches (Wampold, 2013). It is little wonder therefore that, in the face of such strong resistance, the young clinician in training (or the young assistant professor charged with training) might simply question, "Why bother?", when asked to consider exploring a treatment modality that does not meet the EST stamp of approval.

Thankfully, a rapprochement between EST, EBP, and common factors research may be occurring. Hoffman & Barlow (2014), historically strong adherents to the EST model of psychotherapy validation, recently noted the shift when discussing the potential for common factors research to integrate with EST's. They write:

> We are moving away from relatively prescriptive manuals containing slightly different sets of procedures for each individual diagnosis and adopting a

> unified transdiagnostic approach that culls the principal research-supported mechanisms of change contained in effective treatments across large classes of disorders and evaluating these strategies in randomized clinical trials compared with the single-diagnosis approach. (pg. 511)

Therein lies hope for EI. While common factors research and EI are not the same, the growing acceptance of the former bodes well for clinicians who value integrative therapeutic approaches. A hallmark of both common factors research and EI is the emphasis on relationship stances in therapy and the contemplation of universal aspects of the human experience that heal (e.g., hope, empathy, alliance). Instead of asking, "What are the common factors across therapeutic modalities that seem to help?" the operative question for an EI therapist is framed slightly differently as, "What are the universal challenges of existence and anxieties that all humans face regardless of demographic status or presenting concern(s)?" EI argues that questions of meaning, mortality, responsibility, individuality, and guilt confront many, if not all, individuals. While anxiety regarding these existential questions may not be a direct contributor to a client's presenting concerns (though in many cases they certainly are), an awareness of existential concerns and possession of skills and a knowledge base to address these considerations as indicated in therapy would seem to be a critical tool for all clinicians, regardless of primary therapeutic orientation. For certain clinicians who treat adolescents frequently walk away from these encounters feeling that their arsenal of effective change agents is woefully lacking. EI may very well possess the key to unlocking a young client's more deeply rooted anxieties and facilitating a more productive dialogue in this fascinating age group.

There are additional reasons for optimism. Integrative approaches to counseling and therapy are receiving more research attention and general acceptance (Norcross and Goldfried, 2005). Doctoral training programs in counseling psychology are also showing positive attitudes toward therapy integration (Lampropoulus & Dixon, 2007). Closer to home, efforts to integrate existential therapy with other treatment approaches are becoming more commonplace (Shahar & Schiller, 2016). Specifically, existential therapy has been integrated with cognitive therapy (Ottens & Hanna, 1998), CBT (Gebler & Maercker, 2014; Hickes & Mirea, 2012; Sotskova, Carey, & Mak, 2016), multimodal approaches (Rugula & Waldo, 1998), and narrative therapy (Richert, 1999). The similarities between so-called third-wave CBT (e.g., mindfulness, acceptance-based therapy) and existential therapy have been noted as well (Bunting & Hayes, 2008; Claessens, 2010; Masterpasqua, 2016). In fact, given its historical resistance to adopting a rigid, technique-driven conceptualization of the therapy experience, EI may be particularly suited for seamless integration with other practice modalities (Hoffman et al., 2015; Schneider, 2008). As much a subtle adjustment in philosophical stance and increased readiness on the part of the clinician to seize openings in the therapeutic hour is what is required to infuse EI into a treatment protocol as opposed to a radical restructuring of what occurs between client and therapist. This spirit of open readiness forms the basis of this book. The intended audience is not only students and clinicians who identify primarily as existentialist practitioners, but also those who subscribe to other schools of thought yet are seeking to augment their treatment approach. In short, this book offers a road map of sorts to facilitate the effective use of EI with adolescents struggling with a wide range of presenting concerns.

Is It Effective?

Still, as noted by Hoffman and Barlow (2014), one should be hesitant to integrate a therapy that has no demonstrated efficacy. While the field as a whole may be expanding the range of evidence deemed acceptable indicators of therapeutic efficacy, skepticism about the effectiveness of humanistic therapies still pervades. Existential therapy has not been immune to such doubt (Norcross, 1987). In recent years, however, existential therapies have received more research attention, yielding promising results. A few of these efforts are touched upon here.

Of note, Vos et al. (2015) conducted a meta-analytic analysis of 15 randomized controlled studies of existential therapy, subjecting the treatment approach to a type of outcome analysis that has fueled EST research efforts for many years. Their analysis discriminated four types of existential therapies: (1) meaning therapies ($n = 6$ studies); (2) supportive-expressive therapies ($n = 5$ studies); (3) experiential-existential group therapies ($n = 3$); and (4) cognitive-existential therapy ($n = 1$). There were several limitations to the analysis the authors note, including the fact that many of the therapies in the study were conducted in a group format and there were significant differences in the clinical characteristics of the therapies studied. Despite these limitations, the authors found significant positive effects of meaning therapies. Individuals exposed to this particular type of existential therapy tended to "find greater meaning or purpose in life, their level of psychopathology decreases to a moderate extent, and their self-efficacy was strengthened moderately" (Vos et al., 2015, pp. 123–124).

There were other important results reported in the Vos et al. (2015) meta-analytic study. Specifically, the authors found some evidence suggesting supportive-expressive therapies reduce levels of psychopathology. In addition, psychoeducation about existential issues, discussions regarding the meaning of life, and specific experiential exercises seemed to be particularly helpful. It is important to note that the authors of the study also recognized the limitations of their quantitative meta-analysis and recommended future research combine qualitative research with quantitative approaches to increase the external and ecological validity of the findings.

Hoffman and colleagues (2015) also make a compelling argument suggesting that EI already meets the criteria for EBP. Noting the historical difficulties in defining existential therapy, they outlined three "pillars" of existential psychology that appear common to all widely accepted forms of this treatment. These pillars include a (1) relationship focus, (2) an emphasis on emotions, and (3) a meaning-based focus. Systematically drawing upon a wide range of psychotherapy research (including common factors research), they ultimately conclude, "while there are places existential therapy ought strengthen its evidence-based foundation, there is already in place a solid foundation to existential therapy" (pg. 18).

Schneider & Krug (2010) devote a chapter of their book *Existential-Humanistic Therapy* to discussing the research support for existential-humanistic (EH) therapies. They cite common factors research as well as a little known study by Mosher (2001) on the efficacy of existential therapy with patients diagnosed with schizophrenia. Clients in the Mosher study treated with existential therapy achieved better outcomes than those subjected to conventional treatment. In addition, they demonstrate how research conducted by Greenberg (2007) on emotional regulation has implications for EI through their joint emphasis on relationship factors in healing.

Beyond these more nomothetic research efforts, there is an abundance of case study research documenting the effectiveness of EI across a diverse array of clients and wide range of presenting concerns. Schneider and Krug (2010) cite many classic existential case studies, including those reported by Boss (1963), Bugental (1976), May (1983), Spinelli (1997), and Yalom (1989). More recently case study methodology in Schneider's

(2008) landmark work on EI has demonstrated the approach works well with Latino (Comas-Diaz, 2008), African-American (Rice, 2008), Native American (Alsup, 2008), female (Serlin, 2008), and LBGT (Monheit, 2008) clients. Case studies have also demonstrated EI can effectively treat substance abuse (Ballinger et al., 2008), psychosis (Dorman, 2008; Mendelowitz, 2008), and depression (Greening, 2008). Closer to home, Chessick (1996) and Shumaker (2012) have provided case descriptions of effective existential approaches used in the treatment of adolescents. While clearly both quantitative and qualitative, nomothetic and idiographic research should continue to examine the more specific questions of *what* (i.e., what specific features of EI) works with *who* (i.e., specific client characteristics) and *when* (i.e., under what specific circumstances or context), there is already ample data to suggest EI is an effective treatment approach.

EI: An Overview

Cooper (2003) provides arguably the most comprehensive and easily accessible account of different existential approaches to psychotherapy. He delineates six different schools of existential therapy. These include the following: (1) the Daseinsanalytic Approach which calls into question many of the basic assumptions of therapy and psychoanalysis; (2) Victor Frankl's Logotherapy which focuses primarily on the search for meaning; (3) R.D. Laing's work in developing an existential model of schizophrenia; (4) the British School of existential therapy (including Spinelli, 2015; van Deurzen, 2012) that emphasizes relatedness and the dynamic unfolding of each client's being; (5) time-limited approaches to existential therapy; and (6) the EH approach that places particular emphasis on clients discovering their subjective inner experience and summoning the courage to face the challenges of human existence. While there is considerable overlap between these approaches there are important areas of distinction and each have made unique contributions. Though it is beyond the scope of this book to detail the history, similarities and differences, and implications of each approach, the present work incorporates elements of all when considering specific therapeutic stances and techniques that can be used with adolescents when operating from an EI framework. That being said, EI is most closely aligned with EH approaches.

The chief aim of EI is to assist clients in articulating that which is central and vital to their humanity and, in turn, to maximize the individual's freedom (Schneider, 2008). Any serious student of the approach certainly should read Schneider's (2008) *Existential-Integrative Therapy* in full. What follows is a brief review of some of its fundamental concepts. The approach rests upon three important discoveries of the human psyche. First, humans are suspended in mystery, with certain freedoms and limitations that are experienced by all. Second, dread of these freedoms (e.g., choice, will, creative abilities) and limitations (e.g., death, social and natural restraints) can promote dysfunction and extreme counter-reactions in the individual. Third, confronting these dreads and polarities of existence (freedom versus limitation; expansion versus constriction) can lead to a more enriched and fulfilling life experience (Schneider, 2008).

To better understand EI one must contemplate the nature of human consciousness. Schneider (2008) believes human consciousness can be conceptualized as six overlapping layers of increasingly deeper levels of self-awareness and freedom. The simplest layer of consciousness, the *physiological*, is impacted by ancestry, activity level, diet, substance use, genetic and biochemical factors. The second layer, referred to as the *environmental* level of consciousness, involves the basic learning theory principles of operant and classical conditioning. A person who has obtained sufficient awareness at this level of consciousness might appreciate the utility of rewarding oneself with a hot bath at the end of a long, hard day. The *cognitive* level is the third layer of consciousness. Here freedom pertains to one's ability to think logically, detect maladaptive thought patterns, and engage in what is commonly referred to as cognitive therapeutic techniques of thought-stopping, positive reframing, social modeling, etc.

The fourth level of consciousness in the EI framework is the *psychosexual* level (Schneider, 2008). Not surprisingly, the challenges and content area of this level are most responsive to traditionally psychodynamic forms of inquiry (e.g., free association, interpretation of resistance and transference) where the individual's task is to strengthen the ego by increasing one's understanding and mastery of sexual-aggressive tendencies. The *interpersonal* level is the fifth layer or human consciousness. It is yet a step deeper in self-awareness where drives and social inhibition concerns are largely mastered and the focus shifts to identity concerns and one's dependence upon, connectedness with, and separation from others. The therapist-client relationship is a catalyst to promoting interpersonal liberation, where past relationship patterns and attachment formations are activated in the therapeutic relationship and a corrective emotional experience hopefully follows.

At the core of Schneider's (2008) spectrum is the *experiential freedom* level. Schneider also refers to this as the *being level* or *ontological freedom*. This all-encompassing level is described as a "reoccupation project" where clients are able to get in touch with aspects of themselves that have been denied. Experiential freedom extends beyond mere content memories and includes kinesthetic, pre-verbal and intersituational forms of awareness that often lead to profound insights, "aha" moments, and a humbling sense of awe about ourselves and the world we live in. EI argues that Yalom's (1980) four existential givens of human existence – fears of death, meaninglessness, freedom, and isolation – represent a mostly comprehensive, yet incomplete, picture of the array of concerns that define us. Just as fundamental is the human capacity for the aforementioned sense of "awe" and wonder (Schneider, 2008).

More recently Schneider (2014) has used the term "enchanted agnosticism" in conjunction with "awe-based consciousness" to describe these powerful moments that combine fulfillment with mystery. The journey to this deeper level of self-awareness is by no means easy. The client may need to feel previously blocked pain as well as "crushing humiliation and crippling fear" prior to making contact with a deeper sense of wonder and amazement. But for those who can withstand this journey they are rewarded with more vital and enriched existences. They will be more open to taking chances and to appreciating both the profound *and* more mundane aspects of our lives. Emmy van Deurzen (2015) has emphasized this latter point, noting that "the daily routines of caring for and with others is what lends real lustre to life."

Not surprisingly, the moments where one functions at the experiential level of awareness are fleeting and often quite impactful and memorable. As previously alluded to this level of awareness is primarily affect centered but draws upon "four intertwining and overlapping dimensions: 1) the immediate, 2) the kinesthetic, 3) the affective, and 4) the profound or cosmic" (Schneider, 2008, pg. 39). A sense of awe therefore resonates at an even deeper level in humans than the more cerebral contemplation of meaning and meaninglessness. Access to this level of consciousness calls for a *sensitive, present-oriented, and authentic* therapist who gently but persistently encourages the client to explore the constricted and expansive parts of oneself in a safe environment.

Effective EI therapists seem to possess other important attributes. Spinelli (2015) has written extensively on the importance of the concept of relatedness as both a fundamental aspect of being and as a key element in existential therapy. A therapist who engages in *other-focused listening*, who adopts an *attitude of unknowing*, and who pursues *a descriptively focused enquiry* can assist a client in reaching these deeper levels of consciousness. As a client becomes more conscious of his or her limitations and life-limiting patterns of being with the aid of the EI therapist, the individual will paradoxically begin a journey toward greater freedom (Krug, 2009). Thus, *the four central aims of an EI approach* include helping clients (a) *become more present*, (b) *become aware of how they block themselves* from a fuller presence, (c) *take responsibility* for their current life circumstances, and (d) *face existential givens* (e.g., finiteness) in order to self-actualize (Schneider & Krug, 2010).

There are many similarities between Schneider & Krug's (2010) conceptualization of human consciousness and Bugental's (1977) psychotherapeutic goals of EH therapy. Bugental (1977) argues that psychotherapeutic goals range from deficiency motivation and symptom relief levels of focus to increasingly more growth-oriented and ultimately transcendent pursuits. The EH therapist will of course attend to the most pressing and painful client needs that often present in the form of problems related to adjustment and coping through interventions that co-align with EI's focus on the physiological and environmental levels of consciousness. But there will remain an open invitation to clients willing to delve further into more growth-oriented, emancipating, and transcendent levels of being and self-awareness through techniques designed to access one's cognitive, interpersonal, and experiential levels of consciousness.

EI and Psychopathology

Chapter 3 includes a section where a developmental model of adolescent existential anxiety is introduced. Our current focus therefore is limited to a brief overview of the etiology of psychopathology from an EI perspective. Within the EI framework psychopathology is believed to be rooted in constrictive and expansive dread emerging in the context of three types of trauma experiences: (1) *acute trauma*, (2) *chronic trauma*, and (3) *implicit trauma*. Schneider (2008) writes, "dread of constrictive and expansive polarities promotes dysfunction, extremism, polarization, the degree and frequency to which is generally proportional to the degree and frequency of one's dread" (pg. 42). An example of an acute trauma is when a child suffers a serious illness or injury where the threat of nonbeing and smallness jolts the child into compensatory efforts at expansion. Chronic trauma may occur after repeated failed efforts on the part of the child to recover from an acute trauma through expansion. These efforts are rebuffed by the environment resulting in a denial and overcompensation effort of the child that takes the form of a retreat in the opposite direction toward smallness. The final type of trauma posited in this framework is implicit trauma. This is an "indirect, vicariously trauma of family and caretakers" in which a caretaker's chronic trauma coping strategies are modeled for the child and imparted accordingly in an implicit manner. Quite obviously we may be seeing all three forms of this trauma playing out in the lives of the adolescents who appear before us in therapy.

While EI argues psychopathology is rooted in trauma, it is important to remember that individuals differ in their capacity to cope with trauma and the support systems available to them. Regarding one's capacity, Tillich (1952) argues that some individuals are particularly sensitive to the universal threat of nonbeing. This observation is confirmed in clinical practice. The author receives a steady stream of referrals where younger clients between the ages of 7 and 10 years old present in therapy with acute fears of death and life that appear to have no obvious roots in acute and/or chronic trauma. Their attachment formation and support systems seem solid, perhaps reducing the likelihood of implicit trauma occurring. Here biology, temperament, and/or cognitive development may assume an increased role in the manifestation of neurotic levels of anxiety. This potential is explored in greater detail in our developmental model of adolescent existential anxiety introduced in Chapter 3.

EI: Principles and Process

Chapter 4 of this book describes some of the more common EI therapeutic stances, methods, and techniques that can be used with adolescents. Prior to closing this introductory chapter, however, it seems important to include a broader overview of the process of conducting EI and discussion of the general areas of treatment focus. Again, we return to Schneider's (2008) conceptualization of the therapy process and expand from there.

EI unfolds in the context of an initial assessment by the clinician highlighted by particular focus regarding a client's readiness and capacity for change (Schneider, 2008). Conventional assessment methodology is certainly relied upon but EI pays special attention to a clinician's *lived* engagement with the client by adopting a sense of wonder and openness to the therapist's clinical intuitions. Depending upon the outcome of this initial assessment the clinician will then tailor the treatment approach to the level of client functioning that appears most conducive to increasingly deeper levels of engagement. An offer of *nonexperiential liberation* utilizes intervention strategies that contact clients on the physiological, behavioral, and cognitive levels of consciousness. Crisis intervention and cognitive-behavioral strategies such as cognitive restructuring, deep breathing, exposure techniques, etc., are hallmarks of this level of intervention.

Offers of *semiexperiential liberation* constitute intervention strategies designed to access the psychosexual and interpersonal levels of client functioning. These interventions incorporate but are not rooted in experiential interventions. Classic psychoanalytic and psychodynamic techniques such as attending to transference and countertransference, as well free association are utilized. Empathy and "optimal frustration" inducing strategies may be used if the symptomatology seems to reside at the interpersonal level of consciousness.

While offers of nonexperiential and semiexperiential liberation are critical components of an EI approach, the deepest and arguably most unique feature of an EI intervention occurs at the *experiential liberation* level of client functioning. This level of intervention meets clients who are ready to explore trauma and hurts at a deeper kinesthetic-affective level of being. Clients who are capable of contemplating their relative greatness/smallness in the scheme of life, who are ready to repair ontological wounds, and who can withstand shorter-term distress and discomfort to achieve untapped potentials are the targets of this level of intervention.

Schneider (2008) incorporates four basic therapeutic processes in the quest to assist clients in achieving experiential liberation. These include the following: (1) *Presence*: The therapist remains open to all aspects of the client and his or her own being at a deeper level than simply attentive listening. (2) *Invoking the actual:* The therapist encourages the client to attend to their immediate experience as well as their particular struggles with aspects of smallness and greatness. (3) *Vivifying and confronting resistances:* The therapist demonstrates for the client how they block themselves from existential encounters with dreaded polarities and revert to more protective stances. (4) *Rediscovering meaning and awe:* The therapist assists the client in cultivating a sense of intentionality in their approach to life that results in stronger connections to what really matters and a sense of awe and wonderment. Each of these processes utilizes specific therapeutic techniques to achieve their ends and each will be discussed in considerably greater detail in Chapter 4.

It is important to note that the process of EI also aligns well with Spinelli's (2015) three-phase process of conducting existential therapy from a relational perspective. Recall again that Spinelli is associated with the British School of existential therapy, so his approach to existential therapy is not an EI approach. Yet it is helpful to briefly consider his model when attempting to gain a deeper perspective on some of the fundamental aspects of the existential therapy.

The first phase of Spinelli's (2015) "Structural Model" consists of co-creating a therapy world between the client and the clinician. The therapist and client establish a therapeutic contract that outlines the rules and expectations of therapy. All competent therapists, regardless of orientation, will have discussions with new clients about expected frequency of sessions, financial obligations, limits of confidentiality, etc. This is providing informed consent. Beyond these basics, however, the existential therapist will also consider the client's journey to making the initial appointment and will listen very attentively to the client's initial statements upon entering a session. The therapist will always offer an "acceptance-focused" response to the client's initial statements because Spinelli (2015) believes, "this initial willingness to accept the 'rightness' of the client's worldview statements opens the way for the existential therapist to begin to explore descriptively that which the client has chosen to bring to the encounter" (pg. 142).

The first phase also consists of efforts to attune oneself with the client's worldview through a focus on *being with* and *being for* their client. *Being with* consists of the therapist's intent to respect the client's current worldview. *Being for* consists of the therapist's attempts to join the client's worldview through the use of dialogue. As trust and a sense of acceptance is established, clients during Phase One will typically share the story of the problematic and disturbing life events that have led them to therapy. An attitude of "unknowing" is conveyed by the therapist through the use of other-focused listening, strategic questioning, and adherence to the phenomenological method of investigation. All of these therapeutic stances and strategies are consistent with EI.

Phase Two of Spinelli's (2015) model is referred to as "Co-habitating the Therapy-World." The client's worldview and conceptualization of his or her concerns are presumably well understood by the therapist at the time this phase commences. The listening stance of the therapist begins to shift from one of unknowing and uncritical acceptance of the validity of all client statements and stances, to a more pointed and focused effort to, "clarify the implicit or covert existential insecurities that maintain the explicit or overt tensions and disturbances being presented by the client" (pg. 125). Put more simply, the therapist begins to challenge the client's narrative strategically to increase the client's awareness of the stances and attitudes that contribute to their distress. The therapist focuses closely on the client's struggles with various existential polarities, such as those pertaining to attachment versus separation, control versus letting go, power versus impotence, and self-centeredness versus other-focused attention. There are a wider range of therapist techniques utilized during this stage designed to draw out the client's inner struggles, including therapist disclosure, dream work, and discussions about the client's inner daimonic. It is beyond the scope of the present chapter to describe these techniques in detail. Each will be discussed in Chapter 4. For now it is important to note again the close similarities between this phase and Schneider's (2008) focus on the polarities of a client's existence.

The third phase of Spinelli's (2015) model is referred to as the "Closing Down of the Therapy-World" phase. It includes the more obvious focus of ensuring the therapeutic contract has been satisfied. Beyond that, however, is a discussion of how and to what extent will the gains made within the therapeutic hour impact the client's world outside of the therapy setting. Spinelli, citing the work of Leslie Farber (1966), is cognizant of "more complex and disquieting" implications of change that occurs in clients. A client who develops new ideas about freedom, choice, and responsibility may impart these attitudinal shifts upon those around him or her with potentially enriching or devastating consequences. This shift in attention is referred to as "They-focus." In the author's opinion this last phase remains one of the most critical yet overlooked aspects of a meaningful and impactful therapy experience. For certain, therapy has the potential to facilitate important changes in the lives of our clients. These gains, however, do not occur in a vacuum. A client, for example, who reaches the conclusion that they have drifted too far in the direction of "others" on the self- versus other-focused continuum of existence, may accordingly decide that they want to pursue more individual interests that will reduce their focus and time spent with an intimate partner, a child, or a close friend. In more extreme cases they may decide to pursue a divorce or career change that radically impacts his or her family's financial status. While the client may experience these changes positively, is it truly a positive gain if those significant others in the client's life do not experience these changes as positives? While most existential therapists do not offer opinions on these major life choices or provide answers to these hard questions, they at least ask the client to consider them closely during this closing phase of therapy and will challenge a client who is painting an unrealistic representation of how matters will likely play out.

Finally, the third phase of existential therapy within Spinelli's Structural Framework also includes a consideration of the ending of the therapeutic relationship. Here Spinelli argues that, above all, the critical question for a therapist to ask at the time an ending occurs is, "What is it about a particular ending that permits or prevents me from embracing it as appropriate to this particular relationship?" Spinelli notes that, while planned therapeutic endings are the norm and often times most appropriate way to conclude a therapy relationship, unexpected and more abrupt endings as times may also be appropriate.

In closing, Spinelli's three-phase model of existential therapy is included here in an effort to provide the reader with greater insight into the major components of most existential therapy experiences. There are important differences among the various schools of thought that fall under the umbrella of existential therapy, but the author believes the similarities are greater and it is helpful to consider all schools of thought when working with adolescents. To that end, the author believes it is also helpful to consider the work of Adams (2014), Craig (2008), and Leontiev (2015) to further enrich one's understanding of existential therapeutic process, principles, and focal points. As previously stated, a common criticism of existential therapy approaches is a lack of clarity on how it unfolds and what it focuses on. Each of the authors considered below provide additional scaffolding and direction for clinicians who aspire to engage adolescents from an EI perspective. Again, however, what is shared below are more general existential approaches to counseling.

Adams's (2014) on Existential Counseling

Martin Adams (2014) perhaps best describes the challenge of incorporating existential theory into a coherent and practical therapy approach with clients. He writes,

> The overall aim of the existential counselling psychologist is to make this philosophical questioning practical and to work with the client in their search for their own truth throughout their life with an open mind and an attitude of wonder, rather than fitting the client overtly or covertly into established frameworks of interpretation. (pg. 34)

Practical application of existential theory would seem to be a priority for an age group that is still developing the patience, self-regulation, and higher-order cognitive skills to contemplate life at deeper levels. To achieve this aim Adams (2014) draws upon Warnock's (1970) work entitled *Existentialism*. Both argue a clinician should remain mindful of the three essential elements of all existential theories. First, they believe it is incumbent upon an existential therapist to remember that a key aspect of our humanity and consciousness is an appreciation for the "*throwness*" of our lives. What is referenced here is Sartre's (1975) point that "existence comes before essence." That is, we come into this world not of our choosing and strong arguments can be made that our existence is filled with absurdities. Thus, it remains each individual's challenge in life to search for and discover that which has meaning to him or her. A clinician who can convey this concept to adolescents who are struggling with a sense of meaninglessness and/or identity concerns will be on good footing.

The second principle is one of *personal responsibility*. Here Adams (2014) writes,

> When Sartre wrote (2003, p.129) that "To be free is to be condemned to be free", he meant that we have responsibility for our lives, whether we like it or not. Existentially, our autonomy is this fundamental. We are born into it. We are obviously not free to be anything we like, we are constrained by circumstance and context – what existentialists call facticity – but our stance to this is ours and ours alone. (pg. 36)

This principle ties in very closely with Schneider's (2008) discussion of vivifying and confronting resistances. It is tempting to abdicate one's responsibility for one's actions and the life which we are given. We did not ask to be here. We know we will die. The world can be an absurd, unjust, and unforgiving place. Those charged with power and/or our care can break promises and ooze hypocrisy. Adolescents have a wonderful capacity to ferret out all of these disappointments and the failures of the world they inhabit. The EI therapist accepts these observations and mourns the loss of innocence with the adolescent – but for a time only. A challenge is eventually laid out to the adolescent (presumably when the therapeutic relationship is strong enough) where the young person is offered the support to find the courage within themselves to forge ahead with his or her life, find their own meaning, and perhaps even dare to try and leave this world a better place than that which they were born into. Adams (2014) points out the paradox that, by shouldering one's responsibility for one's choices in life, the individual actually frees themselves from feeling stuck or adrift in a world filled with chaos. A life endowed with purpose and meaning is freeing. Thus, when an adolescent asks, "What's the use?" or shrugs "It just doesn't matter" or "Whatever…" these can be golden opportunities for the EI therapist to engage those toss away questions and comments on a deeper level.

The third and final principle of existential theory that Adams (2014) and Warnock (1970) speak of is *phenomenology*. They remind us that we, as clinicians, are "participant observers" in the lives of our clients as opposed to objective scientists in possession of ultimate truths. There should be a humility and openness in a clinician's work as well as a healthy appreciation for the limitations and biases associated with our investigations into our client's lives. A mindful therapist, regardless of therapeutic orientation, constantly tries to shrink his or her blind spots but simultaneously knows that no matter how hard one's tries there will always be some blindness. Adolescents appreciate clinicians who are candid regarding their limitations as therapists and who do not come across as authority figures or experts on living a singular way. The phenomenological perspective fits this spirit of inquiry nicely.

Craig's (2008) Existential Commitments

While attention to the process and immediately felt experience of EI is critical, there is the not so small matter of the content of what one says and areas of client experience that are explored. Here a cursory review of an EI transcript might result in one reaching the conclusion that the approach closely resembles client-centered, psychodynamic, and even aspects of cognitive-behavioral therapies. One would be correct in this assessment to a certain extent. Clients in EI discuss their anxieties and fears, their losses and traumas, things that anger, sadden, and excite them, as well as their most cherished and challenging interpersonal relations. Distant memories, present circumstances, and future aspirations are all subject to examination. Schneider (2008) acknowledges that a good deal of therapy focus and intervention occur at the nonexperiential (physiological, behavioral, cognitive) and semiexperiential (psychosexual, interpersonal) levels of consciousness which respond well to behavioral, cognitive-behavioral, and psychodynamic approaches. Thus, when the therapist speaks in therapy he or she may sound at times very much like cognitive-behavioral, client-centered, and psychodynamic clinicians. So what is the focus of therapy and/or content of discussion that distinguishes an existential approach from other treatment modalities?

Most clinicians who are posed with this question – even those less familiar with existential therapy – possess a general understanding that Yalom's (1980) questions of meaning, life, death, and identity are the main course of an existential approach. Without a doubt these four questions certainly represent a great starting point for existential discussions with clients. For those seeking additional guidance and greater breadth, Craig (2008) has identified several "existential commitments" that he believes "all if not close to all" existential therapists agree upon when considering the focus of existential therapy. His review of these shared commitments can help anchor the content of a clinician's discussions with adolescent clients who appear ready to work at the experiential level of consciousness. Each commitment is listed briefly in bullet points here:

- *The question of what it means to be a human being:* What makes an individual human and how humans differ from other beings is perhaps the most fundamental question of existence explored in existential therapy. Existential therapists are not alone in asking this question, but the way in which they seek answers is unique. The search itself can remind us of what truly has meaning and value. It can cause us to redirect our psychic resources, instill a sense of purpose and intentionality, and inject meaning into our daily existence. The questions that follow give a better sense of the existential search process.
- *The question of mineness:* This query reminds us that the aforementioned question of what it means to be a human being is one that belongs to, and ultimately can only be answered by, the individual. The meaning of what it is to be human is a personal search. There are aspects of our humanity that we may share with others, but our

humanity is unique unto ourselves. The existential therapist does not impose their reality onto the client but aids the client in defining their humanity.

- *The question of existence:* Existential therapists are concerned not just with understanding a person's individual psyche, but his or her "being in the world." One's total existence is not confined to one's physical body. It includes his or her relations with the world. The existential therapist tries to understand a client holistically and dynamically. We are each constantly emerging and unfolding within, interacting with, and impacting the world around us. One cannot be understood in isolation.
- *The question of grounding:* In the quest to better understand existence no priority is given to the experience of one individual over another, or one aspect of an individual's experience over another aspect of that same individual's experience. An existentialist is concerned with "the whole of human existing as it is actually lived, experienced, and endured." Any and all first-person descriptions of humans by humans are given equal weight.
- *The question of method:* As was noted by Adams (2014), the phenomenological method of inquiry is preferred by existential therapists. Every effort is made to avoid turning a client's experience into an abstract conceptual or diagnostic experience. A client's lived experience is respected on its own terms, described with minimal jargon or diagnostic labeling, and studied with an understanding that the search process is limited and biased.
- *The question of wholeness:* Existential therapists attempt to view the client as a whole and avoid reducing our understanding of another to drives or a series of singular motivations. Clients are complex and therapists strive to capture their complexity in a holistic manner.
- *The question of truth and authenticity:* Craig points out that existential therapists strive to be "midwives" of the real, authentic, and true. They believe that humans may need to renounce aspects of their true selves in order to survive in society. An existential therapist helps a client come to terms with aspects of their existence that we have an ambivalent relationship with or avoid.

Several important questions seem to naturally flow from these commitments. Who are we? What defines us? What has meaning? What is truly important? How is our meaning different and similar to other humans? What is our relation to the world in which we exist? Where lies the separation between us and the world? What have we disowned, avoided, and/or ignored in ourselves in our struggle to survive and get along? Questions like these strike at the heart of existential thinking.

In practice it is common for adolescents to experience high levels of anxiety about the future as it pertains to their occupation and chances for success and security. "What will I do?", "Where will I live?", "Will I be a success?", "What will others think of me?", "Will I be accepted?", and "Will I find love?" are frequent concerns voiced by adolescents in therapy. These questions should be attended to with vigilance and sensitivity by a therapist. But they are not the same questions that stem from Craig's existential commitments. *Doing* and *being* are related but different. Recognition, acceptance, achievement can feel wonderful and may have some bearing upon our survival, but are they our essence? An EI therapist who works with adolescents is able to strategically introduce concepts and questions that facilitate self-examination of a deeper kind. The search may not produce easy answers or any answers at all. In the shorter term posing deeper existential questions can actually increase an adolescent's contact with anxiety and uncertainty. So care must be taken by the therapist to not introduce them prematurely to a client who is too vulnerable. But when existential questions are posed at a proper pace and with sufficient therapeutic support, the end result of rigorous discourse and individual contemplation may be a young person emerging from a therapeutic encounter in possession of a deeper sense of intentionality, will, and purpose in life. People who achieve experiential liberation are more likely to become powerful forces of positive change in the world that we all inhabit. Most would agree the world is in desperate need of as many positive forces for change as can be nurtured.

Leontiev's (2015) Targets of Life Enhancement Work

Dimitry Leontiev (2015) recently outlined an existential methodology of life enhancement therapy that can be utilized in individual psychotherapy sessions or small-group work. It is based in part upon Bugental's (1965) two-stage description of existential psychotherapy where an analytical analysis of resistances and blockages (that resembles psychoanalysis and is more cure-oriented) gives way to a more growth-oriented phase where the client is assisted in understanding themselves at a deeper level in order to reach his or her fullest potential. Questions pertaining to meaning form the basis of the life enhancement approach. There are certainly similarities between Leontiev's (2015) life enhancement targets and Craig's (2008) commitments, but there are enough differences to merit the complete listing of the former reported below:

- *The curiosity and courage to know and understand:* This is a very important target pertaining to breadth of knowledge and exposure to the world around us. It echoes Craig's (2008) commitment to truth and authenticity. While the existential therapist recognizes there can be valid reasons for shielding young people from too much knowledge too soon, the basic stance of life enhancement work is that "one is taught not to be afraid of knowledge." What matters is what one does with this knowledge. The life enhancement or EI therapist who works with adolescents does not believe shielding or escaping knowledge is a healthy pursuit.
- *Coherence of the world:* Attention is paid to how the individual makes sense of the world and connects the dots of what happens both to them and around them. If the world seems fragmented to the adolescent, attention is paid to why this may be the case and what are the structural links and meaning they are chaining together to provide a sense of coherence to their lives.
- *Reflective awareness:* This includes not only awareness of the world around us but self-awareness and how we relate to the world around us. The closest parallel to Craig (2008) here would perhaps be the commitment to understanding existence. Existential therapists encourage clients to take a moment to deliberately detach themselves from their typical stimulus-response action patterns and, instead, *really* contemplate the choices they make and alternatives that exist.
- *Involvement:* Authentic individuals are truly involved with and committed to their choices, actions, and lives. Clients are encouraged not to let things go or to let life simply happen to them, but to remain engaged, controlled, and challenged. A committed person retains the ability to self-regulate and remain goal-directed even in under heavy duress.
- *The scale of the life world:* Attention is paid to helping the client differentiate that which is truly important to them from that which is less important or unimportant. False values are discarded in favor of what really matters.

- *Objectivity as the counterpart of narcissism and insult:* This is perhaps best likened to an existential dose of humble pie. It echoes Ellis's rational-emotive-therapy (RET) cognitive restructuring technique of distinguishing needs from wants. It reminds us that the world proceeds according to its own will and laws and does not adhere to our personal wants, desires, or creeds. Another individual does not owe us the courtesy of pleasing us or catering to our needs. When they do, it is a gesture that should be greatly appreciated.
- *Time integration and time mastery:* This is a more complex target of intervention that essentially states the individual should strive to live within time as opposed to out of time. It reminds us to value the precious time we have and can effectively integrate the past, present, and future.
- *Essential contact with life:* This target reminds us that our "surface" contact with reality and life really only scratches the surface of our existence. On rare occasions we are able to get in touch with the "aha" moments in life as described by Schneider (2008) and Leontiev here. A therapist cannot directly cause a client to have such an experience, but the therapist can help a client remain aware and ready to discriminate such an experience when it occurs.
- *Authenticity:* The therapist encourages a client to not mindlessly play out the script of his or life that may be primed for us genetically and due to early conditioning. The client is exhorted to become *alive*, is reminded of his or her ability to change, and is supported when appropriate to summon the courage to experiment with new ways of living that had previously only been the stuff of fantasy.
- *The provision of mediating mental tools:* Here clients are provided tools to help examine themselves and their experience in a self-detached manner. In doing so the client increases their sense of self-determination and self-control.

Conclusion

This chapter presented a brief overview of EI, how EI conceptualizes psychopathology, the basic process of EI, and common focal points of focus and discussion. While EI has been used primarily with adults and the approach is therefore geared toward this population, the author and others have found many adolescents in clinical practice can not only follow the main tenets of EI, but crave exposure to them, and flourish when they are integrated into the treatment protocol. Still, there are some who may question the extent to which adolescents experience existential anxiety and/or can comprehend some of the basic concepts associated with existential theory and EI. Chapters 2 and 3 offer a response to these concerns. Chapter 2 focuses on the prevalence of existential anxiety during adolescence and risk factors that appear to exacerbate the experience of existential anxiety and/or make a successful resolution to existential concerns less likely. Chapter 3 examines protective factors that may help to mitigate the experience of existential anxiety during adolescence and then offers a developmental model of existential anxiety. The model is based upon research indicating the presence of these concerns in this age group, theoretical and case study analyses of adolescents who experience existential anxiety, and an analysis of existential anxiety predictors and protective factors.

References

Adams, M. (2014). Human development and existential counselling psychology. *Counselling Psychology Review*, *29*(2), 34–42.

Alsup, R. (2008). Existentialism of personalism: A Native American perspective. In K. J. Schneider (Ed.), *Existential-integrative psychotherapy: Guideposts to the core of practice* (pp. 121–127). New York, NY, US: Routledge/Taylor & Francis Group.

Ballinger, B., Matano, R. A., & Amantea, A. C. (2008). A perspective on alcoholism: The case of Charles. In K. J. Schneider (Ed.), *Existential-integrative psychotherapy: Guideposts to the core of practice* (pp. 177–185). New York, NY, US: Routledge/Taylor & Francis Group.

Bassett-Short, A., & Hammel, G. A. (2008). A student point of view: Existential psychotherapy from within the training process. In K. J. Schneider (Ed.), *Existential- integrative psychotherapy: Guideposts to the core of practice* (pp. 23–29). New York, NY, US: Routledge/Taylor & Francis Group.

Boss, M. (1963). *Psychoanalysis and Daseinsanalysis.* Oxford, England: Basic Books.

Bugental, J. F. (1965). The existential crisis in intensive psychotherapy. *Psychotherapy: Theory, Research & Practice*, *2*(1), 16–20. doi:10.1037/h0088602

Bugental, J. F. (1976). *The search for existential identity.* San Francisco: Jossey-Bass.

Bugental, J. (1977). The Far Side of Despair. In D. Nevill (Ed.), *New Frontiers of Humanistic Psychology* (pp. 133–156). New York: Gardner Press.

Bugental, J. F. (1978). *Psychotherapy and process: the fundamentals of an existential-humanistic approach.* Reading, MA: Addison-Wesley Pub. Co.

Bunting, K., & Hayes, S. C. (2008). Language and meaning: Acceptance and commitment therapy and the EI model. In K. J. Schneider (Ed.), *Existential-integrative psychotherapy: Guideposts to the core of practice* (pp. 217–234). New York, NY, US: Routledge/Taylor & Francis Group.

Chambless, D. L., Crits-Christoph, P., Wampold, B. E., Norcross, J. C., Lambert, M. J., Bohart, A. C., &…Johannsen, B. E. (2006). What Should Be Validated?. In J. C. Norcross, L. E. Beutler, R. F. Levant (Eds.), *Evidence-based practices in mental health: Debate and dialogue on the fundamental questions* (pp. 191–256). Washington, DC, US: American Psychological Association. doi:10.1037/11265-005

Chambless, D. L., & Hollon, S. D. (1998). Defining empirically supported therapies. *Journal Of Consulting And Clinical Psychology, 66*(1), 7–18. doi:10.1037/0022-006X.66.1.7

Chessick, R. D. (1996). Heidegger's 'authenticity' in the psychotherapy of adolescents. *American Journal Of Psychotherapy, 50*(2), 208–216.

Claessens, M. (2010). Mindfulness based-third wave CBT therapies and existential-phenomenology. Friends or foes?. *Existential Analysis, 21*(2), 295–308.

Comas-Díaz, L. (2008). Latino psychospitituality. In K. J. Schneider (Ed.), *Existential-integrative psychotherapy: Guideposts to the core of practice* (pp. 100–109). New York, NY, US: Routledge/Taylor & Francis Group.

Cooper, M. (2003). *Existential therapies.* London: Sage.

Craig, E. (2008). A brief overview of existential depth psychotherapy. *The Humanistic Psychologist, 36*(3–4), 211–226. doi:10.1080/088732608023 49958

Dorman, D. (2008). Dante's cure: Schizophrenia and the two-person journey. In K. J. Schneider (Ed.), *Existential-integrative psychotherapy: Guideposts to the core of practice* (pp. 236–245). New York, NY, US: Routledge/Taylor & Francis Group.

Erikson, E. (1968). *Identity: youth and crisis.* Oxford, England: Norton & Co.

Evidence-based practice in psychology. (2006). *American Psychologist, 61*(4), 271–285. doi:10.1037/0003-066X.61.4.271

Farber, L. H. (1966). *The Ways of the Will.* New York: Harper & Row.

Fitzgerald, B. (2005). An existential view of adolescent development. *Adolescence, 40*(160), 793–799.

Gebler, F. A., & Maercker, A. (2014). Effects of including an existential perspective in a cognitive-behavioral group program for chronic pain: A clinical trial with 6 months follow-up. *The Humanistic Psychologist, 42*(2), 155–171. doi:10.1080/08873267.2013.865188

Greenberg, L. S. (2007). Emotion coming of age. *Clinical Psychology: Science And Practice*, *14*(4), 414–421. doi:10.1111/j.1468-2850.2007.00101.x

Greening, T. (2008). Reflections on the depressed and dying: The case of Carol. In K. J. Schneider (Ed.), *Existential-integrative psychotherapy: Guideposts to the core of practice* (pp. 342–345). New York, NY, US: Routledge/Taylor & Francis Group.

Hickes, M., & Mirea, D. (2012). Cognitive behavioural therapy and existential-phenomenological psychotherapy: Rival paradigms or fertile ground for therapeutic synthesis?. *Existential Analysis*, *23*(1), 15–31.

Hofmann, S. G., & Barlow, D. H. (2014). Evidence-based psychological interventions and the common factors approach: The beginnings of a rapprochement?. *Psychotherapy*, *51*(4), 510–513. doi:10.1037/a0037045

Hoffman, L., Vallejos, L., Cleare-Hoffman, H. P., & Rubin, S. (2015). Emotion, relationship, and meaning as core existential practice: Evidence-based foundations. *Journal Of Contemporary Psychotherapy*, *45*(1), 11–20. doi:10.1007/s10879-014-9277-9

Krug, O. T. (2009). James Bugental and Irvin Yalom: Two masters of existential therapy cultivate presence in the therapeutic encounter. *Journal Of Humanistic Psychology*, *49*(3), 329–354. doi:10.1177/0022167809334001

Lampropoulos, G. K., & Dixon, D. N. (2007). Psychotherapy integration in internships and counseling psychology doctoral programs. *Journal Of Psychotherapy Integration*, *17*(2), 185–208. doi:10.1037/1053-0479.17.2.185

Lantz, J. (2004). Research and Evaluation Issues in Existential Psychotherapy. *Journal Of Contemporary Psychotherapy*, *34*(4), 331–340. doi:10.1007/s10879-004-2527-5

Laska, K. M., Gurman, A. S., & Wampold, B. E. (2014). Expanding the lens of evidence-based practice in psychotherapy: A common factors perspective. *Psychotherapy*, *51*(4), 467–481. doi:10.1037/a0034332

Leontiev, D. A. (2015). Experience processing as an aspect of existential psychotherapy: Life enhancement methodology. *Journal Of Contemporary Psychotherapy*, *45*(1), 49–58. doi:10.1007/s10879-014-9284-x

Marcia, J., & Josselson, R. (2013). Eriksonian personality research and its implications for psychotherapy. *Journal Of Personality*, *81*(6), 617–629. doi:10.1111/jopy.12014

Masterpasqua, F. (2016). Mindfulness mentalizing humanism: A transtheoretical convergence. *Journal Of Psychotherapy Integration*, *26*(1), 5–10. doi:10.1037/a0039635

May, R. (1981). *Freedom and destiny*. New York, NY, US: W W Norton & Co.

May, R. (1983). Socrates and God. *Contemporary Psychology*, *28*(5), 412–413. doi:10.1037/022069

Mendelowitz, E. (2008). Meditations on dissociation: Kristina and the enigmatic self. In K. J. Schneider (Ed.), *Existential-integrative psychotherapy: Guideposts to the core of practice* (pp. 245–266). New York, NY, US: Routledge/Taylor & Francis Group.

Monheit, J. (2008). A lesbian and gay perspective: The case of Marcia. In K. J. Schneider (Eds.), *Existential-integrative psychotherapy: Guideposts to the core of practice* (pp. 140–146). New York, NY, US: Routledge/Taylor & Francis Group.

Mosher, C. M. (2001). The social implications of sexual identity formation and the coming-out process: A review of the theoretical and empirical literature. *The Family Journal*, *9*(2), 164–173. doi:10.1177/1066480701092011

Norcross, J. C., & Goldfried, M. R. (2005). The future of psychotherapy integration: A roundtable. *Journal Of Psychotherapy Integration*, *15*(4), 392–471. doi:10.1037/1053-0479.15.4.392

Norcross, J. C. (1987). A rational and empirical analysis of existential psychotherapy. *Journal Of Humanistic Psychology*, *27*(1), 41–68. doi:10.1177/0022167887271005

Ottens, A. J., & Hanna, F. J. (1998). Cognitive and existential therapies: Toward an integration. *Psychotherapy: Theory, Research, Practice, Training*, *35*(3), 312–324. doi:10.1037/h0087832

Rice, D. L. (2008). An African American perspective: The case of Darrin. In K. J. Schneider (Ed.), Existential-integrative psychotherapy: Guideposts to the core of practice (pp. 110–121). New York, NY, US: Routledge/Taylor & Francis Group.

Richert, A. J. (1999). Some thoughts on the integration of narrative and humanistic/existential approaches to psychotherapy. *Journal Of Psychotherapy Integration*, *9*(2), 161–184. doi:10.1023/A:1023295309766

Rugala, S. A., & Waldo, M. (1998). An integration of existential psychology and the multimodal model. *Journal Of Humanistic Psychology*, *38*(4), 65–79. doi:10.1177/00221678980384005

Sartre, J.P. (1975). *Being and nothingness*. New York, NY: Washington Square Press.

Schneider, K. J., & Krug, O. T. (2010). *Existential–humanistic therapy*. Washington, DC, US: American Psychological Association.

Schneider, K. J. (2008). *Existential-integrative psychotherapy: Guideposts to the core of practice*. New York, NY, US: Routledge/Taylor & Francis Group.

Schneider, K. J. (2014). Enchanted agnosticism, awe, and existential-integrative therapy. *Spirituality In Clinical Practice*, *1*(1), 71–73. doi:10.1037/scp0000007

Serlin, I. (2008). Women and the midlife crisis: The Anne Sexton complex. In K. J. Schneider (Ed.), *Existential-integrative psychotherapy: Guideposts to the core of practice* (pp. 146–163). New York, NY, US: Routledge/Taylor & Francis Group.

Shahar, G., & Schiller, M. (2016). A conqueror by stealth: Introduction to the special issue on humanism, existentialism, and psychotherapy integration. *Journal Of Psychotherapy Integration*, *26*(1), 1–4. doi:10.1037/int0000024

Shumaker, D. (2012). An existential–integrative treatment of anxious and depressed adolescents. *Journal Of Humanistic Psychology*, *52*(4), 375–400. doi:10.1177/0022167811422947

Sotskova, A., Carey, T., & Mak, B. (2016). Applying Goldfried's concept of assimilative psychotherapy integration: The process of synthesizing existential and cognitive behavioral therapy models. *Journal Of Psychotherapy Integration*, *26*(1), 36–48. doi:10.1037/a0040040

Spinelli, E. (1997). Human sexuality and existential-phenomenological inquiry. *Counselling Psychology Review*, *12*(4), 170–178.

Spinelli, E. (2015). Experiencing change: A phenomenological exploration. *Existential Analysis*, *26*(1), 4–20.

Tillich, P. (1952). Anxiety, religion, and medicine. *Pastoral Psychology*, *3*11–17. doi:10.1007/BF01769082

Tillich, P. (1967). The eternal now. In Scott, N.A., Jr. (Ed.), *The Modern Vision of Death* (pp. 97–106). Richmond, VA: John Knox Press.

van Deurzen, E. (2012). Reasons for living: Existential therapy and spirituality. In L. Barnett, G. Madison (Eds.), *Existential therapy: Legacy, vibrancy and dialogue* (pp. 171–182). New York, NY, US: Routledge/Taylor & Francis Group.

van Deurzen, E. (2015). Structural existential analysis (SEA): A phenomenological method for therapeutic work. *Journal Of Contemporary Psychotherapy*, *45*(1), 59–68. doi:10.1007/s10879-014-9282-z

Vos, J., Craig, M., & Cooper, M. (2015). Existential therapies: A meta-analysis of their effects on psychological outcomes. *Journal Of Consulting And Clinical Psychology*, *83*(1), 115–128. doi:10.1037/a0037167

Wampold, B. E. (2013). The good, the bad, and the ugly: A 50-year perspective on the outcome problem. *Psychotherapy*, *50*(1), 16–24. doi:10.1037/a0030570

Warnock, M. (1970). Existentialism. New York: Oxford University Press.

Yalom, I. D. (1980). *Existential psychotherapy*. New York, NY, US: Basic Books.

Yalom, I. D. (1989). *Love's executioner: And other tales of psychotherapy*. New York, NY, US: Basic Books.

CHAPTER 2

The Incidence, Prevalence, and Risk Factors Associated with Debilitating Existential Anxiety in Adolescents

Introduction

How common is existential anxiety in adolescence? How intensely do adolescents contemplate their fate, questions of meaning, of life, and of death? What predicts the emergence of debilitating existential anxiety in certain teens? Why do some adolescents experience these worries while others not so much? These are critical questions that merit the attention of any clinician intent upon treating adolescents. This chapter explores these questions in detail and ultimately concludes that (a) existential anxiety is experienced by many adolescents, (b) some experience this manner of anxiety to debilitating degrees, and (c) there are several probable predictors of existential anxiety in this age group. Chapter 3 will continue the discussion with an examination of several protective factors that may reduce the risk of an adolescent experiencing debilitating levels of existential anxiety followed by a developmental model of existential anxiety based upon the review of risk and protective factors.

How Common Is Existential Thinking and Anxiety in Adolescence?

Existential anxiety is thought to be a universal phenomenon that manifests in the lifespan of every individual (May, 1977; Rank, 1936; Tillich, 1952). Faced with the certainty of death, the responsibility of finding meaning in one's life, and guilt stemming from our unlived potentials and/or impact

D. Shumaker, *Existential-Integrative Approaches to Treating Adolescents*, DOI 10.1057/978-1-349-95211-3_2

upon others and the world around us, no one is thought to be spared the experience of existential anxiety. Still, until fairly recently there has been little empirical evidence beyond case study reports to confirm this supposition. This state of affairs is changing. Though the empirical evidence is still limited there are strong suggestions that existential concerns are frequently experienced by adolescents (Shumaker, 2012). The body of research on this topic is reviewed here.

To date, Berman and colleagues' (2006) investigation into the presence of existential concerns in a sample of 139 high-school-age youth perhaps provides the most compelling evidence in support of this assertion. The participants completed the existential anxiety questionnaire (EAQ; Weems et al., 2004) which is a 13-item, true-false rating scale designed to measure the critical domains of anxiety outlined by Tillich (1952) (i.e., fate/death, meaninglessness/emptiness, guilt/condemnation). The mean age of the participants was 16.7 years with a range between 15 to 18 years and a standard deviation of 0.9 years. Seventy percent of the sample were female. Seventy-eight percent were Euro-American, with 5% African-American, 4% Hispanic American, 1% Asian, 3% mixed ethnic background, and 9% choosing not to endorse an ethnic background. Importantly, the authors found no statistically significant associations between EAQ scores and age, grade level, gender, or ethnicity. The prevalence of existential anxiety in the sample was notably high. Specifically nearly half the youth surveyed expressed death apprehension, while concerns regarding fate (64%), meaninglessness (30%), emptiness (70%), condemnation (53%), and guilt (59%) were also endorsed with high frequency. Ninety-six percent of the sample endorsed at least one significant area of existential anxiety, leading the study authors to conclude that "it may be reasonable to consider [existential anxiety] a normative phenomenon" (Berman et al., 2006, pg. 308).

The author has recently replicated Berman et al.'s (2006) major findings regarding prevalence of existential anxiety concerns in a sample of college students. Sixty-nine participants ranging in age from 19 to 25 years old (mean age = 19.9; SD = 1.7) were administered the EAQ (Shumaker et al., in press). The participants in this study are, on average, slightly older than those sampled in the Berman et al. (2006) study. In regard to gender, 64% of the sample were female. The majority of the sample identified as Euro-American (61%), followed by Hispanic (13%), Asian (12%), Mixed or Other Ethnicity (9%), and African-American (4%) ethnic groups. As was found in the Berman et al. (2006) all but one participant (99%) endorsed at least one form of existential anxiety. In terms of Tillich's subcategories of existential anxiety, 84% endorsed at least one fate item, 72% endorsed at least one emptiness, and 93% endorsed at least one meaningless item. A notable percentage of participants endorsed all items in subcategories. Specifically, nearly 8% endorsed all fate items, 3% endorsed all emptiness items, and approximately one out of every five participants endorsed every meaninglessness item. This suggests that a sizable portion of young, college students of various ethnic and religious backgrounds are experiencing intense concerns regarding the universal existential concerns of fate and guilt, emptiness, and meaninglessness.

Existential concerns appear common to adolescents across the world. For example, Winston et al. (2013) measured the presence of existential thinking in a sample of 567 adolescents between the ages of 14 and 18 years in India where a collectivistic culture predominates. They note that existential thinking is different from existential anxiety, the former defined simply as "the extent to which a person thinks about such issues" (Winston et al., 2013). The researchers measured this construct using the Existential Thinking Scale, a 14-item measure developed by Shearer (2006) to assess an individual's propensity for existential thinking. The authors found that 75% of their sample demonstrated a moderate to strong propensity to engage in existential thinking. They also found a significant positive correlation between one's propensity to engage in existential thinking and the presence of symptomatology as measured by the Symptom Check List-90-Revised (SCL-90R) (Derogatis & Lazurus, 1994). Adolescents in India who think more about existential issues tend to report higher levels of psychiatric distress.

In a study of 426 Eastern European adolescents (Transylvania, Romania) between the ages of 15 and 18 years, Brassai and colleagues (2012) assessed the presence of existential attitudes related to the search for meaning (SFM) and presence of meaning (POM). Steger and colleagues' (2006) Meaning in life questionnaire (MLQ) was used to assess these constructs while measures of problem and health-related behaviors were also administered. The authors found that individuals who reported elevated levels of SFM and POM were less likely to self-report antisocial and aggressive problem behaviors. Further the average SFM score on the MLQ was quite high, suggesting a high percentage of participants were attempting to find meaning in their lives. Shek et al. (1994) found similar results in a sample of adolescents in China. These findings are consistent with Damon and colleagues' (2003) contention that a SFM and purpose is a central task of adolescence with important positive prognostic implications. This SFM certainly falls under the broader rubric of existential concerns.

Finally, several studies indicate adolescents think about death and fear their demise. This finding has been replicated across a wide range of American (Ollendick et al., 1985, 2001), European (Ollendick et al., 1991), Asian (Dong et al., 1994), and African (Ollendick et al., 1996; Ingman et al., 1999) samples, suggesting a universality of this fear in adolescence. In summary, there is a growing body of evidence that existential concerns are experienced by a high percentage of youth across a variety of cultures and that gender, ethnicity, and religious preference does not seem to predict the presence of these apprehensions. Further, there appear to be a smaller but far from insubstantial percentage of these youth who may experience these concerns to an intense degree.

What Are Predictors of Existential Anxiety and Concerns in Adolescence?

The range of research that arguably should be reviewed when considering predictors of existential anxiety is quite broad. There are, of course, limited empirical analyses, several case studies, and extensive theoretical discussions of existential anxiety that should arguably first be taken into account. In addition, research on both normative and pathological adolescent bio-psycho-socio development has much to offer. Finally, predictors of Diagnostic and Statistical Manual (DSM) anxiety disorders may also shed important light upon the development of debilitating existential anxiety, in part because the high comorbidity between generalized anxiety and existential anxiety suggests possible common etiological factors (Weems et al., 2004). The following discussion touches upon several predictors suggested across these sources of data. The review likely does not capture the entire spectrum of possible predictors as existential anxiety remains relatively understudied, the aforementioned range of data sources is far reaching, and there are likely additional untapped data sources to be considered. Readers therefore are encouraged to view this effort as an initial venture that will hopefully stimulate additional discussion and empirical analysis. Recognizing in advance there may be a fair degree of overlap across categories, the predictors discussed below are classified into the following four subgroups: (1) biological; (2) psychological/individual; (3) social/familial; and (4) cultural/historical/contextual.

Biological

Genetic Vulnerability/Heritability: Might there be a genetic component to the experience of existential anxiety? Is there a heritable component to the same? Put differently (to say the least), is there a collective unconscious transmitted across generations through blood-lines that fosters a deeper appreciation for existential concerns in certain individuals? These are fascinating questions that have no clear answers at this point in time. There are no known studies that investigate the genetic markers of and/or heritability of existential anxiety. What little that can be said on the topic comes from research on DSM classified anxiety disorders.

DSM anxiety disorders – phobias, generalized anxiety disorder (GAD), panic disorder (PD), and obsessive compulsive disorder (OCD) – are commonly experienced by youth. Approximately 3–12% of children and adolescents likely have a diagnosable anxiety disorder at any given time (Rice & Thapar, 2009). Research suggests a strong heritability component in these disorders. Drake and Ginsburg's (2012) excellent review of family factors in the development of anxiety disorders suggests the heritability component may explain as much as 30% of the variance in the development of anxiety disorders. Turner and colleagues (1987), for example, found that children whose parents had been diagnosed with an anxiety disorder were seven times more likely to be diagnosed with an anxiety disorder compared to children who did not have a parent diagnosed with a disorder. Recently, Ask and colleagues (2016) studied nearly fourteen hundred monozygotic and dizygotic twins reared together. They estimated the heritability component of child and adolescent anxiety disorders in the sample at 44%, with shared environmental variance at 25% and nonshared environmental variance at 31%. Thus, it is quite clear that anxiety disorders have a strong genetic and heritable component.

In a review of heritability research on anxiety, Gregory and Eley (2007) suggest that a genetic marker for "anxiety sensitivity" may account for at least a portion of the heritable component of anxiety disorders. Anxiety sensitivity pertains to an individual's fear of the physical sensations associated with anxiety. It is estimated that up to half the variance in anxiety sensitivity is accounted for by genes (Stein et al., 1999). But more research needs to be conducted to pinpoint the specific genetic risk factors for the development of anxiety disorders. While informative, can a connection be made between anxiety sensitivity and existential anxiety? Perhaps one can. Fitzgerald (2005) and Hacker (1994) suggest in their developmental models of existential anxiety that adolescence is characterized by the introduction of several life stressors that can give rise to existential anxiety. Adolescents who have a general vulnerability to stress and who possesses an anxiety sensitivity may more acutely feel the stress associated with the existential concerns contemplated more deeply during this stage of life. Panic-related symptomatology (heart racing, choking sensations) could give way to catastrophic misinterpretations ("I might die") which in turn could lead to deeper concern regarding the core existential fear of death and nothingness.

Temperament/Personality: There are no known empirical studies that examine the relationship between temperament and existential anxiety. Research on the relationship between temperament and DSM anxiety disorders suggests that elevated levels of behavioral inhibition (BI) appear to predict anxiety disorders in preschool-aged youth (Degnan et al., 2010; Wichstrom et al., 2013) and middle-school-aged youth (Hudson and Dodd, 2012). Tincas and colleagues (2006), in a review of the relationship between temperament and anxiety disorders, defines BI as "a reluctance to approach novel situations or unfamiliar persons" (pg. 492). Approximately 15% of children display elevated BI (Fox et al., 2005). Children with this temperament tend to slow their motor activity and demonstrate long latencies when confronted with novelty. Later in childhood these children often demonstrate social anxiety and tend to withdraw from new situations. Increased amygdala activity and associated enhanced physiological reactivity may be the underlying biological cause of this temperament typology (Kagan & Snidman, 1999). Sensitivity to change and novelty would make conceptual sense as a risk factor for increased levels of existential anxiety in adolescence. Adolescence is certainly a time of change and transition. Behaviorally inhibited individuals may feel the impact of these changes on a deeper level, leading to increased awareness and contemplation of the dynamic, fragile, and temporary nature of one's existence. Attachment, parenting style, and maternal psychopathology may mediate the connection between BI and the development of anxiety disorders (Dengan et al., 2010).

Negative affectivity has also been associated with the development of both anxiety and depressive disorders (Ask et al., 2016). Clark and Watson's (1991) tripartite models of anxiety and depression suggest that negative affectivity in combination with somatic arousal may lead to the development of anxiety while negative affect along with low positive affect may correlate more with depression. Here again, while highly speculative, a vulnerability to experiencing higher levels of negative affect in conjunction with physiological anxiety and related discomfort may lead to more questioning of the meaning of one's existence and perhaps in even extreme cases, despair and suicidal ideation.

In regard to personality type, there is an abundance of research that suggests highly anxious individuals experience elevated levels of neuroticism and lower levels of extraversion on measures of Big Five personality traits (Bienvenu et al., 2004; Rector et al., 2012; Vreeke & Muris, 2012). Elevated neuroticism is characterized by a tendency to experience unpleasant emotions easily, emotional instability, and a low tolerance for stress. Lower levels of extraversion are associated with a more quiet, withdrawn, and deliberate approach to life. Until recently, however, there were no studies examining the relationship between Big Five personality traits and existential anxiety. The author has attempted to fill this gap in research in a study investigating these factors in a college-aged population (Shumaker et al., in press). Preliminary results suggest a strong positive association between neuroticism and existential anxiety. More specifically, the N4 subscale of self-consciousness seems to be the personality subtype that most strongly predicts existential anxiety. Individuals scoring highly on this subscale are prone to shyness and social inhibition. This finding has very important implications for the assessment and detection of existential anxiety in individuals seeking mental health services. Further, it offers tantalizing clues into the personality features of individuals who may be vulnerable to existential anxiety. An individual who may struggle with venturing into the world and intimate relationships may contemplate and struggle with the existential givens of life at a deeper level than most.

Ojala (2005) suggests that a stronger sense of responsibility may be associated with existential anxiety. One might therefore expect to see a relationship between the Big Five personality trait of conscientiousness and existential anxiety. In fact, such was evidenced in the aforementioned study conducted by the author (Shumaker et al., in press). Specifically, lower levels of conscientiousness (and lower levels of extraversion) also seemed to predict increased levels of existential anxiety. Individuals who demonstrate lower levels of conscientiousness may be lacking in motivation, a sense of direction, and a belief in one's self-efficacy. Perhaps these individuals feel vulnerable and less capable of effectively contending with life tasks and existential concerns, resulting in elevated existential anxiety. Certainly more research is needed to further clarify the relationship between personality and existential anxiety. But it seems quite clear that a connection does, in fact, exist.

Medical and Lifespan Developmental Concerns: Significant health concerns appear to predict existential anxiety. Simony and colleagues (2015) found that individuals being treated for coronary heart disease demonstrated elevated levels of existential anxiety and required encouragement and education to overcome their fears of engaging in rehabilitative exercise. A fear of death seemed ever present for many of the study participants. One participant, for example, described his experience of physical exertion at one point in the following manner:

> I feel uncomfortable and the sensation extends into my arm, and I start thinking "Ooh really." It was much like that in the beginning. I was afraid to die. Is it time to go for good now, or what is it? (pg. 2585)

Interestingly, the author (DMS) had a very similar experience when he was 15 years old and suffered a compound fracture of his left arm. While objectively not life threatening, upon seeing the horribly disfigured arm, two thoughts rushed into the forefront of the author's consciousness: "Boy, this is going to hurt like heck" and "Is some sort of blood clot going to kill me here?"

There is a strong link between DSM anxiety disorders and physical health conditions as well. El-Gabalawy and colleagues (2011), for example, found that health concerns increased the odds of one experiencing anxiety. Further, the combination of anxiety and health concerns was associated with poorer self-reported health in participants than when anxiety problems or medical concerns were experienced alone. Thus, physical illness and health concerns likely increase the risk of a wide range of anxieties, including fears of death, incapacitation, pain and suffering, and a loss of meaning/purpose/connections in life.

In a related area of inquiry, Benton et al. (2007) have investigated the relationship between existential death anxiety and aging. They argue that, as humans age, their awareness of their mortality and impending annihilation increases. It is natural at this stage of life for individuals to experience increased levels of existential death anxiety. An individual's experience of their own physical decline may produce the most intense levels of existential anxiety. But the individual who is aging may not be the only one impacted by the march of time. Martens and colleagues (2005) suggest that mere exposure to the elderly and physical signs of aging and deterioration may increase existential death anxiety in younger individuals. More than a few adolescents and young adults in the author's clinical practice have commented on the fact that they feel "uncomfortable," "weird," and even "freaked out" when in close contact with elderly relatives, especially those near death. When asked to further explain what freaks them out, several report that this contact reminds them of their own mortality. Benton et al. (2007) suggest that a fear of losses (e.g., losing meaning, friendships, self-sufficiency) may be the driving force associated with increased existential anxiety in young adults who contemplate aging.

Cognitive Factors/Intelligence: There are no empirical studies that investigate the relationship between intelligence and existential anxiety. There are suggestions in the literature however that higher levels of intelligence may be associated with increased existential anxiety. For example, Ellsworth (1999), citing a client in her clinical practice, suggested that "giftedness" may predict existential anxiety in adolescents. She argued that knowing too much and feeling too much may create a burden for the adolescent where they are more acutely sensitive to existential dreads. Chessick (1996) has similarly noted a readiness on the part of "certain rather cerebral adolescents" to contemplate Heidegger's concept of "resoluteness" in therapy and benefit from existential treatment approaches. He argues that certain adolescents struggle with living an inauthentic existence and that this can lead to stress, a sense of meaninglessness, and other forms of maladjustment. Here again, while conceptually compelling, his empirical evidence seems mostly based upon a case report of an adolescent he successfully treated using existential concepts in therapy.

The research on anxiety and intelligence has yet to yield a definitive picture of the relationship between the two constructs (Eussen et al., 2013). Several studies report higher levels of intelligence predict more severe anxiety (e.g., Sukhodolsky et al., 2005; Witwer & Lecavalier, 2010) while others have found low intelligence predicts elevated anxiety (Flensborg-Madsen et al., 2012; White & Roberson-Nay, 2009). Eussen and colleagues (2013) argue that the assumption that higher intelligence is associated with increased self-awareness which, in turn, can lead to more increased anxiety about one's deficits appears to not be supported. Koenen and colleagues (2009) explain the relationship between lower intelligence and increased risk of adult anxiety disorders as due to a deficit in cognitive reserves. Adding to an already murky picture it is hardly surprising that a meta-analysis found a quadratic relationship between intelligence and anxiety where extremes on both ends of the general intelligence continuum may predict elevated anxiety (van Steensel et al., 2012). In short, individuals with low, normative, and high levels of general intelligence are vulnerable to experiencing more severe anxiety throughout their lifespans.

It is important to remember that there are multiple intelligences. Emotional intelligence, in particular, may better predict severe anxiety. Specifically, there appears to be an inverse relationship between emotional intelligence and anxiety (Lizeretti & Extremera, 2011; Summerfeldt et al., 2011). Emotional intelligence involves one's abilities to perceive, manage, regulate, and understand emotions in oneself and others. Individuals with advanced abilities in this area of functioning tend to demonstrate more refined self-regulation and social skills. The emotional and social world of an individual may be less clear and frankly scarier when one's emotional intelligence is less developed; in turn leading to more intense anxiety levels (Lizeretti & Extremera, 2011). Could it be that higher levels of emotional intelligence protect one against more debilitating levels of existential anxiety? Though fascinating clues from research on emotional intelligence related to anxiety suggest this possibility, clearly more direct study of the relationship is needed before definitive conclusions can be drawn.

Psychological/Individual Factors

Identity Formation: Erikson famously characterized adolescence as a critical phase of identity development (Erikson, 1959). Adolescents struggle to form a coherent sense of identity and experience role confusion. Many of Erikson's views on this phase of life development have been supported by Marcia's (1993) impressive body of research. Marcia argues that there are four identity statuses that adolescents and young adults may experience and progress through. These include identity diffusion, identity foreclosure, identity moratorium, and identity achievement, and are based upon the cross-tabulation of the two dimensions of choice and commitment. Identity diffusion (low choice, low commitment) and identity foreclosure (low choice, high commitment) are thought to represent relatively less mature stages of identity development, while identity moratorium (high crisis-making choices, low commitment) is thought to be more complex. Most importantly for the present discussion, adolescents who fall within the identity-moratorium range of functioning tend to experience more severe anxiety (Cote, 2009; Kidwell et al., 1995) and uncertainty (Meeus, 1996; Meeus Iedema et al., 1999). Closer to home, Berman and colleagues (2006) found that adolescents who fell within the identity-moratorium category demonstrated elevated levels of existential anxiety as compared to adolescents falling with the other three categories of identity formation. The authors speculate that adolescents in the identity moratorium stage of development experience elevated existential anxiety, "because individuals in this status are exploring different options for their core beliefs but have not yet chosen from the available alternatives or committed themselves" (pg. 309).

Identity achievement (post-crisis-producing choices, high commitment) is the final category of identity formation falling in Marcia's framework. It is seen as the most complex and mature of the four options. Not surprisingly, this condition correlates with more mature interpersonal relationships (Dyk & Adams, 1990; Kroger, 2003), balanced thinking (Boyes and Chandler, 1992), and higher levels of personal agency (Cote, 1996). As will be noted in the chapter on protective factors, it appears that identity achievement may be associated with lower levels of existential anxiety (Berman et al., 2006). Overall, it seems clear that greater identity uncertainty predicts elevated levels of existential anxiety.

Search for Meaning/Presence of Meaning: Frankl (1965) has suggested that a frustrated SFM life can lead to feelings of distress and existential anxiety. He conceptualized a "will to meaning" as an essential component of human existence that can provide a sense of purpose and authenticity to one's existence even under the harshest of circumstances (Frankl, 1963). Frankl argued that a frustrated will to meaning can lead to adolescents experiencing an existential vacuum resulting in feelings of boredom, apathy, neurosis, aggression, addiction, and depression. As discussed in the first chapter, the question of meaning is viewed as a fundamental existential concern (Yalom, 1980).

Frankl's thinking about the importance of meaning for healthy development has been borne out by empirical studies. Specifically, individuals who struggle to find a sense of meaning are more likely to experience anxiety and depression (Debats et al., 1993). Steger and colleagues (2006) developed the MLQ to test for the presence of two constructs related to an individual's experiencing of meaning in his or her life. The POM subscale measures the extent to which one's believe life to be meaningful. The SFM subscale measures one's drive and orientation toward finding meaning in one's life (Steger et al. 2006). Steger and colleagues (2006) cogently note that the POM and SFM constructs may run parallel to Marcia's identity development model. They found that participants in their study who demonstrated higher levels of SFM were significantly more likely to demonstrate anxiety and depressive symptomatology (Steger et al., 2006). Individuals who experience a lower sense of meaning in their lives may be more vulnerable to experiencing anxiety disorders (Flensborg-Madsen et al., 2012). Indeed, there is increasing evidence suggesting that a higher sense of meaning leads to a more proactive health orientation in the individual, which in turn can increase physical health and subjective happiness and well-being (Steger et al., 2015). Overall, like identity development, the SOM and POM in one's life seem to mediate the experience of existential anxiety during adolescence.

Self-esteem: Self-esteem can also serve as a risk and protective factor in relation to existential anxiety. Klackl and colleagues (2014) looked at the relationship between self-esteem and death anxiety in young adults and found lower levels of self-esteem were associated with increased concerns about death. Their neuroimaging analyses of participants identified lower activity in the middle and posterior insular brain regions in individuals processing death-related cues, but that self-esteem levels may mediate this effect. Enhanced levels of self-esteem appear to protect individuals against the impact of negative life events by increasing their sense of self-efficacy and belief in one's ability to cope with stress (Hobfoll & Leiberman, 1987). It may therefore be that a lower level of self-esteem is associated with a more vulnerable and ineffective response to stress, which in turn leads to higher levels of anxiety and depression (Mann et al., 2004; Rosenfield et al., 2005).

Rosenfield and colleagues (2005) suggest that a related construct – self-salience – may predict internalizing problems as well. Self-salience refers to a cognitive schema that reflects the relative importance of the self versus others in social relationships. Individuals who score lower on self-salience (i.e., tend to stress the needs of others at the expense of oneself) tend to be more vulnerable to experiencing internalizing disorders. This is believed to be the case because these individuals tend to have more negative cognitions about themselves and may rely on others excessively. This, in turn, could lead to feelings of insecurity, disappointment, and frustration. It is unclear whether the same relationship between self-salience and existential anxiety exists. This merits further exploration.

Intolerance of Uncertainty: Intolerance of uncertainty has been defined as "the tendency to react negatively on an emotional, cognitive, and behavioral level to uncertain situations and events" (Buhr & Dugas, 2009, p. 216). Individuals with this sensitivity find uncertain events upsetting and stressful. They tend to assume negative outcomes in these situations, interpret ambiguity in a negative manner, and find it difficult to perform in uncertain situations (Boulter et al., 2014). It appears that two subfactors form the basis of this larger character trait: *desire for predictability* and *uncertainty paralysis*. Intolerance of uncertainty predicts a gamut of internalizing disorders, including GAD, OCD, social anxiety disorder, PD, and agoraphobia (Carleton et al., 2012; McEvoy & Mahoney, 2012). More pertinent to the present focus, this construct also predicts increased worry in adolescents (Laugesen et al., 2003). Excessive worrying can actually serve as a form of cognitive avoidance that suppresses more adaptive and healing emotional and physiological responses to anxiety. Attempts to suppress or control worry can lead to intrusive thoughts, which results in increased suppression attempts, even more intrusive thoughts, and ultimately more anxiety (Mineka & Zinbarg, 2006).

While no studies have investigated the relationship between intolerance of uncertainty, excessive worrying, and existential anxiety, it makes conceptual sense that a strong relationship would exist. Specifically, a hallmark of existential anxiety is a personal struggle with the contingent nature of one's existence and appreciation for the fragile and fleeting nature of the same. Faced with a myriad of life uncertainties and the unpredictable nature of one's life course and inevitable demise (i.e., we do not know when or how we will die), adolescents who have greater difficulty tolerating uncertainty would appear more likely to struggle with these existential givens of our existence.

Perceived Controllability: Though there have been no studies reported in the literature examining the social learning bases of existential anxiety, Mineka and Zinbarg (2006) offer a compelling learning theory account of GAD and post-traumatic stress disorder (PTSD) that may have implications for our understanding of the etiology of debilitating existential anxiety. They cite evidence indicating individuals who experience uncontrollable adverse events early in life may be more vulnerable to developing GAD and PTSD. In a related finding, individuals who report lower levels of perceived controllability of events are at increased risk for experiencing clinically significant anxiety (Mineka & Zinbarg, 2006). Individuals who perceive their world as less predictable are also highly vulnerable to the experiencing PTSD symptoms following a traumatic event (Mineka & Zinbarg, 2006). Thus, both the experience of actual uncontrollable adverse events and the perception of a lower ability to control events increase risk for these debilitating anxiety disorders and a perpetual sense of foreboding doom. Again, however, it is unclear whether debilitating levels of existential anxiety are related to a lower locus of control, a lower tolerance for uncertainty, and/or excessive worrying tendencies that serve an avoidance function. Clearly these are important and compelling areas of future study.

Values and Moral Reasoning: There has been some exploration and discussion of the relationship between values, macro-level concerns, well-being, and existential anxiety (Shaffer, 1978; Ojala, 2005). Values are defined as desirable goals that serve as guiding principles in humans lives (Schwartz, 1992). Erikson (1963) wrote extensively about the development of a worldview and coherent ideology as a critical component of adolescent identity development. May (1950) noted that existential anxiety occurs when one senses a threat to one's core values and being. Thus, in a time of life where one becomes more in tune with his or her core values *and* more aware of threats to these core values, it would seem reasonable that adolescents who experience this threat more acutely may be vulnerable to increased levels of existential anxiety.

There are suggestions in the research that this may just be the case. However, the relationship is complicated and mitigated by a sense of meaning and faith in the likelihood that solutions will be forthcoming to resolve threats to one's values. Specifically, Ojala (2005) investigated the relationship between environmental worries, well-being, and existential anxiety in a large cohort of adolescents ($N = 253$). A sense of meaningfulness and faith in science and institutions was associated with enhanced well-being in participants who demonstrated high levels of environmental concern. Conversely, those participants who scored lower on meaningfulness and hopefulness demonstrated lower levels of well-being. Thus, how one appraises threats to one's values system seems to impact the level of distress they will experience related to existential concerns. In summary, awareness of threats to one's existence or core values will inevitably increase existential anxiety, but other factors can mitigate the level of distress associated with this form of anxiety.

Social/Familial

Trauma/Loss/Death: In an insightful theoretical discussion, Stolorow (2007) illuminates the connection between trauma and existential anxiety related to Heidegger's (1927/1962) concept of "Being toward death." He supports Heidegger's contention that the realization that one is thrown against their will into an inevitable encounter with nonbeing shatters the seeming significance of everyday tasks and generates a feeling of uncanniness. In these "aha" moments the individual who comes to realize their potential nonbeing will experience intense levels of existential anxiety concerning their ultimate demise. The individual feels an acute sense of being alone in this world and questions whether all attempts in this life to actualize something or achieve a level of permanent distinction may be for naught. This realization can be understandably overwhelming, even debilitating, and thus individuals under normal circumstances find ways to conceal this reality through their absorption in daily life tasks. Trauma, however, can wreak havoc on these defense systems (i.e., the illusion of predictability and controllability) and any belief in the permanency of our existence.

In the specific case of trauma pertaining to the loss of a loved one, Stolorow (2007) observes a loss such as this also "shatters the absolutisms of everyday life, which, like the illusions of the 'they,' evade and cover-up the finitude, contingency, and embeddedness of our existence" (pp. 378–379). He argues that the existential anxiety in these cases can be so intense as to become unendurable, resulting in dissociative states. He cites his own personal experience with the loss of his spouse as evidence of the extreme destabilization one can experience in these situations.

Stolorow's (2007) account of the relationship between trauma and existential anxiety is indirectly supported by empirical research showing a strong link between early childhood trauma and the development of anxiety disorders in childhood, adolescence, and adulthood. Hovens and colleagues (2012), for example, conducted a longitudinal study on the development of mental health disorders in a large sample (N = 1209) adults who had experienced childhood trauma (i.e., losses, neglect, psychological, physical and sexual abuse). They determined that childhood trauma was associated with an increased persistence of both comorbidity and chronicity in childhood anxiety and depressive disorders. Emotional neglect, psychological and physical abuse, but not sexual abuse, was associated with persistence of comorbid anxiety and depressive disorders. Maniglio (2013), in a comprehensive review of meta-analytic studies investigating the relationship between childhood sexual abuse and anxiety disorders, uncovered convincing evidence suggesting that this form of abuse is a significant, though nonspecific, risk factor for anxiety disorders. In fact, it appears that trauma exposure can increase the risk of a wide range of Axis I pathology, not just anxiety disorders (Brown et al., 2014). The final chapter of this book explores EI approaches to working with adolescents who experienced trauma.

Familial and Parental Factors: There appears to be a striking lack of research on the relationship between existential anxiety and parent-child relationships, parenting behaviors, and parental psychopathology. Problematic attachment formation resulting in tenuous parent-child bonding, the experience of excessively restrictive or permissive discipline, and/or exposure to parents suffering from chronic and debilitating psychopathology all would seem critical risk factors for the development of debilitating existential anxiety during childhood and adolescence. All of these factors could contribute to a sense of uncertainty and fragility in the child and adolescent, in turn, making existential concerns more prominent and resolutions to this anxiety source less likely. A lack of family stability and parental acceptance and presence could discourage critical dialogue that might normally occur between the adolescent and parent regarding existential concerns, leaving the adolescent to suffer in silence with questions of meaning, mortality, and one's self-worth. Hollis (2013), in *Hauntings,* notes the importance of parental and other historical influences on the child's experience of existential anxiety. He rhetorically asks, "So who would contend, then, that the primary haunting of adult life is not the internalization of those parental presences that drive, deflect, repeat, and necessarily distort our voyage through this essentially unknowable universe?" (pg. 32). He cites several examples of how disconnected, limited, and/or abusive parents can fail to provide essential support for a child contemplating the "existential horror" of disconnect and abandonment.

Once again the literature on the relationship between familial and parent factors and general anxiety provides indirect support for the premise of a possible connection between these same factors and existential anxiety. Anxiety disorders seem to run in families. As previously discussed, genetic influences may account for as much as 30% of the variance in the development of anxiety disorders (Drake & Ginsburg, 2012). Still, that leaves as much as 70% of the variance due to shared and nonshared environmental influences. Parenting factors seem to account for a good deal of these environmental influences.

Perhaps the most critical parenting factor that influences the development of anxiety disorders in childhood and adolescence is whether a strong bond forms between parent and child. There is a wealth of evidence linking insecure parent-child attachment to the development of anxiety disorders (Colonnesi et al., 2011; Warren et al., 1997). If the infant and toddler's formative life experiences are lacking in warmth and caretaker responsivity to needs, it obviously could result in a hypersensitivity to the fragility of one's existence and sense of aloneness that will set the stage for chronic anxiety symptomatology later in life.

There may be a host of parent and/or familial factors that could negatively influence the development of a secure attachment. For example, child exposure to early family adversity – including elevated maternal stress, multiple maternal partner changes, and total life adversities – predicts the development of anxiety disorders in adolescence (Phillips et al., 2005). Phillips and colleagues (2005) have speculated that early life adversity that is perceived as threatening may be the most likely form of adversity to increase the risk of later anxiety disorders. It is important to remember that the child is not the only family member affected by these life adversities. The primary attachment figure will be impacted as well. A parent who endures significant life adversities may become preoccupied with navigating these adversities at the expense of the child. Both the parent and child may be traumatized in the process of contending with these life adversities, increasing the risk for the development of anxiety disorders.

A host of other parental factors predicts the development of anxiety disorders in childhood and adolescence. Parental anxiety appears to increase the risk of anxiety disorders in preschool-aged youth (Wichstrom et al., 2013). It may be that these parents model avoidance behaviors and increased threat perception. Maternal overprotectiveness and parental control may also increase the risk of a child experiencing an anxiety disorder (Ballash et al., 2006; Hudson and Dodd, 2012). Parents who are overprotective and overcontrolling may reinforce their child functioning at a lower level, thus leading to a child who feels less capable. Ultimately this could increase anxiety in the child, especially when separated from a parent (Wood et al, 2003). Overall, it seems clear that insecure attachment formation, family instability, parental psychopathology, and negative parenting factors all can increase the risk for the development of anxiety disorders. It seems quite likely, if not yet empirically supported, that these same factors will increase the likelihood of a child and/or adolescent experiencing elevated existential anxiety.

Peer Victimization/Bullying: While there are no investigations into the relationship between peer victimization and existential anxiety, there are strong suggestions that being subjected to bullying can increase one's susceptibility to developing an anxiety disorder during childhood and adolescence (Hawker & Boulton, 2000; Stapinski et al., 2015; Wichstrom et al., 2013). This is hardly surprising since there is an abundance of evidence to suggest that bullying has long-term, pervasive, and confounding negative effects (e.g., anxiety, depression, suicide) that last well into adulthood (Takizawa et al., 2014). In fact, there is a growing body of data to suggest that bullying may have long-term and permanent negative effects upon an individual's physiological reactivity to stress (Murray-Close, 2013; Ouellet-Morin et al., 2013). Suffice to say that if one's chemistry is altered by a bullying experience, then this social stressor is profoundly influential in the life course of an individual.

Stapinski and colleagues (2015) argue that peer victimization during adolescence may be particularly damaging. This is a time where youth increasingly seek autonomy from their parents and peers become even more important for one's social adjustment. Adolescents who are already anxious and/or may have less developed social skills may be particularly vulnerable to the impact of bullying. Thus, mistreatment by peers can be especially hurtful, increasing the individual's sense of isolation and reducing self-esteem. A critical self-referent attribution of the victimization can increase social withdrawal and lead to depressive symptoms in addition to anxiety (Prinstein et al., 2005).

Given the strong evidence supporting a connection between peer-victimization and anxiety, what bearing may this social influence have on the experience of existential anxiety? While speculative, a connection seems very likely and perhaps similar to that posited by Stolorow (2007) in his discussion of the impact that trauma and loss has on existential anxiety. For certain exposure to chronic and/or intense bullying can be conceptualized as a specific type of trauma. Not only can one's physical integrity and safety be threatened and/or harmed, but as discussed it can also lead to profound feelings of isolation and devaluation of one's self-worth. Therefore, perhaps as many as three existential concerns are activated as a result of a bullying experience. To begin, the existential concern of one's mortality and *being toward death* is stirred because the individual is enduring threats and harms, often on a chronic basis. One may understandably fear for their life if they are told they will be killed and/or are physically assaulted. Second, the existential awareness of one's fundamental aloneness and isolation in the world is triggered through the systematic isolation from others and devaluation that bullying entails. Finally, at a time when connection with peers seems so essential and meaningful to the individual, it is hardly a stretch to assume the isolated bully victim may come to question whether life truly has anything meaningful to offer. Thus, bullying is very likely a powerful factor that can increase existential anxiety in adolescent victims. In the absence of other support systems and appropriate intervention, these young victims may not be able to find the resources within themselves to successfully resolve an existential crisis stimulated by a peer-victimization experience, leading again to debilitating anxiety, depression, and increased risk of suicide.

Cultural/Contextual

Man-Made and Natural Disasters: There is considerable research on the impact of man-made and natural disasters. One study devoted to this research area examined the relationship between natural disasters and existential anxiety. Specifically, Scott and Weems (2013) investigated the relationship between natural disasters and existential anxiety in a sample of Gulf Coast adults who were exposed to Hurricane Katrina. They found that those residents who were more closely exposed to the effects of the disaster had significantly higher levels of existential anxiety than those who were not exposed to the disaster. The threat to one's existence, the senselessness of the event, the lack of control and predictability experienced when one is exposed to natural disasters may activate existential concerns related to meaninglessness, death, and even guilt. The relationship could also be bi-directional in that those individuals who experience elevated existential anxiety may be particularly vulnerable to exposure to natural disasters.

Beyond the research specific to existential anxiety, there are strong indications that exposure to man-made (e.g., terrorism) and natural disasters increases the risk for development of PTSD and other anxiety disorders in children and adolescents (Brown & Goodman, 2005; Brown et al., 2011; Priebe et al., 2011). Weems and colleagues (2007) note that pre-disaster emotional functioning and the amount of exposure to a disaster likely impacts whether a given individual will go on to experience long-term negative effects of a disaster. Trait anxiety and anxiety sensitivity may influence the likelihood of a child experiencing a long-term negative outcome (Hensley & Varela, 2008). Certainly familial factors also impact a youth's response to a disaster. For example, maternal overprotectiveness following a disaster may augment the child's trauma response and increase the likelihood of maladjustment (Bokszczanin, 2008). A parent's development of PTSD symptoms following exposure to a disaster independently predicts an adolescent's development of PTSD symptomatology as well (Polusny et al., 2011). Overall there are strong indications that, while the impact on a youth can be mediated by a host of factors, disasters strike at the core of existential concerns related to mortality, meaning, guilt, our fundamental aloneness, and limited controllability of our lives.

Societal Injustice and Group Membership Status: While there is admittedly a lack of empirical research in support of the proposed connection between societal injustice and group membership status with existential anxiety, at a minimum it seems necessary here to at least propose the influence of these factors. There are harmful societal factors that fall short of being labeled "disasters" that may still impact an adolescent's experience of existential anxiety. Racism, sexism, and other systemic marginalization and mistreatment of minority groups are a glaring example of this form of chronic macro-level trauma where nonmembership in the predominate group can lead to maladjustment (Williams & Mohammed., 2013). A lack of employment opportunity, the unaffordable nature of higher education, inequality in access to health care, and other critical services are additional examples of societal ills that potentially can impact an adolescent's development of debilitating existential anxiety. Exposure to these societal injustices can promote a worldview where life seems so arbitrary, unfair, and cruel that one's existence feels essentially meaningless.

Frankl (1969/1988) offers arguably the most cogent existential perspective on the impact of societal injustice on existential anxiety. He believed an individual's will to meaning is one of three essential pillars that forms the basis of his Logotherapy (the other two are freedom of will and the meaning of life). He argued that an individual experiences fulfillment when there is a sense of intentionality to his or her existence. Existential anxiety is mediated by a sense of purpose and direction. A misdirected focus on becoming self-actualized or happy will not achieve the desired ends. These experiences are the inevitable by-product of a life focus on pursuing meaning.

Frankl (1969/1988) spent a great deal of time discussing the negative impact that experiencing a frustrated will to meaning can have upon the individual. He noted that many young individuals in society live in an existential vacuum where there are (a) no clear answers as to what the individual should do to find meaning, and (b) a striking lack of opportunity or access to meaningful pursuits available to members of society. The youth who cannot find meaning in his or her existence or lacks access to potentially meaningful experiences will likely suffer from boredom, apathy, and neurosis. In addition, Frankl believed that a provisional and/or fatalistic attitude toward life, aggression, addiction, anxiety, and depression are often the symptoms of living in an existential vacuum where one experiences a frustrated will to meaning. van Deurzen (2012) points out that adolescents often become disillusioned with exploitation and disregard for human values. Here an argument is being put forth that simply bearing witness to societal failings can lead to existential angst. Ultimately, however, it is important to remember that Frankl (and most existential theorists) believed it is up to the individual to find meaning for themselves even under the harshest of conditions where society may not be affirming their inherent dignity and worth. In the case of the individual who witnesses and/or experiences societal injustice it just may be harder to do so.

Maercker and Horn (2013) appear to agree with this line of thinking. They have proposed a socio-personal perspective on the development and maintenance of PTSD. Their model accounts for distal social effects on the individual's trauma reactions that include such factors as a collectivist experience of a trauma and societal acknowledgment of injustice. In short, they argue that an individual who has the experience of "in-group" membership may be buffered against the negative impact of trauma. Those individuals who feel marginalized and who are the subject of discrimination will have a harder time coping with trauma.

In a related line of research, Yair (2014) suggests that cultural trauma can increase existential anxiety. In a theoretical paper he refers to the Israeli culture as experiencing elevated fears of annihilation due to the history of persecution and genocide experienced within their culture. More specifically, he argues that "narratives and stories about historical massacres coalesce with contemporary threats and future insecurities in creating existential Israeli anxiety" (pg. 349).

Conclusions

Existential anxiety seems to be intensely felt by many adolescents and a portion of individuals in this age range experience debilitating levels of this emotion and life concerns. This supports the contention by existential theorists that existential anxiety is a universal "given" of human existence. Further, a host of individual, familial, and societal factors appear to impact both the extent to which an adolescent will make contact with their existential anxiety *and* the extent to which an adolescent struggles to resolve the distress associated with the reflective awareness of existential concerns. The next chapter examines the protective factors that promote a successful resolution of existential anxiety during adolescence and introduces a developmental model of existential anxiety based upon an analysis of existing models of anxiety development and consideration of both risk and protective factors.

References

Ask, H., Waaktaar, T., Seglem, K. B., & Torgersen, S. (2016). Common etiological sources of anxiety, depression, and somatic complaints in adolescents: A multiple rater twin study. *Journal Of Abnormal Child Psychology, 44*(1), 101–114. doi:10.1007/s10802-015-9977-y

Ballash, N., Leyfer, O., Buckley, A. F., & Woodruff-Borden, J. (2006). Parental Control in the Etiology of Anxiety. *Clinical Child And Family Psychology Review, 9*(2), 113–133. doi:10.1007/s10567-006-0007-z

Bienvenu, O. J., Samuels, J. F., Costa, P. T., Reti, I. M., Eaton, W. W., & Nestadt, G. (2004). Anxiety and depressive disorders and the five-factor model of personality: A higher- and lower-order personality trait investigation in a community sample. *Depression And Anxiety, 20*(2), 92–97. doi:10.1002/da.20026

Benton, J. P., Christopher, A. N., & Walter, M. I. (2007). Death anxiety as a function of aging anxiety. *Death Studies, 31*(4), 337–350. doi:10.1080/07481180601187100

Berman, S. L., Weems, C. F., & Stickle, T. R. (2006). Existential Anxiety in Adolescents: Prevalence, Structure, Association with Psychological Symptoms and Identity Development. *Journal Of Youth And Adolescence, 35*(3), 303–310. doi:10.1007/s10964-006-9032-y

Bokszczanin, A. (2008). Parental support, family conflict, and overprotectiveness: Predicting PTSD symptom levels of adolescents 28 months after a natural disaster. *Anxiety, Stress & Coping: An International Journal, 21*(4), 325–335. doi:10.1080/10615800801950584

Boulter, C., Freeston, M., South, M., & Rodgers, J. (2014). Intolerance of uncertainty as a framework for understanding anxiety in children and adolescents with autism spectrum disorders. *Journal Of Autism And Developmental Disorders, 44*(6), 1391–1402. doi:10.1007/s10803-013-2001-x

Boyes, M. C., & Chandler, M. (1992). Cognitive development, epistemic doubt, and identity formation in adolescence. *Journal Of Youth And Adolescence, 21*(3), 277–304. doi:10.1007/BF01537019

Brassai, L., Piko, B. F., & Steger, M. F. (2012). Existential attitudes and Eastern European adolescents' problem and health behaviors: Highlighting the role of the search for meaning in life. *The Psychological Record, 62*(4), 719–734.

Brown, E. J., & Goodman, R. F. (2005). Childhood Traumatic Grief: An Exploration of the Construct in Children Bereaved on September 11. *Journal Of Clinical Child And Adolescent Psychology, 34*(2), 248–259. doi:10.1207/s15374424jccp3402_4

Brown, T. H., Mellman, T. A., Alfano, C. A., & Weems, C. F. (2011). Sleep fears, sleep disturbance, and PTSD symptoms in minority youth exposed to Hurricane Katrina. *Journal Of Traumatic Stress, 24*(5), 575–580.

Brown, R. C., Berenz, E. C., Aggen, S. H., Gardner, C. O., Knudsen, G. P., Reichborn- Kjennerud, T., &...Amstadter, A. B. (2014). Trauma exposure and Axis I psychopathology: A cotwin control analysis in Norwegian young adults. *Psychological Trauma: Theory, Research, Practice, And Policy, 6*(6), 652–660. doi:10.1037/a0034326

Buhr, K., & Dugas, M. J. (2009). The role of fear of anxiety and intolerance of uncertainty in worry: An experimental manipulation. *Behaviour Research And Therapy, 47*(3), 215–223. doi:10.1016/j.brat.2008.12.004

Carleton, R. N., Mulvogue, M. K., Thibodeau, M. A., McCabe, R. E., Antony, M. M., & Asmundson, G. G. (2012). Increasingly certain about uncertainty: Intolerance of uncertainty across anxiety and depression. *Journal Of Anxiety Disorders, 26*(3), 468–479. doi:10.1016/j.janxdis.2012.01.011

Chessick, R. D. (1996). Heidegger's 'authenticity' in the psychotherapy of adolescents. *American Journal Of Psychotherapy, 50*(2), 208–216.

Clark, L. A., & Watson, D. (1991). Tripartite model of anxiety and depression: Psychometric evidence and taxonomic implications. *Journal Of Abnormal Psychology, 100*, 316–336.

Colonnesi, C., Draijer, E. M., Jan J. M. Stams, G., Van der Bruggen, C. O., Bögels, S. M., & Noom, M. J. (2011). The relation between insecure attachment and child anxiety: A meta-analytic review. Journal Of Clinical Child And Adolescent Psychology, 40(4), 630–645. doi:10.1080/15374416.2011.581623

Côté, J. E. (1996). Sociological perspectives on identity formation: The culture–identity link and identity capital. *Journal Of Adolescence, 19*(5), 417–428. doi:10.1006/jado.1996.0040

Côté, J. E. (2009). Identity formation and self-development in adolescence. In R. M. Lerner, L. Steinberg (Eds.), *Handbook of adolescent psychology: Individual bases of adolescent development, Vol. 1*, 3rd *ed.* (pp. 266–304). Hoboken, NJ, US: John Wiley & Sons Inc.

Damon, W., Menon, J., & Bronk, K. C. (2003). The development of purpose during adolescence. *Applied Developmental Science, 7*(3), 119–128. doi:10.1207/S1532480XADS0703_2

Debats, D. L., Van der Lubbe, P. M., & Wezeman, F. R. (1993). On the psychometric properties of the Life Regard Index (LRI): A measure of meaningful life: An evaluation in three independent samples based on the Dutch version. *Personality And Individual Differences, 14*(2), 337–345. doi:10.1016/0191-8869(93)90132-M

Degnan, K. A., Almas, A. N., & Fox, N. A. (2010). Temperament and the environment in the etiology of childhood anxiety. *Journal Of Child Psychology And Psychiatry, 51*(4), 497–517. doi:10.1111/j.1469-7610.2010.02228.x

Derogatis, L. R., & Lazarus, L. (1994). SCL-90—R, Brief Symptom Inventory, and matching clinical rating scales. In M. E. Maruish, (Ed.), *The use of psychological testing for treatment planning and outcome assessment* (pp. 217–248). Hillsdale, NJ, US: Lawrence Erlbaum Associates, Inc.

Dong, Q., Yang, B., & Ollendick, T. H. (1994). Fears in Chinese children and adolescents and their relations to anxiety and depression. *Child Psychology & Psychiatry & Allied Disciplines, 35*(2), 351–363. doi:10.1111/j.1469-7610.1994.tb01167.x

Drake, K. L., & Ginsburg, G. S. (2012). Family factors in the development, treatment, and prevention of childhood anxiety disorders. *Clinical Child And Family Psychology Review, 15*(2), 144–162. doi:10.1007/s10567-011-0109-0

Dyk, P. H., & Adams, G. R. (1990). Identity and intimacy: An initial investigation of three theoretical models using cross-lag panel correlations. *Journal Of Youth And Adolescence, 19*(2), 91–110. doi:10.1007/BF01538715

El-Gabalawy, R., Mackenzie, C. S., Shooshtari, S., & Sareen, J. (2011). Comorbid physical health conditions and anxiety disorders: A population-based exploration of prevalence and health outcomes among older adults. *General Hospital Psychiatry, 33*(6), 556–564. doi:10.1016/j.genhosppsych.2011.07.005

Ellsworth, J. (1999). Today's adolescent: Addressing existential dread. *Adolescence, 34*(134), 403–408.

Erikson, E. H. (1959). Identity and the life cycle: Selected papers. *Psychological Issues*, 11–171.

Erikson, E. H. (1963). The Golden Rule and the cycle of life. In R. W. White (Ed.), *The study of lives: Essays on personality in honor of Henry A. Murray* (pp. 412–428). New York, NY, US: Atherton Press. doi:10.1037/12238-018

Eussen, M. M., Van Gool, A. R., Verheij, F., De Nijs, P. A., Verhulst, F. C., & Greaves-Lord, K. (2013). The association of quality of social relations, symptom severity and intelligence with anxiety in children with autism spectrum disorders. *Autism, 17*(6), 723–735. doi:10.1177/1362361312453882

Fitzgerald, B. (2005). An existential view of adolescent development. *Adolescence, 40*(160), 793–799.

Flensborg-Madsen, T., Tolstrup, J., Sørensen, H. J., & Mortensen, E. L. (2012). Social and psychological predictors of onset of anxiety disorders: Results from a large prospective cohort study. *Social Psychiatry And Psychiatric Epidemiology, 47*(5), 711–721. doi:10.1007/s00127-011-0373-9

Fox, N. A., Henderson, H. A., Marshall, P. J., Nichols, K. E., & Ghera, M. M. (2005). Behavioral Inhibition: Linking Biology and Behavior within a Developmental Framework. *Annual Review Of Psychology, 56*235–262. doi:10.1146/annurev.psych.55.090902.141532

Frankl, V. (1963). *Man's search for meaning: an introduction to logotherapy.* Oxford, England: Washington Square Press.

Frankl, V. E. (1965). The concept of man in logotherapy. *Journal Of Existentialism, 6*(21), 53–58.

Frankl, V. E. (1969). *The will to meaning: Principles and application of logotherapy.* New York: World.

Gregory, A. M., & Eley, T. C. (2007). Genetic influences on anxiety in children: What we've learned and where we're heading. *Clinical Child And Family Psychology Review, 10*(3), 199–212. doi:10.1007/s10567-007-0022-8

Hacker, D. J. (1994). An existential view of adolescence. *The Journal Of Early Adolescence, 14*(3), 300–327. doi:10.1177/0272431694014003001

Hawker, D. J., & Boulton, M. J. (2000). Twenty years' research on peer victimization and psychosocial maladjustment: A meta-analytic review of cross-sectional studies. *Journal Of Child Psychology And Psychiatry, 41*(4), 441–455. doi:10.1111/1469-7610.00629

Heidegger, M. (1927). *Sein und Zeit.* Gesamtausgabe Volume 2. [trans. by John Macquarrie and Edward Robinson (London: SCM Press, 1962)]

Hensley, L., & Varela, R. E. (2008). PTSD symptoms and somatic complaints following Hurricane Katrina: The roles of trait anxiety and anxiety sensitivity. *Journal Of Clinical Child And Adolescent Psychology, 37*(3), 542–552. doi:10.1080/15374410802148186

Hobfoll, S. E., & Leiberman, J. R. (1987). Personality and social resources in immediate and continued stress resistance among women. *Journal Of Personality And Social Psychology, 52*(1), 18–26. doi:10.1037/0022-3514.52.1.18

Hollis, J. (2013). *Hauntings: dispelling the ghosts who run our lives.* Asheville, NC: Chiron Publications.

Hovens, J. M., Giltay, E. J., Wiersma, J. E., Spinhoven, P., Penninx, B. H., & Zitman, F. G. (2012). Impact of childhood life events and trauma on the course of depressive and anxiety disorders. *Acta Psychiatrica Scandinavica, 126*(3), 198–207. doi:10.1111/j.1600-0447.2011.01828.x

Hudson, J. L., & Dodd, H. F. (2012). Informing early intervention: Preschool predictors of anxiety disorders in middle childhood. *Plos ONE, 7*(8). doi:10.1371/journal.pone.0042359

Ingman, K. A., Ollendick, T. H., & Akande, A. (1999). Cross-cultural aspects of fears in African children and adolescents. *Behaviour Research And Therapy, 37*(4), 337–345. doi:10.1016/S0005-7967(98)00108-9

Kagan, J., & Snidman, N. (1999). Early childhood predictors of adult anxiety disorders. *Biological Psychiatry*, *46*(11), 1536–1541. doi:10.1016/S0006-3223(99)00137-7

Kidwell, J. S., Dunham, R. M., Bacho, R. A., Pastorino, E., & Portes, P. R. (1995). Adolescent identity exploration: A test of Erikson's theory of transitional crisis. *Adolescence*, *30*(120), 785–793.

Klackl, J., Jonas, E., & Kronbichler, M. (2014). Existential neuroscience: Self-esteem moderates neuronal responses to mortality-related stimuli. *Social Cognitive And Affective Neuroscience*, *9*(11), 1754–1761. doi:10.1093/scan/nst167

Koenen, K. C., Moffitt, T. E., Roberts, A. L., Martin, L. T., Kubzansky, L., Harrington, H., &... Caspi, A. (2009). Childhood IQ and adult mental disorders: A test of the cognitive reserve hypothesis. *The American Journal Of Psychiatry*, *166*(1), 50–57. doi:10.1176/appi.ajp.2008.08030343

Kroger, J. (2003). Identity development during adolescence. In G. R. Adams, M. D. Berzonsky, (Eds.), *Blackwell handbook of adolescence* (pp. 205–226). Malden: Blackwell Publishing.

Laugesen, N., Dugas, M. J., & Bukowski, W. M. (2003). Understanding Adolescent Worry: The Application of a Cognitive Model. *Journal Of Abnormal Child Psychology*, *31*(1), 55–64. doi:10.1023/A:1021721332181

Lizeretti, N. P., & Extremera, N. (2011). Emotional intelligence and clinical symptoms in outpatients with generalized anxiety disorder (GAD). *Psychiatric Quarterly*, *82*(3), 253–260. doi:10.1007/s11126-011-9167-1

Maercker, A., & Horn, A. B. (2013). A socio-interpersonal perspective on PTSD: The case for environments and interpersonal processes. *Clinical Psychology & Psychotherapy*, *20*(6), 465–481. doi:10.1002/cpp.1805

Maniglio, R. (2013). Child sexual abuse in the etiology of anxiety disorders: A systematic review of reviews. *Trauma, Violence, & Abuse*, *14*(2), 96–112. doi:10.1177/1524838012470032

Mann, M., Hosman, C. H., Schaalma, H. P., & de Vries, N. K. (2004). Self-esteem in a broad- spectrum approach for mental health promotion. *Health Education Research*, *19*(4), 357–372. doi:10.1093/her/cyg041

Marcia, J. E. (1993). The relational roots of identity. In J. Kroger, (Ed.), *Discussions on ego identity* (pp. 101–120). Hillsdale, NJ, US: Lawrence Erlbaum Associates, Inc.

Martens, A., Goldenberg, J. L., & Greenberg, J. (2005). A Terror Management Perspective on Ageism. *Journal Of Social Issues*, *61*(2), 223–239. doi:10.1111/j.1540-4560.2005.00403.x

May, R. (1950). *The meaning of anxiety*. New York, NY, US: Ronald Press Company. doi:10.1037/10760-000

May, R. (1977). *The meaning of anxiety*., Rev. *ed*. New York, NY, US: W W Norton & Co.

McEvoy, P. M., & Mahoney, A. E. (2012). To be sure, to be sure: Intolerance of uncertainty mediates symptoms of various anxiety disorders and depression. *Behavior Therapy, 43*(3), 533–545. doi:10.1016/j.beth.2011.02.007

Meeus, W. (1996). Studies on identity development in adolescence: An overview of research and some new data. *Journal Of Youth And Adolescence, 25*(5), 569–598. doi:10.1007/BF01537355

Meeus, W., Iedema, J., Helsen, M., & Vollebergh, W. (1999). Patterns of adolescent identity development: Review of literature and longitudinal analysis. *Developmental Review, 19*(4), 419–461. doi:10.1006/drev.1999.0483

Mineka, S., & Zinbarg, R. (2006). A contemporary learning theory perspective on the etiology of anxiety disorders: It's not what you thought it was. *American Psychologist, 61*(1), 10–26. doi:10.1037/0003-066X.61.1.10

Murray-Close, D. (2013). Psychophysiology of adolescent peer relations I: Theory and research findings. *Journal Of Research On Adolescence, 23*(2), 236–259. doi:10.1111/j.1532-7795.2012.00828.x

Ojala, M. (2005). Adolescents' Worries about Environmental Risks: Subjective Well-being, Values, and Existential Dimensions. *Journal Of Youth Studies, 8*(3), 331–347. doi:10.1080/13676260500261934

Ollendick, T. H., Matson, J. L., & Helsel, W. J. (1985). Fears in children and adolescents: Normative data. *Behaviour Research And Therapy, 23*(4), 465–467. doi:10.1016/0005-7967(85)90174-3

Ollendick, T. H., Yule, W., & Ollier, K. (1991). Fears in British children and their relationship to manifest anxiety and depression. *Child Psychology & Psychiatry & Allied Disciplines, 32*(2), 321–331. doi:10.1111/j.1469-7610.1991.tb00310.x

Ollendick, T. H., Yang, B., King, N. J., Dong, Q., & Akande, A. (1996). Fears in American, Australian, Chinese, and Nigerian children and adolescents: A cross-cultural study. *Child Psychology & Psychiatry & Allied Disciplines, 37*(2), 213–220. doi:10.1111/j.1469-7610.1996.tb01393.x

Ollendick, T. H., Langley, A. K., Jones, R. T., & Kephart, C. (2001). Fear in children and adolescents: Relations with negative life events, attributional style, and avoidant coping. *Journal Of Child Psychology And Psychiatry, 42*(8), 1029–1034. doi:10.1111/1469-7610.00801

Ouellet-Morin, I., Wong, C. Y., Danese, A., Pariante, C. M., Papadopoulos, A. S., Mill, J., & Arseneault, L. (2013). Increased serotonin transporter gene (SERT) DNA methylation is associated with bullying victimization and blunted Cortisol response to stress in childhood: A longitudinal study of discordant monozygotic twins. *Psychological Medicine, 43*(9), 1813–1823. doi:10.1017/S0033291712002784

Phillips, N. K., Hammen, C. L., Brennan, P. A., Najman, J. M., & Bor, W. (2005). Early Adversity and the Prospective Prediction of Depressive and Anxiety Disorders in Adolescents. *Journal Of Abnormal Child Psychology, 33*(1), 13–24. doi:10.1007/s10802-005-0930-3

Polusny, M. A., Ries, B. J., Meis, L. A., DeGarmo, D., McCormick-Deaton, C. M., Thuras, P., & Erbes, C. R. (2011). Effects of parents' experiential avoidance and PTSD on adolescent disaster-related posttraumatic stress symptomatology. *Journal Of Family Psychology, 25*(2), 220–229. doi:10.1037/a0022945

Priebe, S., Marchi, F., Bini, L., Flego, M., Costa, A., & Galeazzi, G. (2011). Mental disorders, psychological symptoms and quality of life 8 years after an earthquake: Findings from a community sample in Italy. *Social Psychiatry And Psychiatric Epidemiology, 46*(7), 615–621. doi:10.1007/s00127-010-0227-x

Prinstein, M. J., Cheah, C. L., & Guyer, A. E. (2005). Peer Victimization, Cue Interpretation, and Internalizing Symptoms: Preliminary Concurrent and Longitudinal Findings for Children and Adolescents. *Journal Of Clinical Child And Adolescent Psychology, 34*(1), 11–24. doi:10.1207/s15374424jccp3401_2

Rank, O. (1936). *Will therapy. An analysis of the therapeutic process in terms of relationship*. Oxford, England: Knopf.

Rector, N. A., Bagby, R. M., Huta, V., & Ayearst, L. E. (2012). Examination of the trait facets of the five-factor model in discriminating specific mood and anxiety disorders. *Psychiatry Research, 199*(2), 131–139. doi:10.1016/j.psychres.2012.04.027

Rice, F., & Thapar, A. (2009). Depression and anxiety in childhood and adolescence: Developmental pathways, genes and environment. In Y. Kim, (Ed.), *Handbook of behavior genetics* (pp. 379–396). New York, NY, US: Springer Science + Business Media. doi:10.1007/978-0-387-76727-7_26

Rosenfield, S., Lennon, M. C., & White, H. R. (2005). The self and mental health: Self-salience and the emergence of internalizing and externalizing problems. *Journal Of Health And Social Behavior, 46*(4), 323–340. doi:10.1177/002214650504600402

Schwartz, S. H. (1992). Universals in the content and structure of values: Theoretical advances and empirical tests in 20 countries. In M. P. Zanna, (Ed.), *Advances in experimental social psychology, Vol. 25* (pp. 1–65). San Diego, CA, US: Academic Press. doi:10.1016/S0065-2601(08)60281-6

Scott, B. G., & Weems, C. F. (2013). Natural disasters and existential concerns: A test of Tillich's theory of existential anxiety. *Journal Of Humanistic Psychology, 53*(1), 114–128. doi:10.1177/0022167812449190

Shaffer, J. B. (1978). *Humanistic psychology*. New Jersey: Prentice-Hall.

Shearer, C. B. (2006). Development and validation of a scale for existential thinking. *Unpublished manuscript. Kent State University, OH.*

Shumaker, D. (2012). An existential–integrative treatment of anxious and depressed adolescents. *Journal Of Humanistic Psychology, 52*(4), 375–400. doi:10.1177/0022167811422947

Shumaker, D., Killian, K., Cole, C., Hruby, A., & Grimm, J. (in press). Existential anxiety, personality type, and therapy preference in young adults. *Journal of Humanistic Psychology.*

Simonÿ, C. P., Pedersen, B. D., Dreyer, P., & Birkelund, R. (2015). Dealing with existential anxiety in exercise-based cardiac rehabilitation: A phenomenological-hermeneutic study of patients' lived experiences. *Journal Of Clinical Nursing, 24*(17–18), 2581–2590. doi:10.1111/jocn.12867

Stapinski, L. A., Araya, R., Heron, J., Montgomery, A. A., & Stallard, P. (2015). Peer victimization during adolescence: Concurrent and prospective impact on symptoms of depression and anxiety. *Anxiety, Stress & Coping: An International Journal, 28*(1), 105–120. doi:10.1080/10615806.2014.962023

Steger, M. F., Frazier, P., Oishi, S., & Kaler, M. (2006). The meaning in life questionnaire: Assessing the presence of and search for meaning in life. *Journal Of Counseling Psychology, 53*(1), 80–93. doi:10.1037/0022-0167.53.1.80

Steger, M. F., Fitch-Martin, A. R., Donnelly, J., & Rickard, K. M. (2015). Meaning in life and health: Proactive health orientation links meaning in life to health variables among American undergraduates. *Journal Of Happiness Studies, 16*(3), 583–597. doi:10.1007/s10902-014-9523-6

Stein, M. B., Jang, K. L., & Livesley, W. J. (1999). Heritability of anxiety sensitivity: A twin study. *The American Journal Of Psychiatry, 156*(2), 246–251.

Stolorow, R. D. (2007). Anxiety, authenticity, and trauma: The relevance of Heidegger's existential analytic for psychoanalysis. *Psychoanalytic Psychology, 24*(2), 373–383. doi:10.1037/0736-9735.24.2.373

Sukhodolsky, D. G., do Rosario-Campos, M. C., Scahill, L., Katsovich, L., Pauls, D. L., Peterson, B. S., &... Leckman, J. F. (2005). Adaptive, Emotional, and Family Functioning of Children With Obsessive-Compulsive Disorder and Comorbid Attention Deficit Hyperactivity Disorder. *The American Journal Of Psychiatry, 162*(6), 1125–1132. doi:10.1176/appi.ajp.162.6.1125

Summerfeldt, L. J., Kloosterman, P. H., Antony, M. M., McCabe, R. E., & Parker, J. A. (2011). Emotional intelligence in social phobia and other anxiety disorders. *Journal Of Psychopathology And Behavioral Assessment, 33*(1), 69–78. doi:10.1007/s10862-010-9199-0

Takizawa, R., Maughan, B., & Arseneault, L. (2014). Adult health outcomes of childhood bullying victimization: Evidence from a five-decade longitudinal British birth cohort. *The American Journal Of Psychiatry, 171*(7), 777–784. doi:10.1176/appi.ajp.2014.13101401

Tillich, P. (1952). Anxiety, religion, and medicine. *Pastoral Psychology, 3*11–17. doi:10.1007/BF01769082

Ţincaş, I., Benga, O., & Fox, N. A. (2006). Temperamental predictors of anxiety disorders. *Cogniţie Creier Comportament, 10*(4), 489–515.

Turner, S. M., Beidel, D. C., & Costello, A. (1987). Psychopathology in the offspring of anxiety disorders patients. *Journal Of Consulting And Clinical Psychology*, *55*(2), 229–235. doi:10.1037/0022-006X.55.2.229

van Deurzen, E. (2012). Reasons for living: Existential therapy and spirituality. In L. Barnett, G. Madison, (Eds.), *Existential therapy: Legacy, vibrancy and dialogue* (pp. 171–182). New York, NY, US: Routledge/Taylor & Francis Group.

van Steensel, F. J., Bögels, S., & Dirksen, C. (2012). Anxiety and quality of life: Clinically anxious children with and without autism spectrum disorders compared. *Journal Of Clinical Child And Adolescent Psychology*, *41*(6), 731–738. doi:10.1080/15374416.2012.698725

Vreeke, L. J., & Muris, P. (2012). Relations between behavioral inhibition, Big Five personality factors, and anxiety disorder symptoms in non-clinical and clinically anxious children. *Child Psychiatry and Human Development*, *43*(6), 884–894. doi:10.1007/s10578-012-0302-5

Warren, S. L., Huston, L., Egeland, B., & Sroufe, L. A. (1997). Child and adolescent anxiety disorders and early attachment. *Journal Of The American Academy Of Child & Adolescent Psychiatry*, *36*(5), 637–644. doi:10.1097/00004583-199705000-00014

Weems, C. F., Costa, N. M., Dehon, C., & Berman, S. L. (2004). Paul Tillich's theory of existential anxiety: A preliminary conceptual and empirical examination. *Anxiety, Stress & Coping: An International Journal*, *17*(4), 383–399. doi:10.1080/10615800412331318616

Weems, C. F., Pina, A. A., Costa, N. M., Watts, S. E., Taylor, L. K., & Cannon, M. F. (2007). Predisaster trait anxiety and negative affect predict posttraumatic stress in youths after Hurricane Katrina. *Journal Of Consulting And Clinical Psychology*, *75*(1), 154–159. doi:10.1037/0022-006X.75.1.154

White, S. W., & Roberson-Nay, R. (2009). Anxiety, social deficits, and loneliness in youth with autism spectrum disorders. *Journal Of Autism And Developmental Disorders*, *39*(7), 1006–1013. doi:10.1007/s10803-009-0713-8

Wichstrøm, L., Belsky, J., & Berg-Nielsen, T. S. (2013). Preschool predictors of childhood anxiety disorders: A prospective community study. *Journal Of Child Psychology And Psychiatry*, *54*(12), 1327–1336. doi:10.1111/jcpp.12116

Williams, D. R., & Mohammed, S. A. (2013). Racism and health I: Pathways and scientific evidence. *American Behavioral Scientist*, *57*(8), 1152–1173. doi:10.1177/0002764213487340

Winston, C. N., Sumathi, D., & Maher, H. (2013). Existential inquiries and pathological correlates among Indian adolescents. *Psychology Of Religion And Spirituality*, *5*(4), 263–271. doi:10.1037/a0032643

Witwer, A. N., & Lecavalier, L. (2010). Validity of comorbid psychiatric disorders in youngsters with autism spectrum disorders. *Journal Of Developmental And Physical Disabilities*, *22*(4), 367–380. doi:10.1007/s10882-010-9194-0

Wood, J. J., McLeod, B. D., Sigman, M., Hwang, W., & Chu, B. C. (2003). Parenting and childhood anxiety: Theory, empirical findings, and future directions. *Journal Of Child Psychology And Psychiatry, 44*(1), 134–151. doi:10.1111/1469-7610.00106

Yair, G. (2014). Israeli existential anxiety: Cultural trauma and the constitution of national character. *Social Identities: Journal For The Study Of Race, Nation And Culture, 20*(4–5), 346–362. doi:10.1080/13504630.2014.1002390

Yalom, I. D. (1980). *Existential psychotherapy.* New York, NY, US: Basic Books.

CHAPTER 3

A Developmental Model of Existential Anxiety During Adolescence

Introduction

The previous chapter established that existential anxiety is a critical component of adolescent emotional development and that the degree of acuity, distress, and debilitation caused by existential anxiety during adolescence appears to be mediated by several individual, familial, and sociocultural risk factors. Utilizing the same data sources (i.e., the research on existential anxiety and DSM anxiety disorders) as well as research on resilience, this chapter first discusses protective factors that may mitigate the level of distress and/or impairment an adolescent will experience when they make contact with existential questions, concerns, and anxiety. The term "resilience" encapsulates multiple protective factors including personal dispositions, family cohesion, and personal resources outside of one's family (Gamerzy, 1993; Werner, 1993). Rutter (2006) defines it broadly as reduced vulnerability to environmental stressors, the ability to overcome adversity, and/or positive outcomes in the face of increased adversity. Adolescents who demonstrate higher levels of resilience are less likely to develop anxiety and depressive symptoms (Hjemdal et al., 2011). It follows that these same individuals may be better equipped to resolve existential concerns and crises. Following the discussion of possible protective factors, the author proposes a developmental model of existential anxiety that will hopefully guide future research on this topic and assist clinicians who work with adolescents in their efforts to both assess and treat existential anxiety.

D. Shumaker, *Existential-Integrative Approaches to Treating Adolescents*, DOI 10.1057/978-1-349-95211-3_3

What Are the Protective Factors That May Reduce the Risk for Experiencing Debilitating Existential Anxiety?

A survey of theoretical discussions and research uncovers several possible protective factors that likely play a role in promoting a successful resolution to an adolescent's experience of existential anxiety. To be clear, given that existential anxiety is likely a universal and normative aspect of human functioning, successful adolescent socio-emotional development is not defined by avoidance of existential anxiety. Rather it is how the adolescent copes with this type of anxiety and resolves the existential questions that form the basis of this emotional experience that distinguishes adjustment from maladjustment. Rank, Tillich, May, and other prominent existential theorists have argued that the ability to channel existential anxiety into energy for creative pursuits and a worldview that emphasizes a zest for life and deeper appreciation for the given day are indicators of a healthy response to the experience of existential anxiety. Similarly Frankl believed individuals who embrace the pursuit of meaning even in the face of great odds or invalidation by society are more likely to resolve existential concerns and angst. But what aspects of the individual, his or her family, and society facilitate and support the young person in meeting the burden of responsibility of facing life head-on, with a sense of urgency and solemn responsibility? The list of protective factors introduced below arguably plays important roles in promoting these forms of adaptive coping. Most of the protective factors appear to occur at the individual level of functioning, but familial and sociocultural-level protective factors likely do exist and will be suggested here as well.

Genetic/Biological

As indicated in the prior chapter there are no peer-reviewed empirical studies that investigate a genetic or biological basis of existential anxiety. Not surprisingly, there is also a notable absence of studies that examine whether there is a genetic or biological basis for the development of protective factors that promote the successful resolution of existential concerns and/or reduce the risk of an individual experiencing debilitating existential anxiety. One notable exception exists however. Klackl and colleagues (2014) have investigated the biological mediators of death anxiety and their study will be discussed in some detail below.

Given the relative lack of information on biological protective factors that reduce debilitating existential anxiety what remains are the clues provided by research on the genetic and biological bases of resilience. Here there are strong suggestions of a link between biology and resilience. For example, research suggests the genetic factors that influence resilience may account for as much as 61% of the heritability of generalized anxiety disorder (GAD) (Amstadter et al., 2016). However, biologically focused studies of resilience cover such a broad array, including studies of genomes, neuroendocrinology, immunology, emotion, and neural plasticity, that this research domain has not surprisingly lacked a unifying theoretical framework to guide investigators (Curtis & Cicchetti, 2003). Given this broad and convoluted landscape it is not possible to discuss in detail all of the potential biological and genetic linkages to resilience within the scope of our brief overview. Some of the more prominently cited biological links, however, are introduced briefly here.

At a most foundational level, Caspi and colleagues (2003) believe that the serotonin transporter promoter gene may be implicated in the development of resilience. Rutter (2012) provides an insightful review of the research on this gene and resilience, concluding that there is sufficient evidence suggesting such a connection exists. In addition, Porges (2003) and Calkins and colleagues (2007) argue that the development of one's parasympathetic nervous system is a critical factor in the regulation of motor activity and emotion. They argue individual differences in emotional regulation and expression may be important factors that support social engagement and social functioning. Thus, individuals endowed with a more sophisticated parasympathetic nervous system may be protected against the development of a host of internalizing symptomatology, including anxiety.

Curtis and Cicchetti (2003) also highlight the roles that neural plasticity and advanced cognitive processing abilities have in the development of resilience. These connections make obvious conceptual sense. Intelligence can mitigate environmental and biological challenges to the adolescent's mental health functioning and overall adjustment. In the specific case of an adolescent who experiences existential concerns, the ability to process existential questions at a deeper level of sophistication and the ability to utilize that same intellectual power to pursue adaptive resolutions to these questions can only be enhanced by possessing advanced cognitive abilities. As advances in medical science allow for more specific investigations into the neural basis of emotion and emotion regulation *and* as the biological-environmental interactions that occur within the life course of an individual are more adequately understood, the story of resilience at the genetic and neural level will surely become clearer.

In addition to examining the role of specific genes, neural development, and the nervous system, biologically focused research has also studied the relationship between temperament and resilience. Kim-Cohen and colleagues (2004), for example, have suggested that children who have an "outgoing" temperament are more likely to remain positively adjusted in the face of deprivation and hardship. Children with outgoing temperaments approach novelty eagerly and with confidence. They are seen by others as good-natured and sociable. While highly speculative, individuals who possess this temperament may be able to resolve existential concerns more quickly and with less distress because they embrace novelty (e.g., thoughts about the meaning of one's life, increased awareness of one's mortality) and possess the confidence that they will successfully resolve even the toughest of tasks.

In a related line of research, Penela and colleagues (2015) suggest that engaged emotional regulation strategies may mitigate the negative effects of BI in the development of psychological problems. Emotional regulation refers to the ways in which an individual attends to and controls their emotional reactions. Research suggests three basic emotional regulation strategies: active, passive, and disruptive. Engaged strategies are defined as increased use of active strategies and decreased used of passive strategies. Penela and colleagues (2015) found that children who demonstrated engaged emotional regulation strategies at a young age demonstrated higher levels of social competence at a later stage of development. As previously indicated social competence is a major predictor of resiliency. Again, though highly speculative, it may be the children and adolescents who actively engage in a positive manner with the uncomfortable emotions associated with existential anxiety are more likely to find a resolution in the form of adaptive emotional coping strategies and/or a philosophical outlook that leads to less distress and positive adjustment.

Additional biologically based traits have been identified as potential predictors of resiliency. For example, Boardman and colleagues (2008) have suggested that resiliency is linked to an elevated sense of self-acceptance and a higher degree of environmental mastery. Returning focus to our discussion of existential anxiety it makes conceptual sense that an adolescent who posits tough existential questions and/or experiences existential anxiety will navigate these uncomfortable cognitions and emotions in a more adaptive manner if he or she possesses a positive self-concept and problem-solving skills. This postulate seems to have some empirical backing. Specifically, Klackl and colleagues (2014) have conducted neuroimaging research on the relationship between self-esteem and death anxiety. High self-esteem has been shown to have buffering effects against anxiety. For certain individuals higher in self-esteem tend to be happier and cope better in the face of adversity (Hobfoll & Leiberman, 1987). One hypothesis that explains why high self-esteem individuals may experience less anxiety about death is because "they are temporarily able to down-regulate the intensity of their emotional experience or even a more general form of awareness" through decreased activation in the bilateral insula region of their brains (Klackl, 2014, pg. 1754). In other words, high self-esteem individuals may be able to grapple with death cues in a manner that shifts focus away from the self quickly and effectively. This hypothesis was supported in the (Klackl et al. 2014) study, providing tangible evidence of a brain function that mediates interoceptive awareness and, in the case of individuals with a strong sense of self-esteem, may help them more adaptively process death fears.

In summary, the research on the biological and genetic bases of resilience is broad and rapidly advancing. While most would agree that biological factors contribute to the development of resiliency, there are no studies that directly examine the relationship between biological protective factors that mitigate the distress associated with existential anxiety and/or that promote the successful resolution of existential concerns. We are left to speculate that engaged emotional regulation strategies, an outgoing temperament, advanced cognitive abilities, elevated self-esteem, and other potential biologically based traits may help adolescents better weather the storm and stress of existential angst.

Psychological/Individual Factors

While there are several individual psychological factors that likely protect an adolescent from experiencing debilitating existential anxiety, none has been more discussed and researched than the POM (presence of meaning) in the individual's life. Frankl (1963; 1986) argued that the question of what has meaning in one's life is most pressing during adolescence but that the will to meaning is a fundamental component of human existence at virtually all life stages. In this respect an "adolescent's preoccupation with this question is not a morbid symptom," but rather a naturally occurring phenomenon that is heightened during this stage of development and could be addressed in a therapeutic setting (Frankl, 1986). He argued existential therapy was particularly well suited to address the question of meaning, offering the client an opportunity to better comprehend his or her responsibility for identifying and completing one's task(s) of life. In addition, he believed that there is not a universal meaning to life that is shared by all. Rather each individual is unique, faces a singular context that impacts his or her options, and is further bound by time constraints – all of which combine to make it virtually impossible for any two individuals to identify the exact same meaning. The individual who ultimately understands what life asks of him or her stands the best chance of realizing potential and living a fulfilled existence. It is not surprising therefore that having a sense of purpose in life has been identified by Rutten and colleagues (2013) as a key component of resilience. Nor is it surprising that Frankl believed individuals lacking in a sense of meaning tend to suffer. This hypothesis has been borne out by research efforts that have found those lacking in meaning are at greater risk for anxiety and depression (Debats et al., 1993), as well as substance abuse and suicidal ideation (Harlow, Newcomb & Bentler, 1986).

In more recent times Steger and colleagues (2006; 2009) have researched how meaning impacts human functioning. The authors first developed the meaning in life questionnaire (MLQ), a 10-item self-report measure scored on a Likert scale designed to assess both the presence of meaning (POM) and search for meaning (SFM) in one's life (Steger et al., 2006). In their initial series of investigations they demonstrated the sound psychometric properties of the MLQ and found that greater POM levels seemed to be associated with better adjustment. In a follow-up study conducted with a sample of adults who were attempting to stop smoking, they found "POM seemed to buffer the deleterious relation between SFM and health and anxiety" (Steger et al., 2009, pg. 357). These findings provide additional support for the premise that individuals who are both searching for and lacking in meaning may experience the greatest health-related risks and distress.

In a related line of inquiry, Ojala (2005) studied the relationships between values, meaning, existential anxiety, and well-being in a sample of adolescents. The author noted that the emergence of values is a key aspect of adolescent development and can help define a sense of identity and purpose to one's existence. When one's core values are threatened, existential anxiety could increase and well-being could suffer. But Ojala (2005) cogently noted that this outcome was not necessarily predetermined. Rather, if an adolescent contemplated existential worries in a productive manner the individual could develop a deeper sense of "existential meaning" that could mitigate distress and maladjustment. Specifically, the author argued, "the person has to be able to interpret, process, and link stimulus and values together to create a meaningful integrated whole; otherwise a reduced sense of well-being will occur" (Ojala, 2005, pg. 335). The study results ultimately confirmed this premise. Specifically, two subgroups of adolescents were identified as experiencing a high degree of worry about an existential concern. One subgroup, characterized by higher levels of meaningfulness, hope, and anger, reported enhanced well-being. The second group (high worries and lower well-being) demonstrated lower levels of the same characteristics (i.e., a sense of meaningfulness, hope, and anger). In essence, it is how the adolescent processes the existential worry, as opposed to merely experiencing the worry, that seems to predict well-being. As Ojala (2005) states, "existential dimensions such as experienced meaningfulness and emotions with different appraisal patterns than worry could function as buffers preventing strong existential worry" (pg. 342).

Adolescents who develop a coherent and stable sense of identity may be further protected when existential anxiety is experienced. Identity formation, or lack thereof, was previously conceptualized as a possible risk factor in the experience of debilitating existential anxiety. For certain, Erikson (1959; 1968) identified the establishment of a clear sense of identity as a chief task of adolescence. As also noted in the prior chapter, the specific challenge adolescents experience has been referred to as the identity versus role confusion stage of development and was thought to occur between the ages of 12 to 18 years. Individuals during this stage of life entered into a moral-ideological phase of development where new ideas, idealism, and a sense of fidelity begin to dominate moral thinking (Hoare, 2009). Advances in abstract reasoning during these years facilitate a deeper contemplation of one's future prospects as well as critical thinking about parental and societal shortcomings. Many specific existential questions that one contemplates during this stage of development are also likely related to one's identity (Adamson et al., 1999).

Erikson (1968) also deeply appreciated the burdens adolescents face in assuming the responsibilities of adulthood, noting that mental health problems and maladjustment may be symptomatic of this struggle. Successful resolution of the identity versus role confusion stage was characterized by the individual emerging into young adulthood with a clear and stable sense of identity, a strong prosocial orientation, and a sense of fidelity to a cause, task, and/or belief system. Here an association between meaning and identity occurs. Specifically, a sense of meaning can help inform one's identity. Greater ego stability may, in turn, lead to greater perseverance, clarity, and focus on meaningful pursuits. The result of this reciprocal feedback loop would be an adolescent who more successfully manages existential anxiety and concerns. As discussed in the previous chapter, empirical analyses of the Eriksonian paradigm have generated strong support for these premises. Specifically, individuals who fall within the identity achievement (post-crisis-producing choices, high commitment) classification tend to engage in more mature interpersonal relationships (Dyk & Adams, 1990; Kroger, 2003), demonstrate balanced thinking (Boyes and Chandler, 1992), and possess higher levels of personal agency (Cote, 1996). Having a clear sense of identity therefore seems to protect the individual from maladjustment and existential anxiety (Berman et al., 2006).

More recently, Chen and colleagues (2012) examined identity formation and resilience in a small sample of diverse adolescents. Echoing the sentiments of Erikson, the authors noted that "well-shaped identities guide individuals who act according to their beliefs about who they are as persons and how they might behave under particular circumstances" (Chen et al., 2012, pg. 762). Utilizing a sociocultural ethnographic case study research approach the authors found that the development of adaptive self-identity helped the study participants navigate several life challenges they were facing. In short, having a clear and stable sense of identity seems to serve as a protective factor when existential questions and anxiety is experienced.

Having established that a sense of meaning and coherent identity appears to be protective factors that mitigate the experience of debilitating existential anxiety, our focus shifts to the research Davis and colleagues (2003) have conducted that examines the relationship between spirituality and anxiety in a group of at-risk adolescents. The authors found that those participants who reported higher levels of spirituality and religiosity demonstrated greater levels of existential well-being. In turn, higher levels of existential well-being were associated with lower levels of trait anxiety. The authors emphasized however that the content of one's religious belief determines whether or not existential anxiety is reduced. Specifically, religious beliefs that help the individual find purpose and meaning to his or her existence can alleviate anxiety while religious beliefs that ring hollow to the individual or seem abstract may have no impact. Thus, even in the case of spirituality there remains a strong connection with meaning.

Two final individual factors – humility and shame – may serve as protective factors that reduce the likelihood of the adolescent experiencing debilitating existential anxiety. Each is touched upon briefly here. To begin, Kesebir (2014) studied the relationship between humility and existential anxiety. Humility is defined as the ability to see oneself in a true perspective and has long been considered a positive virtue. It includes an ability to realistically assess one's limits and to appreciate one's place in the scheme of things. Lower levels of self-preoccupation are also associated with the construct. As such, it makes conceptual sense that this personality factor may protect against elevated preoccupation with death and one's annihilation. If one can look beyond oneself in the face of immediate distress, feelings of aloneness, and one's inevitable demise, then the pain of these life experiences is less acute and lasting.

In a series of five studies, Kesebir (2014) examined how trait humility and a sense of entitlement moderate reactions to mortality reminders and how manipulations to one's sense of humility impacts anxiety about death and one's mortality. Across these studies the author built a strong case in support of his basic premise that individuals high in humility are buffered against death anxiety and fear of their own mortality, concluding that "the dark side of death anxiety is brought about by a noisy ego only and not by a quiet ego, revealing self-transcendence as a sturdier, healthier anxiety buffer than self-enhancement" (pg. 610). The concept of self-transcendence is a trait that bears further mention. Kesiber (2014) likens it in part to the ability of the individual to easily remove him- or herself from the middle of whatever is going on at the moment and to direct attention to the greater world beyond the individual, transcending, "egotistical concerns and the attendant urge for defensive, self-serving maneuvers" in the process (pg. 611). Few would argue that a self-transcendent stance requires a level of ego strength, identity formation, and affect regulation achieved by only a handful on anything approaching a regular basis. But clearly, while perhaps aspirational for most, self-transcendence likely remains a state of being that promotes the optimal synthesis and resolution of existential anxiety.

Turning attention now to the relationship between shame and existential anxiety, Stolorow (2011), in a theoretical paper, argues that an individual who experiences higher levels of shame may be "held hostage by the eyes of others" and that this unpleasant emotion may serve as a substitute for existential anxiety. Thus, shame is a reflection of inauthentic living while existential anxiety reflects authentic living. In a paradoxical sense therefore, shame and, more importantly, a preoccupation with worldly concerns and the opinions of others might distract one from his or her finitude and the finitude of those cared for. This hardly appears to be an optimal manner through which an individual can shield oneself from the debilitating effects of existential anxiety. But it does cast light on the possibility that individuals may utilize symptom substitution and denial defense formations to combat existential anxiety. For example, might there also exist a subset of individuals who shield themselves from existential anxiety by adopting an excessively optimistic, Pollyannish outlook upon their existence and prospects of meaning and immortality? The study of defense mechanisms in relation to existential anxiety is a fascinating area of future inquiry.

In summary, it appears that possessing a strong sense of meaning and a clearly formed identity are likely the most robust protective individual-level factors that mitigate the debilitative effects of existential anxiety. Spirituality that connects with the individual in a meaningful manner and a sense of humility/self-transcendence are likely two other protective factors. Defense mechanisms, including denial and symptom substitution, and other avoidant functions may also buffer the individual from the immediate negative affect and worries associated with existential anxiety, but they are associated with a host of negative sequelae and perhaps only forestall a future date with the existential givens of our existence.

Familial/Social

As discussed in the previous chapter, formative parental, familial, and peer experiences can negatively impact the adolescent's processing of existential anxiety. At the same time this broad category of influences may also serve a protective function when the adolescent makes contact with existential concerns. While there are no studies that examine the protective function family and social factors can serve when the adolescent processes existential concerns, the research on familial and social contributors to resilience merits consideration. Specifically, three familial and social factors – a secure attachment, social support, and friendships – likely operate as protective factors that promote health and reduce maladjustment. Each factor is considered briefly here.

The development of a secure attachment between child and primary caregiver has been identified as the first primary source of resilience (Rutten et al., 2013). A parent's empathic attunement, responsivity to child's needs, and overall support of a child promote a sense of security. Secure attachment relations serve as the canvas upon which the children learn to integrate mental and emotional experiences into a single coherent representation. The positive experiences the child has with a primary caregiver stimulate the development of an internal working model of how all relationships should be. As Rutten et al. (2013) describes, "securely attached children form internal working models in which the self is perceived as worthy, others are perceived as being available and reliable, and the environment can be perceived as challenging but manageable with the support of others" (pg. 11). In addition, children who are securely attached to their primary caregiver seem to respond to adversity better. Here is where perhaps a connection can be made to existential anxiety experienced during adolescence. Specifically, it may be that when existential questions, concerns, and angst weigh heavily upon an adolescent, those who have an internal working model of relationships that is positive may be more inclined to reach out to others for guidance and support. They also may, in a more general sense, possess the faith and trust in their own abilities to contemplate the most troubling of existential questions and manage the distress that these questions generate.

There is considerable evidence supporting the premise that social support enhances well-being and promotes the development of coping strategies that can assist the individual in times of crisis. An adolescent's development of a positive sense of self and self-efficacy is based, in part, upon the consistent availability of social support (Brennan, 2008). Social support has been defined as "acts that demonstrate responsivity to another's needs" (Cutrona, 1996, pg. 17). Cutrona and Cole (2000) have identified four general types of social support. These include the following: (1) concrete support – this encompasses practical acts of assistance; (2) emotional support – this encompasses empathy, listening, and consistent emotional availability; (3) advice support – this includes advice giving but also just general reassurance; and (4) esteem support – this refers to the extent to which another person promotes one's self-worth and value. Within families it is the unconditional positive regard and commitment to the adolescent that provides the foundation upon which social support is based. While parents are the most influential source of social support, certainly siblings, peers, relatives, and other adult relations can serve as important resources as well (Biegel et al., 1994). There is also evidence indicating that positive social support by parents increases the likelihood of an adolescent experiencing an easier transition into adulthood (Coleman & Hagell, 2007; McGrath et al., 2014).

In terms of how social support might mitigate the adolescent's negative reaction to existential concerns it would seem that, much like the case of secure attachment formation, an adolescent who perceives a caretaker to be a supportive and accessible resource could potentially lean on this relationship when existential concerns and anxiety are experienced. In the author's clinical practice many adolescents report having suffered in silence for considerable lengths of time prior to entering therapy due to a perception that parents or other potential supportive resources would not understand their existential concerns. Recognizing that the hesitancy on the part of an adolescent to discuss existential fears with a parent or other potential social support may not accurately reflect the sensitivity and empathic attunement of the individual who has been bypassed, the *perception* of social support does seem to play a critical role in whether adolescents will feel comfortable sharing their worries with parents, siblings, friends, and other adults. Thus, where indicated part of the treatment process when working with adolescents who are experiencing existential anxiety involves assisting adolescents and parents in improving their communication about these concerns and normalizing the adolescent's worries for all parties involved.

A third category of possible social protective factors consists of positive peer relations and friendships. It has long been established that friendships are a very important support during adolescence (Hartup & Stevens, 1999). Beyond providing social support, friends can model effective coping and how to access resources that promote well-being (Finkenauer & Righetti, 2011). Close friendships during adolescence support basic needs of acceptance, validation, intimacy, and security (La Guardia, 2008; Mendelson & Aboud, 1999). In a recent review of the literature on the positive effects of friendships during adolescence, Graber and colleagues (2016) posited four major mechanisms through which friends can promote resilience. These include (a) fostering more effective coping, (b) promoting a sense of self-efficacy, (c) enhancing self-esteem, and (d) supporting a self-construct that encourages the individual to view oneself in relation to others. The authors tested the mechanisms through which friendships promote resilience in a large sample of British adolescents and found considerable support for their hypothesized mechanisms of change. Specifically, they concluded supportive friendships facilitate resilience "by supporting development of a constructive coping style (comprised of engaged coping and support-seeking), encouraging effort, using a supportive friendship network, and reducing disengaged and externalizing coping" (Graber et al., 2016, pg. 351). Thus, there are strong indications that positive and close friendships during adolescence promote resilience in a variety of ways that include but are not limited to social support.

As has previously been stated, there are unfortunately no studies that directly examine the adolescent experience of existential anxiety in relation to protective familial and social factors. The research on attachment, social support, and friendships in relation to resilience that has been briefly reviewed here suggests that all these factors may support an adolescent in processing and coping with existential anxiety. Those adolescents who benefitted from a secure attachment relation with their primary caregiver, who experienced consistent social support that was attuned to their particular needs at the time, and who develop close friendships with peers that promote positive coping through modeling likely stand a much better chance of weathering the storms of existential angst confronted at this critical stage of life.

A Developmental Model of Existential Anxiety During Adolescence

Having established the universality of existential anxiety during adolescence and having reviewed predictors and protective factors that likely impact an adolescent's experience of the same, we now propose a developmental model that aims to predict how existential anxiety might be experienced by a particular adolescent. It is important, however, to first re-emphasize that the existential anxiety derived from the "givens" of our existence (e.g., we will die, we are responsible for our choices, we are alone) is present to at least a minimal degree from the first experiences of consciousness. Put differently, the model of adolescent existential anxiety proposed here does not argue that existential anxiety is first experienced during teenage years. It assumes children experience existential anxiety. What *is* proposed is the following: critical bio-psycho-socio developments experienced by the individual both prior to and during adolescence allows for qualitatively different contact with existential anxiety than that achieved during earlier life stages. Coinciding with (and partially because of) these maturational changes, an adolescent has developed a worldview, set of values, identity, and interpersonal stance that are largely influenced by formative attachment and caretaking experiences that will impact how the individual experiences and resolves trauma. These traumas, in conjunction with a more acute awareness of the "givens" of human existence, threaten the adolescent's security and ignite new experiences of existential anxiety. The resolution of the adolescent's existential anxiety is contingent upon how the trauma is resolved and the same cognitive capacities, attachment style, identity formation, prosocial moral development, and support systems that partially fuel this emotional experience in the first place. Thus, the model attempts to account for the diversity of existential anxiety experiences across adolescents while still assuming the universality of the basic emotional experience. The remaining portion of this section explores this basic premise in greater detail (Fig. 3.1).

As depicted in the figure, the proposed model of adolescent existential anxiety argues that existential anxiety is felt to at least a minimal degree within the context of formative attachment relationships in the earliest stages of development prior to the initial experience of consciousness. The trauma of birth and totally dependency an infant has upon the care of others to

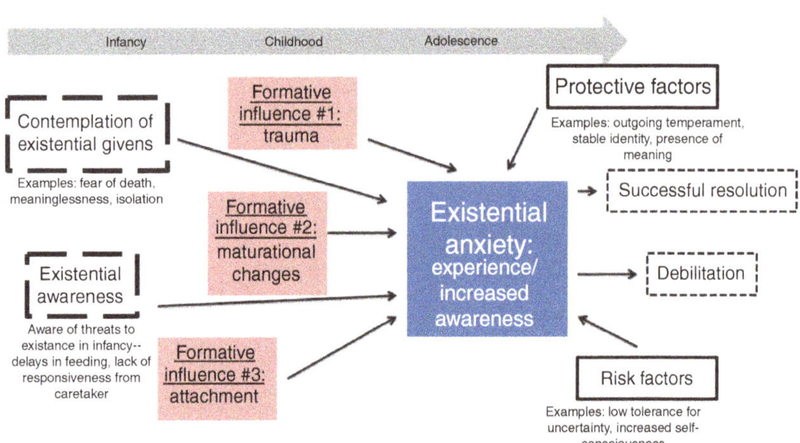

Fig. 3.1 Developmental model of existential anxiety in adolescence

survive certainly is punctuated with intense moments of anxiety, fear, and distress under even the best of circumstances. The infant and then toddler will experience threats to his or her existence ranging from micro-traumas (e.g., delays in receiving feeding, a lack of empathic attunement and responsivity by a primary caretaker) to overt neglect and/or abuse. The frequency and intensity of these threats will be in direct relation to the level of existential anxiety experienced during this life stage. As time passes the maturing child, in possession of both consciousness and basic language skills, develops a basic narrative explaining this core emotional experience. "Life is scary" and "I can't trust anyone" are examples of the type of basic narrative a child of this age (four or five years old) develops who has experienced more trauma than most that both explains these core emotions and reflects a crude philosophy of life. Thus, the existential givens of human existence – fears of death, meaninglessness, freedom, and isolation – are more actively contemplated. As the child continues to mature, three major sources of influence will impact how these existential concerns and anxiety are experienced and resolved in adolescence. These influences are trauma experiences, maturational changes, and the child's attachment style. Each of these formative influences is considered in detail here.

Influence #1: Trauma

As discussed in Chapter 1, EI argues that psychopathology is rooted in trauma. Similarly, the proposed model of adolescent existential anxiety identifies trauma experiences as the first major influence upon the experience of existential anxiety during adolescence. By way of review, acute trauma is the first type of trauma in Schneider's (2008) framework and pertains to immediate but time-limited threats such as physical injury. Chronic traumas are the second typology. They are experienced over longer periods of time and result from failed attempts to overcompensate from the initial acute trauma. The third type, implicit trauma, involves a modeling component in which the wounds of a parent are implicitly transmitted to the child through close observation of the parent's behaviors. It has become increasingly clear that trauma experienced during childhood and adolescence can have a range of negative effects upon the individual that can be evidenced through anxiety, depression, and other Axis I disorders (Hovens et al., 2012; Maniglio, 2013). More intense existential anxiety experiences are likely another outcome of trauma experienced in the early stages of life.

Stolorow's (2007) conceptualization of the relationship between trauma and existential anxiety was introduced in Chapter 2. He argues that trauma represents an unwanted encounter with one's mortality and ultimate experience of nonbeing. The fragility of life, a sense of aloneness, and even a sense of meaninglessness are common reactions of the individual who experiences trauma. These sources of existential anxiety can be particularly acute in children and adolescents who do not possess the coping resources and wisdom of adults to help buffer the impact of the trauma. Whether the adolescent will be subsequently overwhelmed by the negative impact of a trauma and develop neurotic anxiety or other mental health disorders will of course depend upon the intensity and type of trauma, the developmental stage when the trauma was experienced, and the social supports in place at the time and following the trauma. But at a minimum trauma will generate at least some existential anxiety.

While the connections between acute and chronic trauma and existential anxiety may seem inherently more obvious, Schneider's (2008) consideration of implicit traumas should not be overlooked. It is relatively easy to make the argument that physical injury, physical abuse, psychological abuse, and sexual abuse would heighten the young person's experience of existential anxiety. Each of these acute and chronic trauma experiences can present serious and immediate threats to one's existence, and each can cause the individual to question mortality and meaning, and further lead to a profound feeling of aloneness. On the other hand, the implicit traumas are more insidious and subtle. The parent who is not engaging in overt abuse can still devalue or neglect the child and adolescent's experience of the world through the modeling of a value system that is inconsistent with their child's and/or through active dismissal of the child's values and identity. For example, "You shouldn't be crying about that!", "Stop listening to that stupid music!", and "You should be trying out for football instead of cross country" are just a few of the myriad of ways in which an implicit trauma can be experienced. Each, in their own way, represents a negation of what Roger's (1959) refers to as the young person's organismic valuing process (i.e., the inherent tendency of each individual to know what is best for themselves). This lack of understanding and acceptance of the young person can create profound anxiety and depression as the adolescent finds his or her values, identity, friend choice, and/or worldview dismissed, belittled, or, in more extreme instances, attacked. As Hollis (2013) contends, parents possess the ability to deflect and distort their child's voyage in a way that can result in debilitating "hauntings" later in life. Schneider (2008) captures this devaluation and/or distortion process through his inclusion of implicit traumas in his model of developmental psychopathology.

Influence #2: Maturational Changes

The maturational changes in cognitive functioning, prosocial moral reasoning, and identity formation achieved during adolescence represent the second source of influences that impact the adolescent's experience of existential anxiety. For certain, adolescence has long been identified as a distinct period of development from evolutionary (Hall, 1904), psychosocial (Erikson, 1968), psychosexual (Freud, 1905/1953), and cognitive (Piaget, 1951) perspectives. The adolescent undergoes critical and qualitative changes in brain development (Paus, 2009), hormonal make-up (Susman & Dorn, 2009), and neurochemistry (Luciana, 2013) that afford the opportunity for the world and one's existence to be contemplated at a deeper level. Specific changes in brain structure include a thinning of the brain cortex, pruning of certain subcortical structures, and increasing interconnectivity between brain regions (Luciana, 2013). An important result of the increasing efficiency and interconnectivity of the adolescent brain is advances in executive functioning skills that encompass monitoring, organizing, planning, and impulse control (Kuhn, 2009). The myriad of changes seem to support greater exploration of the world and increased sensation-seeking behaviors. Concurrent advances in an adolescent's meta-cognitive abilities may aid the development of executive functioning skills (Best & Miller, 2010). Adolescents think about how they are thinking and start to learn from mistakes. A sense of intentionality and a more disciplined approach to life's demands often follow as well.

Adolescents are not only more cognitively efficient and self-aware, they are also capable of problem-solving and reasoning at a more sophisticated level than children. Complex problem-solving (CPS) abilities, for example, have been shown to rapidly increase during this stage of development (Frickshorn et al., 2014). CPS and metacognitive abilities are perhaps the logical outgrowth of early research efforts by Inhelder and colleagues (1958), who identified adolescence as the *formal operations* or "thinking about thinking" stage of development. Adolescents also seem to experience significant advancements in their introspective abilities, in turn developing a more nuanced understanding to the world around them (Harter, 2006; Harter et al., 1997). They are able to spot inconsistencies in the messages they receive and behaviors they observe in the models and authority figures around them. This enhanced capacity to recognize the contradictions (and even hypocrisy) in others is thought to increase both intrapsychic distress and questions about the authenticity of the world in which they exist. It is hardly surprising, therefore, that Hacker (1994) identified an adolescent's advances in abstract thinking as the critical component to the awakening to existential concerns.

Bering (2002) has also cogently highlighted the adaptive quality that possessing an existential theory of mind (EToM) has on human functioning. He defines EToM as "a biological based, generic explanatory system that allows individuals to perceive meaning in certain life events" (pg. 4). It is based upon the ability of the individual to ascribe intentionality to life events and behaviors of others. EToM's purpose is to help the individual explain what otherwise might seem like meaningless life events, reducing anxiety and promoting adjustment in a world that can seem random and cruel on a regular basis. Bering (2002) argues that the perception of intentionality crystallizes during later stages of childhood and continues to develop during adolescence into adulthood. This enhanced ability to "mind read" plays an important role in developmental models of anxiety. Adolescents who possess advanced abilities to explain the intentions behind life events are more likely to contemplate existential concerns (Warren & Sroufe, 2004; Westenberg et al., 2001). If, for example, the adolescent experiences the death of someone close to him or her, not only is the pain of the loss acutely felt but the meaning and/or meaninglessness of the loss is contemplated as well as the adolescent's mortality. Bering (2003) believes "we are a species whose members are ravenous to understand the drama of our own lives" (pg. 20). Adolescents seem to possess the cognitive hardware to begin to satisfy this appetite. A logical outgrowth is the contemplation of the "givens" of our existence.

Of course, there is great intraindividual and interindividual variability among adolescents as to the age of onset, pace, and extent to which advances in cognitive functioning occur (Kuhn, 2009). It has become increasingly apparent that a narrow window of months or years in early adolescence when this capacity develops does not exist (Keating, 2004). Yet, again, with few exceptions it appears that most adolescents will experience sufficient cognitive advancements that lead to a qualitatively different experience of some of life's most basic questions, such as "What happens after I die?" and "Why am I here on this earth?"

The cognitive advances experienced during adolescence also impact and parallel prosocial moral development. Eisenberg and colleagues (2005) have demonstrated conclusively that adolescents experience major advances in perspective-taking and prosocial moral reasoning. These capacities are closely related to the ability to empathize with the experience of others. The advances in perspective-taking extend beyond merely the ability to empathize, impacting the development of core values, beliefs, social problem-solving skills and attitudes. These gains, in turn, seem to promote altruistic tendencies in adolescents (Eisenberg & Fabes, 1998). Hoffman (2000) even suggested that the ability to sympathize with the chronic distress of disadvantaged groups is another critical outgrowth of this area of development. Thus, prosocial moral reasoning can fuel positive behavior change across multiple levels of human experience.

The implications of the research on adolescent prosocial moral development for the current study of existential anxiety during adolescence are profound and far reaching. Indeed, a connection between existential anxiety and advanced moral reasoning has been posited previously (Scott & Weems, 2013). The connection is straightforward. The increased perspective-taking abilities and associated advances in empathic attunement to both the experience of individuals close to the adolescent but also society as a whole would seem to promote increased awareness of certain existential concerns which, in turn, may lead to higher levels of existential anxiety. For example, an adolescent who is sensitized to issues of discrimination may logically begin to more actively question the meaning of our existence, one's purpose in life, and/or the potential for injustice to impact his or her life at some point in the future. In these moments, the world would appear less sensible and the adolescent's worldview and/or core values would become destabilized and/or threatened. Existential anxiety would ensue. In short, adolescents who develop the ethic of care, see the world through other's eyes (i.e., "mind read"), and develop a deeper sense of empathy will likely be more sensitive to existential concerns pertaining to injustice, meaninglessness, and the fragility of life.

Identity formation is the final subcategory of maturational influences that impact the adolescent's experience of existential anxiety. By way of review, in the previous chapter the construct was discussed as a possible risk factor for the development of debilitating existential anxiety and in the current chapter it has been discussed as a potential protective factor. Now the experience of identity concerns and how these concerns are resolved are conceptualized as a normative part of adolescent development that fosters contact with existential concerns and anxiety.

Erikson (1968), Marcia (1993), and others have demonstrated that a stable identity is associated with positive adjustment while an unstable identity is associated with distress and maladjustment. Adolescents seek to define for themselves and others who they are, and the answers they adopt can profoundly impact their adjustment for both good and bad. An ability to develop a stable sense of identity is dependent in part upon the development of a minimal level of self-awareness that is thought to be reached by most during the second decade of life (Cote, 2009). Thus, the advances in meta cognition and abstract reasoning capacities provide critical hardware from which a more stable sense of identity begins to formulate. In addition, the previously mentioned advances in perspective-taking seem to both fuel and aid the adolescent's search for identity. Specifically, adolescents study the behaviors of peers and adults with a level of careful attentiveness that surpasses their attending behaviors of childhood by a significant margin. This refinement of observation skills allows the adolescent to try on different roles and internalize different values in their personal search for a coherent and stable identity (Peterson, 1987). Waterman (1984) has cogently noted that identity formation is an *act of creation* on the part of the individual, requiring the individual to assume *responsibility* for the choices they make within almost a limitless sea of possibilities. It takes courage to define oneself but the benefits of doing so are far reaching. Adolescents who manage to establish a clear identity formation are able to contemplate existential concerns with a secure foothold in place.

In summary, maturational advances in cognitive functioning, prosocial moral reasoning, and identity formation cause the adolescent to contemplate his or her existence in a qualitatively different manner than what was experienced during childhood. The adolescent finds it increasingly harder to accept "pat" answers to existential questions about life, death, meaning, etc.,. because their cognitive maturation makes it impossible to do so. They ruminate about the "givens" of life because the questions do not have easy answers, speak to core values, and frequently the adolescent has not yet developed the defense mechanisms adults use to put these universal worries aside (Becker, 1973; Shumaker, 2012). As stated previously, the resolution of these deliberations during adolescence seems highly dependent upon the individual's sensitivity to existential concerns, coping resources, and social support.

Influence #3: Attachment Style

Attachment formation is the final major source of influence included in our model of adolescent existential anxiety. Beyond positing a link between trauma, maturational factors, and psychopathology, it is clear individuals differ in the support systems they have in place that can help them weather the storm of adolescence and the existential concerns that arise during this stage of life. Indeed, the most basic support system in existence is the bond that is created between a child and primary caretaker from birth through infancy and childhood. The individual learns life's most basis lessons of trust, responsivity, predictability, control, responsibility, patience, and survival through this relationship. An individual's attachment style is based upon the parent-child bond. It is an expression of the individual's object relations, which is the blue print from which one's basic interpersonal stance is based. By the time the individual reaches adolescence, he or she has developed answers to some very basic questions, such as: Are others to be trusted? Will I always be let down? Do I assume the basic goodness in others? Does it pay to keep my distance from others? The answers to these questions reflect the individual's attachment style and have a profound influence on how the individual navigates the world and interpersonal relations. It seems imperative, therefore, that a comprehensive model of existential anxiety captures the object relations influence as expressed through the individual's attachment style.

As was the case in our discussion of identity formation, we have discussed attachment style as a potential risk and protective factor that impacts their experience and resolution of existential anxiety during adolescence. Specifically, an insecure attachment style is a risk factor for mental health disorders and maladjustment (Colonnesi et al., 2011; Warren et al., 1997), while a secure attachment style is a clear source of resilience and can buffer the individual from the impact of trauma and other stressors (Rutten et al., 2013). There are at least two mechanisms through which an individual's attachment style impacts both the experience of existential anxiety and resolution of the same. Social support seeking and the availability of social support are the first mechanism. Specifically, those with insecure attachment styles may be less likely to seek social supports when existential concerns arise due to a basic distrust of others and tendency to isolate and withdraw when under duress. Even if they were so inclined to pursue support, individuals with insecure attachment styles may have unsatisfactory options available who can provide cogent advice, understanding, and emotional support. Conversely, those with secure attachment styles will likely have more social supports available to them that are eager to provide critical assistance. Individuals with secure attachment styles are also, on average, more comfortable pursuing these resources when existential anxiety arises.

A second, more speculative, means through which attachment style impacts an adolescent's experience of existential anxiety pertains to the interaction between attachment style and the manner through which the existential "givens" are framed. Research indicates that, on average, adolescents with an insecure attachment style will have experienced greater histories of deprivation, inconsistent, distant, neglectful, and/or abusive parenting, and other related traumas than those who demonstrate secure attachment styles. Given these vast differences in life histories, where those who demonstrate insecure attachment styles may have been experiencing micro-traumas literally from birth while their securely attached brethren were spared these small horrors, it stands to reason that those with insecure attachment formations would have made contact with the existential givens of existence in a much harsher and urgent manner. Put simply, not being sure when (or if) one's next meal or hug is coming likely creates intense levels of distress and hypervigilance, as well as a profound distrust for the world. Questions of meaning and mortality are introduced in rapid fire at a time when normally individuals benefit from a level of responsivity and empathic attunement that keep these questions far at bay. The infant and child also does not possess the cognitive hardware to contemplate and resolve these questions in a manner that promotes long-term adjustment. The answers to these questions for the child are incomplete and unsatisfactory. Are other's trustworthy? Perhaps not. Am I safe? I'm not sure. Does the world make sense or have some greater meaning or purpose to it? It doesn't make any sense to me.

Thus, those who experience such early deprivation and chaos have, to at least a minimal extent, likely already developed crude hypotheses about many of the existential concerns that are contemplated normally at later stages of development. By the time the insecurely attached individual reaches adolescence, they may have become defended against existential anxiety and threats to their existence through repressive defense mechanisms, a basic mistrust of others, a sense of hopelessness about the world and one's prospects, and/or a compromised identity formation. All these coping responses lead to psychosocial maladjustment. It could also, of course, be the case that the insecurely attached adolescent may experience existential anxiety much more acutely than most because of their early life histories. A sensitization process is proposed here. Either way, through avoidance, repression, or sensitization, it seems likely that insecurely attached adolescents will be at greater risk for converting existential anxiety into neurotic anxiety.

In summary, trauma experiences, neglect, abuse, and chaotic family environments, as well as poverty and limited access to resources, all increase the risk for the development of existential anxiety through overstimulation of the young person's root fears of death, isolation, guilt, and freedom. The same conditions that give rise to existential anxiety, however, often prohibit the individual from successfully resolving this emotional experience because they simultaneously negatively impact a child's identity and object relations development and prematurely tax coping resources. Thus, a cyclical model may apply here. In brief, trauma is perceived as a threat which generates existential anxiety which summons inadequate coping that results in an insufficient resolution of the anxiety, making the individual more vulnerable when the next trauma is felt. More specifically, if an insecurely attached young person has limited coping resources and support systems, he or she may be more reliant upon the use of less adaptive defense mechanisms (e.g., repression) and coping strategies (e.g., isolation, substance use) to manage these fundamental threats to his or her being. Excessive use of these mechanisms and strategies in combination with sufficient intensity of trauma increases the risk of existential anxiety overwhelming the individual. The young person continues to isolate and/or rely upon maladaptive coping strategies when contact is made with these intense threats and fears. A worldview emphasizing feelings of guilt and fear, the individual's lack of control, a sense of meaninglessness, and/or life's fragility is further reinforced. Under these conditions the risk of neurotic anxiety and maladjustment developing increases greatly.

The Influence of Risk and Protective Factors

While trauma, maturation, and attachment style account for the lion's share of influence on the adolescent's experience of existential anxiety, the proposed model incorporates more specific risk and protective factors that can further mediate the experience. Chapter 2 examined a wide range of risk factors that likely increase existential anxiety and/or decrease the individual's ability to successfully resolve the experience of existential anxiety. Many of these specific risk factors are either directly related to one of the three formative influences in the proposed model (e.g., an insecure attachment style is a direct expression of attachment style) or indirectly related to these major influences (e.g., self-consciousness may be indirectly related to certain maturational factors). The same could be said for the model's consideration of protective factors introduced earlier in this chapter.

Recognizing that some overlap between the formative influences and risk/protective factors exists, it makes sense to present them separately in the proposed model for the following reasons. First, certain risk and protective factors certainly do not easily fit under the umbrella of one of our major sources of influence. For example, an intolerance for uncertainty seems to be a risk factor for increased sensitivity to existential anxiety. Though it may be distantly related to attachment style, trauma experiences, and/or maturational factors, the connection does not appear obvious and, therefore, it should be introduced in the model separate from these major sources of influence. Second, the inclusion of specific risk and protective factors hopefully will facilitate the detective efforts of clinicians working with adolescents whom they suspect may be experiencing existential anxiety and/or concerns. In other words, while we can acknowledge the formative, broad influences of prior trauma history, maturational advances, and attachment style on an adolescent's experience of existential anxiety, the sources of influence impacting a given adolescent's experience of existential anxiety at a specific life stage are so complex and broad-ranging, that it seems imperative to develop a model that attempts to capture some of that complexity and goes beyond a more general rendering of the phenomena. Clinicians with access to a more extensive list of risk and protective factors will be able to more accurately assess and more effectively treat acute existential anxiety presentations in their young clients. Of course, the model is only an initial attempt at capturing the complexity of existential anxiety experienced during this stage of life. It is certainly speculative and by no means definitive.

Having made the argument for including specific risk and protective factors in the model of adolescent existential anxiety, the chapter ends with a brief summary of the risk and protective factors clinicians should consider. To begin, in terms of risk factors clinicians should first assess an adolescent's formative parenting experiences, attachment style, and trauma history when existential concerns and/or debilitating existential anxiety is suspected. After these major sources of influence are measured, the following specific risk factors should be assessed: (1) *elevated anxiety sensitivity* – individuals with prior histories of generalized anxiety symptomatology reflect this construct; (2) *negative affectivity* – this pertains to a pervasive tendency to experience the world negatively at an emotional level; (3) *increased self-consciousness* – individuals who are prone to shyness and withdrawal fall within this category; (4) *decreased conscientiousness* – this reflects a lack of drive, clarity of goals, or belief in one's self efficacy; (5) *history of significant health concerns* – individuals who have experienced health concerns or closely witnessed significant health concerns or the effects of aging in others are included here; (6) *identity-moratorium stage of identity formation* – these individuals are still struggling to define for themselves and others who they are; (7) *higher SFM /lower sense of meaning* – individuals who have not found meaning in their existence and are actively searching for meaning fall into this category; (8) *low self-esteem* – this is perhaps related to low conscientiousness and reflects a negative self-concept and belief in one's ability to navigate life's challenges; (9) *low tolerance for uncertainty* – this includes individuals who struggle when definitive answers are not forthcoming; (10) *low perceived controllability* – this reflects an outlook that views life primarily as unpredictable and events as frequently beyond one's control; (11) *exposure to man-made or natural disasters* – close proximity to large-scale life tragedies such as 9/11 and Hurricane Katrina are examples of this factor; and (12) *experience of societal injustice* – individuals who are the victim of discrimination, prejudice, or other unfair/inequitable societal practices fall into this category. When one, some, or several of these factors are present it can perhaps enrich a clinician's clinical formulation of the sources of a client's difficulties and allow for a more targeted intervention strategy.

Similarly, when an adolescent reports a history of trauma exposure, is making contact with existential concerns, or is going through several life transitions and stressors, an assessment of protective factors can help predict the client's capacities to successfully weather the acute stressors and/or convert existential anxiety into creative pursuits. The specific protective factors clinicians are encouraged to review include the following: (1) *outgoing temperament* – these individuals approach novelty eagerly and with confidence, and they are perceived by others as good-natured and sociable; (2) *engaged emotional regulation* – this refers to the ability to attend to one's emotions actively and effectively with little use of passivity and/or avoidance; (3) *elevated self-acceptance/sense of mastery* – this includes both self-esteem, problem-solving abilities, and a related sense of faith in one's ability to navigate life's obstacles; (4) *POM* – the identification of a set of values and sense of meaning is included here;

(5) *stable identity* – individuals who have reached the identity achievement stage of development fall into this category; (6) *sense of faith/spirituality* – this includes having a sense of faith or belief in a higher purpose and is associated with having a sense of meaning; (7) *humility/transcendence* – this reflects an ability to have a sense of perspective about one's place in the universe and to look beyond one's immediate needs and fears; (8) *secure attachment* – this is an outgrowth of a strong parent-child bond and reflects healthy object relations; (9) *social support* – this encompasses material, emotional, and instructive forms of support forthcoming from family, friends, and other institutions; and (10) *positive peer relations* – this is perhaps a specific form of social support that also is a source of modeling for how to cope with stress and negative emotional experiences.

Conclusions

This chapter began with a review of the protective factors that appear to help mitigate the experience of potentially debilitating existential anxiety during adolescence. They can serve as a reference for clinicians working with adolescents experiencing existential anxiety and may represent untapped sources of resilience that can help the young person weather the general storm and stress of this stage of development in addition to the more specific distress caused by existential concerns. The chapter continued with the introduction of an existential model of anxiety that further elaborated on the formative influences, specific risk and protective factors, and reciprocal impact that these influences and factors have on both the development, maintenance, and resolution of existential concerns. Having more clearly defined how existential anxiety is experienced during adolescence, Chapter 4 introduces some general treatment strategies clinicians should consider utilizing when working with individuals experiencing this manner of concern.

References

Adamson, L., Hartman, S. G., & Lyxell, B. (1999). Adolescent identity—a qualitative approach: Self-concept, existential questions and adult contacts. *Scandinavian Journal Of Psychology*, *40*(1), 21–31. doi:10.1111/1467-9450.00094

Amstadter, A. B., Maes, H. H., Sheerin, C. M., Myers, J. M., & Kendler, K. S. (2016). The relationship between genetic and environmental influences on resilience and on common internalizing and externalizing psychiatric disorders. *Social Psychiatry And Psychiatric Epidemiology, 51*(5), 669–678. doi:10.1007/s00127-015-1163-6

Becker, E. (1973). *The denial of death*. New York, NY, US: Free Press.

Bering, J. M. (2002). The existential theory of mind. *Review Of General Psychology, 6*(1), 3–24. doi:10.1037/1089-2680.6.1.3

Bering, J. M. (2003). Towards a cognitive theory of existential meaning. New Ideas In Psychology, 21(2), 101–120. doi: 10.1016/S0732-118X(03)00014-X

Berman, S. L., Weems, C. F., & Stickle, T. R. (2006). Existential Anxiety in Adolescents: Prevalence, Structure, Association with Psychological Symptoms and Identity Development. *Journal Of Youth And Adolescence, 35*(3), 303–310. doi:10.1007/s10964-006-9032-y

Best, J. R., & Miller, P. H. (2010). A developmental perspective on executive function. *Child Development, 81*(6), 1641–1660. doi:10.1111/j.1467-8624.2010.01499.x

Biegel, D. E., Tracy, E. M., & Corvo, K. N. (1994). Strengthening social networks: Intervention strategies for mental health case managers. *Health & Social Work, 19*(3), 206–216.

Boardman, J. D., Blalock, C. L., & Button, T. M. (2008). Sex differences in the heritability of resilience. *Twin Research And Human Genetics, 11*(1), 12–27. doi:10.1375/twin.11.1.12

Boyes, M. C., & Chandler, M. (1992). Cognitive development, epistemic doubt, and identity formation in adolescence. *Journal Of Youth And Adolescence, 21*(3), 277–304. doi:10.1007/BF01537019

Brennan, M. A. (2008). Conceptualizing resiliency: An interactional perspective for community and youth development. *Child Care In Practice, 14*(1), 55–64. doi:10.1080/13575270701733732

Calkins, S. D., Blandon, A. Y., Williford, A. P., & Keane, S. P. (2007). Biological, behavioral, and relational levels of resilience in the context of risk for early childhood behavior problems. *Development And Psychopathology, 19*(3), 675–700. doi:10.1017/S095457940700034X

Caspi, A., Sugden, K., Moffitt, T. E., Taylor, A., Craig, I. W., Harrington, H., & . . . Poulton, R. (2003). Influence of life stress on depression: Moderation by a polymorphism in the 5 - HTT gene. *Science, 301*(5631), 386–389. doi:10.1126/science.1083968

Chen, J., Lau, C., Tapanya, S., & Cameron, C. A. (2012). Identities as protective processes: Socio-ecological perspectives on youth resilience. *Journal Of Youth Studies, 15*(6), 761–779. doi:10.1080/13676261.2012.677815

Coleman, J., & Hagell, A. (2007). *Adolescence, risk and resilience: Against the odds* (Vol. 3). New York: John Wiley & Sons.

Colonnesi, C., Draijer, E. M., Jan J. M. Stams, G., Van der Bruggen, C. O., Bögels, S. M., & Noom, M. J. (2011). The relation between insecure attachment and child anxiety: A meta-analytic review. *Journal Of Clinical Child And Adolescent Psychology*, 40(4), 630–645. doi:10.1080/15374416.2011.581623

Côté, J. E. (1996). Sociological perspectives on identity formation: The culture–identity link and identity capital. *Journal Of Adolescence*, *19*(5), 417–428. doi:10.1006/jado.1996.0040

Côté, J. E. (2009). Identity formation and self-development in adolescence. In R. M. Lerner, L. Steinberg, (Eds.), *Handbook of adolescent psychology: Individual bases of adolescent development, Vol. 1*, 3rd *ed.* (pp. 266–304). Hoboken, NJ, US: John Wiley & Sons Inc.

Curtis, W., & Cicchetti, D. (2003). Moving research on resilience into the 21st century: Theoretical and methodological considerations in examining the biological contributors to resilience. *Development and Psychopathology*, 15, 773–810.

Cutrona, C. E. (1996). *Social support in couples: Marriage as a resource in times of stress.* Thousand Oaks, CA, US: Sage Publications, Inc. doi:10.4135/9781483327563

Cutrona, C. E., & Cole, V. (2000). Optimizing support in the natural network. In S. Cohen, L. G. Underwood, B. H. Gottlieb, (Eds.), *Social support measurement and intervention: A guide for health and social scientists* (pp. 278–308). New York, NY, US: Oxford University Press. doi:10.1093/med:psych/9780195126709.003.0009

Davis, T. L., Kerr, B. A., & Kurpius, S. R. (2003). Meaning, Purpose, And Religiosity In At- Risk Youth: The Relationship Between Anxiety And Spirituality. *Journal Of Psychology And Theology*, *31*(4), 356–365.

Debats, D. L., Van der Lubbe, P. M., & Wezeman, F. R. (1993). On the psychometric properties of the Life Regard Index (LRI): A measure of meaningful life: An evaluation in three independent samples based on the Dutch version. *Personality And Individual Differences*, *14*(2), 337–345. doi:10.1016/0191-8869(93)90132-M

Dyk, P. H., & Adams, G. R. (1990). Identity and intimacy: An initial investigation of three theoretical models using cross-lag panel correlations. *Journal Of Youth And Adolescence*, *19*(2), 91–110. doi:10.1007/BF01538715

Eisenberg, N., & Fabes, R. A. (1998). Prosocial development. In N. Eisenberg, (Ed.), *Handbook of child psychology: Social, emotional, and personality development, Vol. 3*, 5th *ed.* (pp. 701–778). Hoboken, NJ, US: John Wiley & Sons Inc.

Eisenberg, N., Cumberland, A., Guthrie, I. K., Murphy, B. C., & Shepard, S. A. (2005). Age Changes in Prosocial Responding and Moral Reasoning in Adolescence and Early Adulthood. *Journal Of Research On Adolescence*, *15*(3), 235–260. doi:10.1111/j.1532-7795.2005.00095.x

Erikson, E. H. (1959). Identity and the life cycle: Selected papers. *Psychological Issues*, *1*1–171.

Erikson, E. (1968). *Identity: youth and crisis.* Oxford, England: Norton & Co.

Finkenauer, C., & Righetti, F. (2011). Understanding in close relationships: An interpersonal approach. *European Review Of Social Psychology, 22*(1), 316–363. doi:10.1080/10463283.2011.633384

Frankl, V. (1963). *Man's search for meaning: an introduction to logotherapy.* Oxford, England: Washington Square Press.

Frankl, V. E. (1986). Logotherapy and the challenge of suffering. *Review Of Existential Psychology & Psychiatry, Spec Issue 20*(1–3), 63–67.

Freud, S. (1905/1953). Three essays on the theory of sexuality. *Se, 7*, 125–243.

Frischkorn, G. T., Greiff, S., & Wüstenberg, S. (2014). The development of complex problem solving in adolescence: A latent growth curve analysis. *Journal Of Educational Psychology, 106*(4), 1007–1020. doi:10.1037/a0037114

Gamerzy, N. (1993). Children in poverty: Resilience despite risk. *Psychiatry, 56*(1), 127–136.

Graber, R., Turner, R., & Madill, A. (2016). Best friends and better coping: Facilitating psychological resilience through boys' and girls' closest friendships. *British Journal Of Psychology, 107*(2), 338–358. doi:10.1111/bjop.12135

Hacker, D. J. (1994). An existential view of adolescence. *The Journal Of Early Adolescence, 14*(3), 300–327. doi:10.1177/0272431694014003001

Hall, G. S. (1904). *Adolescence: Its psychology and its relations to physiology, anthropology, sociology, sex, crime, religion and education, Vol. I.* New York, NY, US: D Appleton & Company. doi:10.1037/10616-000

Harlow, L. L., Newcomb, M. D., & Bentler, P. M. (1986). Depression, self-derogation, substance use, and suicide ideation: Lack of purpose in life as a mediational factor. *Journal Of Clinical Psychology, 42*(1), 5–21. doi:10.1002/1097-4679(198601)42:1<5::AID-JCLP2270420102>3.0.CO;2-9

Harter, S., Bresnick, S., Bouchey, H. A., & Whitesell, N. R. (1997). The development of multiple role-related selves during adolescence. *Development And Psychopathology, 9*(4), 835–853. doi:10.1017/S0954579497001466

Harter, S. (2006). The Self. In N. Eisenberg, W. Damon, R. M. Lerner, (Eds.), *Handbook of child psychology: Social, emotional, and personality development, Vol. 3*, 6th *ed.* (pp. 505–570). Hoboken, NJ, US: John Wiley & Sons Inc.

Hartup, W. W., & Stevens, N. (1999). Friendships and adaptation across the life span. *Current Directions In Psychological Science, 8*(3), 76–79. doi:10.1111/1467-8721.00018

Hjemdal, O., Vogel, P. A., Solem, S., Hagen, K., & Stiles, T. C. (2011). The relationship between resilience and levels of anxiety, depression, and obsessive–compulsive symptoms in adolescents. *Clinical Psychology & Psychotherapy, 18*(4), 314–321. doi:10.1002/cpp.719

Hoare, C. (2009). Identity and spiritual development in the papers of Erik Erikson. *Identity: An International Journal Of Theory And Research, 9*(3), 183–200. doi:10.1080/15283480903344497

Hobfoll, S. E., & Leiberman, J. R. (1987). Personality and social resources in immediate and continued stress resistance among women. *Journal Of Personality And Social Psychology, 52*(1), 18–26. doi:10.1037/0022-3514.52.1.18

Hoffman, M. L. (2000). *Empathy and moral development: Implications for caring and justice*. New York, NY, US: Cambridge University Press. doi:10.1017/CBO9780511805851

Hollis, J. (2013). *Hauntings: dispelling the ghosts who run our lives*. Asheville, NC: Chiron Publications.

Hovens, J. M., Giltay, E. J., Wiersma, J. E., Spinhoven, P., Penninx, B. H., & Zitman, F. G. (2012). Impact of childhood life events and trauma on the course of depressive and anxiety disorders. *Acta Psychiatrica Scandinavica, 126*(3), 198–207. doi:10.1111/j.1600-0447.2011.01828.x

Inhelder, B., Piaget, J., Parsons, A., & Milgram, S. (1958). *The growth of logical thinking: From childhood to adolescence*. New York, NY, US: Basic Books. doi:10.1037/10034-000

Keating, D. P. (2004). Cognitive and brain development. In R. M. Lerner, L. Steinberg, (Eds.), *Handbook of adolescent psychology*, 2nd *ed*. (pp. 45–84). Hoboken, NJ, US: John Wiley & Sons Inc.

Kesebir, P. (2014). A quiet ego quiets death anxiety: Humility as an existential anxiety buffer. *Journal Of Personality And Social Psychology, 106*(4), 610–623. doi:10.1037/a0035814

Kim-Cohen, J., Moffitt, T. E., Caspi, A., & Taylor, A. (2004). Genetic and Environmental Processes in Young Children's Resilience and Vulnerability to Socioeconomic Deprivation. *Child Development, 75*(3), 651–668. doi:10.1111/j.1467-8624.2004.00699.x

Klackl, J., Jonas, E., & Kronbichler, M. (2014). Existential neuroscience: Self-esteem moderates neuronal responses to mortality-related stimuli. *Social Cognitive And Affective Neuroscience, 9*(11), 1754–1761. doi:10.1093/scan/nst167

Kroger, J. (2003). Identity development during adolescence. In G. R. Adams, M. D. Berzonsky, (Eds.), *Blackwell handbook of adolescence* (pp. 205–226). Malden: Blackwell Publishing.

Kuhn, D. (2009). Adolescent thinking. In R. M. Lerner, L. Steinberg, (Eds.), *Handbook of adolescent psychology: Individual bases of adolescent development, Vol. 1*, 3rd *ed*. (pp. 152–186). Hoboken, NJ, US: John Wiley & Sons Inc. doi:10.1002/9780470479193.adlpsy001007

La Guardia, J. G. (2008). On the role of psychological needs in healthy functioning: Integrating a self-determination theory perspective with traditional relationship theories. In J. V. Wood, A. Tesser, J. G. Holmes, (Eds.), *The self and social relationships* (pp. 27–48). New York, NY, US: Psychology Press.

Luciana, M. (2013). Adolescent brain development in normality and psychopathology. *Development And Psychopathology, 25*(4,Pt 2), 1325–1345. doi:10.1017/S095457941300064

Maniglio, R. (2013). Child sexual abuse in the etiology of anxiety disorders: A systematic review of reviews. *Trauma, Violence, & Abuse, 14*(2), 96–112. doi:10.1177/1524838012470032

Marcia, J. E. (1993). The relational roots of identity. In J. Kroger, (Ed.), *Discussions on ego identity* (pp. 101–120). Hillsdale, NJ, US: Lawrence Erlbaum Associates, Inc.

McGrath, B., Brennan, M. A., Dolan, P., & Barnett, R. (2014). Adolescents and their networks of social support: Real connections in real lives?. *Child & Family Social Work, 19*(2), 237–248. doi:10.1111/j.1365-2206.2012.00899.x

Mendelson, M. J., & Aboud, F. E. (1999). Measuring friendship quality in late adolescents and young adults: McGill Friendship Questionnaires. *Canadian Journal Of Behavioural Science /Revue Canadienne Des Sciences Du Comportement, 31*(2), 130–132. doi:10.1037/h0087080

Ojala, M. (2005). Adolescents' Worries about Environmental Risks: Subjective Well-being, Values, and Existential Dimensions. *Journal Of Youth Studies, 8*(3), 331–347. doi:10.1080/13676260500261934

Paus, T. (2009). Brain development. In R. M. Lerner, L. Steinberg, (Eds.), *Handbook of adolescent psychology: Individual bases of adolescent development, Vol. 1*, 3rd ed. (pp. 95–115). Hoboken, NJ, US: John Wiley & Sons Inc. doi:10.1002/9780470479193.adlpsy001005

Penela, E. C., Walker, O. L., Degnan, K. A., Fox, N. A., & Henderson, H. A. (2015). Early behavioral inhibition and emotion regulation: Pathways toward social competence in middle childhood. *Child Development, 86*(4), 1227–1240. doi:10.1111/cdev.12384

Peterson, G. W. (1987). Role transitions and role identities during adolescence: A symbolic interactionist view. *Journal Of Adolescent Research, 2*(3), 237–254. doi:10.1177/074355488723005

Piaget, J. (1951). *The child's conception of the world* (No. 213). Lanham, MD: Rowman & Littlefield.

Porges, S. W. (2003). Social Engagement and Attachment: A Phylogenetic Perspective. In J. A. King, C. F. Ferris, I. I. Lederhendler, (Eds.), *Roots of mental illness in children* (pp. 31–47). New York, NY, US: New York Academy of Sciences.

Rogers, C. R. (1959). The Way to do is to Be. *Contemporary Psychology, 4*(7), 196–198. doi:10.1037/006081

Rutten, B. F., Hammels, C., Geschwind, N., Menne-Lothmann, C., Pishva, E., Schruers, K., & ... Wichers, M. (2013). Resilience in mental health: Linking psychological and neurobiological perspectives. *Acta Psychiatrica Scandinavica, 128*(1), 3–20. doi:10.1111/acps.12095

Rutter, M. (2006). The Promotion of Resilience in the Face of Adversity. In A. Clarke-Stewart, J. Dunn, (Eds.), *Families count: Effects on child and adolescent development* (pp. 26–52). New York, NY, US: Cambridge University Press. doi:10.1017/CBO9780511616259.003

Rutter, M. (2012). Resilience as a dynamic concept. *Development And Psychopathology*, *24*(2), 335–344. doi:10.1017/S0954579412000028

Schneider, K. J. (2008). *Existential-integrative psychotherapy: Guideposts to the core of practice*. New York, NY, US: Routledge/Taylor & Francis Group.

Scott, B. G., & Weems, C. F. (2013). Natural disasters and existential concerns: A test of Tillich's theory of existential anxiety. *Journal Of Humanistic Psychology*, *53*(1), 114–128. doi:10.1177/0022167812449190

Shumaker, D. (2012). An existential–integrative treatment of anxious and depressed adolescents. *Journal Of Humanistic Psychology*, *52*(4), 375–400. doi:10.1177/0022167811422947

Steger, M. F., Frazier, P., Oishi, S., & Kaler, M. (2006). The meaning in life questionnaire: Assessing the presence of and search for meaning in life. *Journal Of Counseling Psychology*, *53*(1), 80–93. doi:10.1037/0022-0167.53.1.80

Steger, M. F., Mann, J. R., Michels, P., & Cooper, T. C. (2009). Meaning in life, anxiety, depression, and general health among smoking cessation patients. *Journal Of Psychosomatic Research*, *67*(4), 353–358. doi:10.1016/j.jpsychores.2009.02.006

Stolorow, R. D. (2007). Anxiety, authenticity, and trauma: The relevance of Heidegger's existential analytic for psychoanalysis. *Psychoanalytic Psychology*, *24*(2), 373–383. doi:10.1037/0736-9735.24.2.373

Stolorow, R. D. (2011). Toward greater authenticity: From shame to existential guilt, anxiety, and grief. *International Journal Of Psychoanalytic Self Psychology*, *6*(2), 285–287. doi:10.1080/15551024.2011.552411

Susman, E. J., & Dorn, L. D. (2009). Puberty: Its role in development. In R. M. Lerner, L. Steinberg, (Eds.), *Handbook of adolescent psychology: Individual bases of adolescent development, Vol. 1*, 3rd *ed.* (pp. 116–151). Hoboken, NJ, US: John Wiley & Sons Inc. doi:10.1002/9780470479193.adlpsy001006

Warren, S. L., & Sroufe, L. A. (2004). Developmental Issues. In T. H. Ollendick, J. S. March, (Eds.), *Phobic and anxiety disorders in children and adolescents: A clinician's guide to effective psychosocial and pharmacological interventions* (pp. 92–115). New York, NY, US: Oxford University Press. doi:10.1093/med:psych/9780195135947.003.0004

Warren, S. L., Huston, L., Egeland, B., & Sroufe, L. A. (1997). Child and adolescent anxiety disorders and early attachment. *Journal Of The American Academy Of Child & Adolescent Psychiatry*, *36*(5), 637–644. doi:10.1097/00004583-199705000-00014

Waterman, A. S. (1984). Identity formation: Discovery or creation?. *The Journal Of Early Adolescence*, *4*(4), 329–341. doi:10.1177/0272431684044004

Werner, E. E. (1993). Risk, resilience, and recovery: Perspectives from the Kauai Longitudinal Study. *Development And Psychopathology*, 5(4), 503–515. doi:10.1017/S095457940000612X

Westenberg, P. M., Siebelink, B. M., & Treffers, P. A. (2001). Psychosocial developmental theory in relation to anxiety and its disorders. In W. K. Silverman, P. A. Treffers, (Eds.), *Anxiety disorders in children and adolescents: Research, assessment and intervention* (pp. 72–89). New York, NY, US: Cambridge University Press.

CHAPTER 4

Core Existential Treatment Approaches with Adolescents

Introduction

In a chapter devoted to reviewing potentially helpful techniques, tools, and areas of focus that therapists working with adolescents from an EI framework should consider, it is perhaps wise to first remember the cautionary words of Rollo May about how a therapist should approach his or her craft. May, in a broad-ranging interview with Kirk Schneider, emphasized the importance of the therapeutic relationship in creating positive change (Schneider et al., 2009). Specific techniques or "gimmicks" (as May referred to them) held relatively less value as compared to creating an honest and open dialogue based upon trust where clients were encouraged to accept responsibility for their lives. May was not alone in his wariness of relying too heavily on therapeutic "gimmicks." Indeed, as discussed in Chapter 1, existential therapy enjoys a long and rich history of resisting a manualized, technique-driven, or symptom-based approach. The phenomenological approach that underlies the practice of existential therapy hinges upon the therapist's ability to study and come to understand the client's unique worldview, and to also tailor a treatment approach accordingly. Existential therapists, as much as any therapeutic school of thought, therefore seem to have a keen grasp of two basic foundations upon which good therapy is based. First, they appreciate that, aside from perhaps taking into account certain pre-existing client factors, the therapeutic relationship common factor is the driving force behind positive change in therapy (Beutler et al., 2012). Second, existential therapists understand

D. Shumaker, *Existential-Integrative Approaches to Treating Adolescents*, DOI 10.1057/978-1-349-95211-3_4

the importance of a flexible and nuanced approach to therapy. Or, more simply, they understand that one size does not fit all.

At the risk of oversimplifying the experience, it is arguably the very acts of (a) engaging in empathically attuned, active-listening, (b) approaching clients from a humanistic place of unconditional positive regard, and (c) modeling the humility, grace, openness, and courage that is needed to face life's "givens" that have the most profound impact upon clients as opposed to the teaching of a specific technique or set of techniques. Schneider (2008) certainly reflects this basic stance, maintaining it is *presence* or the act of "being there" that constitutes the therapist's fundamental experiential task. More focus will be devoted to Schneider's discussion of this aspect of therapy in our review of core techniques. Wampold's (2012) Tripartite Model of the therapeutic relationship also speaks to this notion. The model states that the establishment of a strong therapeutic bond can lead to (a) the experience of a real positive relationship, (b) the expectation of hope and positive change, and (c) the encouragement of increased engagement in positive activities. Indeed, the establishment of a strong rapport can have a multitude of beneficial effects.

Validation is another by-product of a strong therapeutic relationship. A therapist's empathically attuned presence facilitates the development of a strong therapeutic bond which, in turn, can serve as a trusted source of critical validation. In the author's experience it is especially important when working with adolescents to validate their dreams, their fledging identities, and their reactions to trauma. The increased urgency to validate stems from an appreciation that these young people may have not yet experienced true unconditional acceptance of their reactions, their thoughts, their feelings, and ultimately . . . their being. Adults, of course, can present in therapy with horrid histories of deprivation and negation as well. But, in the case of the adolescent, one often senses the precipice the individual is peering over where a final window of opportunity exists for the young person to achieve a corrective emotional experience with the aid of an empathically attuned therapist. That window of opportunity is, unfortunately, often mostly shut by the time a therapist makes contact with adult-aged clients who have suffered from long-term maladjustment due to early trauma experiences and/or whose personality formation is deeply entrenched. Simply receiving active confirmation that one is not "crazy" and that one's likes, dislikes, fears, and fantasies are not the same is, in the author's opinion, among the most curative aspects of therapy for this age group.

Still, validation is hardly considered by most to be a therapeutic technique or tool. Further, its natural development in the context of a solid therapeutic alliance between client and therapist is perhaps assumed by most clinicians, researchers, and students new to the field. The author and others disagree with this line of thinking. Demonstrating empathic attunement and validating client's experiences are *difficult* and *complex* tasks when performed at the highest levels of efficiency and there is considerable variation among therapists in their capacities to do this effectively on a consistent basis (Shea, 1998). There is also a fine line between validation and collusion, especially when working with adolescents. Unconditional acceptance of a client's being however does not mean that a therapist has to unconditionally accept all of their actions and/or attitudes (Barrett-Lennard, 1993). This nuance, too, is hard for many therapists to appreciate and delineate in their treatment stances.

Thus the author would encourage therapists in training to devote the majority of their focus and self-development efforts to refining their listening and core counseling skills (e.g., open-ended questioning, reflection of feelings, summarizing) that are designed to help the client tell their story as richly and accurately as possible. To be an engaged *presence* for a typical 45–60-minute session requires a high level of concentration, openness, stamina, and insulation from both internal and external distractions that may be easy for some to do on a single occasion, but is very hard to do consistently across multiple hours per day and multiple days per week. Attendance to self-care, the pursuit of both supervision and one's own therapeutic support, and critical analysis of one's in-session decision-making, verbalizations, and behavioral cues through audiotape and videotape analysis are all essential training components.

This advice may seem underwhelming and unfulfilling to some. Beginning therapists, in particular, crave techniques because possession of these tools can instill confidence and a sense of mastery, provide a more concrete roadmap of what will occur in the session, and help fill the uncomfortable void of silence by arming the therapist with a task to accomplish and things to say in session. In short, knowledge of techniques reduces a beginning therapist's anxiety. Indeed, it is tempting to do all that one can to avoid panic moments in therapy by loading up on tasks, tools, and/or assessment measures to administer to our clients. But those panic moments, too, serve as critical learning experiences for therapists and can increase one's empathic attunement with clients' moments of terror in therapy when they are at a loss for what to say or feel under the microscope and painfully exposed. These moments cannot and should not be artificially by-passed by loading up on techniques and tasks designed to, in part, keep the therapeutic hour flowing at a constantly brisk and uninterrupted pace. Stops and starts, struggles, and moments of discomfort for both the beginning therapist and one's clients are to some extent to be expected and constitute a healthy and natural evolution of the relationship and therapy experience. They are moments of true intimacy and vulnerability. The therapist who is at a loss for words and has the courage to admit it for his or her client without shame or terror likely strengthens the therapeutic bond in a way that far exceeds any of the techniques or interpretations at his or her disposal. It is not the task of a beginning therapist to be perfect and all-knowing. Rather, it is to be authentic, open, interested, *present,* and humble.

Having emphasized the importance of fostering a strong therapeutic alliance through one's presence and mastery of core counseling skills, the remainder of this chapter provides an overview of several EI counseling tools and techniques that are commonly utilized by therapists working within this framework. Included in the review are specific areas of focus and/or philosophical discussions that may also commonly occur within the context of an EI approach. The majority of these intervention strategies have been utilized with adults, and thus it is possible that some may have limited applicability with adolescents. However, in general this seems unlikely given the previously cited research indicating existential concerns are common in this population and evidence suggesting adolescents possess the cognitive capacities to reflect on these concerns at a deeper level.

The techniques and tools that are introduced are based upon a close review of the following data sources: (1) Schneider's (2008) discussion of the therapeutic implications of EI; (2) several landmark works on existential therapy treatment approaches conducted by prominent existential theorists and clinicians including Rollo May, James Bugental, Emmy Van Deurzen, and Ernesto Spinelli; (3) a literature review of peer-reviewed studies of existential treatment approaches; and (4) the author's own clinical experiences and previous research on this topic. The discussion is divided into two parts – "core" and "specific" techniques. This division, however, is admittedly imperfect and somewhat subjective. The "core" techniques section consists of key intervention strategies that are either used by Schneider (2008) or seem to have the potential to assist a wider array of adolescents suffering from a variety of presenting concerns. By contrast, those falling into the specific category seem to be useful in more isolated cases and/or have received relatively less consideration by EI therapists and researchers. As will be discussed in greater detail in future chapters devoted to EI applications with adolescents experiencing specific challenges, the following tools and techniques are most often utilized within the context of an evidenced-based approach as an adjunctive/ supplemental intervention.

Core Techniques and Focal Areas

Presence

This therapeutic stance was discussed briefly in the introduction and is expanded upon here. Schneider (2008) introduced the concept of presence in his more general discussion of "Offerings of Experiential Liberation" that occur within the context of attending to a client's ontological wounds. He describes these wounds as "kinesthetic-affective" in nature. These are deep injuries that strike at the core of one's being and speak to one's smallness/greatness in life. Presence, which he identifies as the first of four nutrients that promote experiential liberation, is the "immediate, kinesthetic, affective, and profound – *attention*" that a therapist conveys in the context of listening and communicating with a client (Schneider, 2008, pg. 60). The therapist who establishes a sense of presence remains open to all aspects of the client and his or her own being at a deeper level than simply attentive listening. For example, Schneider will study a client's physiological constrictive or expansive points by contemplating the following types of questions when meeting with the client: *What kind of the world is this man trying to hold together? What kind of life design do his muscles, gestures, and breathing betray? What does he bring up in my body?*

Schneider (2008) and Craig (1986) note the ability to consistently attend to a client's experience with this level of attentiveness and precision requires a great deal of effort and discipline. Remaining open to one's entire experience of being with a client, deciding what aspects of a client's experience one should attend to in a given moment, and transcending one's own personal biases and belief systems to see a client's experience through their eyes are just some of the challenges associated with remaining a positive presence for clients (Craig, 1986). The therapist must remain impervious to a range of distractions such as becoming consumed with nonclient-related thoughts, excessive attention to one's own physical experience and/or discomfort, overidentification with less important aspects of the client experience, or a failure to remain in the present moment due to a premature focus on the next question or topic of discussion.

Truly "being there" for adolescent clients can be challenging at times. Clients in this age range frequently are reluctant participants in therapy and many report a lack of positive experiences with the adults in their lives. They may have been told by their caretakers, teachers, coaches, siblings, etc., that not only do they have a problem but they *are* the problem, when in actuality nothing could be further from the truth. Often these clients enter the therapy room with complex personal histories and a guarded approach to new encounters because they have been deceived, smothered, neglected, and/or misunderstood. They may have every reason to question the legitimacy or helpfulness of talking to a "stranger" because doing so seems meaningless and generates anxiety (Don't we tell our kids not to talk to strangers?), they are suspicious of the evidence presented to them that it could be helpful, they are concerned about confidentiality, and/or they fear that their participation will be interpreted as a tacit self-endorsement of possessing a major problem or being "crazy." Thus, both overt resistance (e.g., "I'm not talking," "This is a waste of time," providing only "Yes" "No" or "Don't know" answers to all questions) and more passive forms of resistance (e.g., "Everything is fine," missing appointments) are commonly seen. Janet Sasson Edgette (2006) does a remarkable job of describing how adolescents often experience therapy, noting several assumptions they hold that can account for resistance in therapy. Therapists working with this age range should familiarize themselves with her work.

Resistance combined with a mercurial presentation can make it hard for a therapist to attend to the essential aspects of an adolescent client's experience in anything approximating a sustained manner. The young person's style of dress, mannerisms, gait, preferred manner of sitting, use of cosmetics and jewelry, attitude toward the therapist, language and speech patterns can often overwhelm the sensibilities of a therapist. It is truly remarkable how contradictory at times an adolescent's stated aims (e.g., "I want to blend in") can be with their presentation. The therapist's sensibilities can easily be overwhelmed by a myriad of oftentimes contradictory and provocative stimuli. Distinguishing what needs to be attended to within and across sessions can be truly challenging. At times the result is a therapist who becomes fixated on a single component of the adolescent's presentation or does not truly remain open to the client because of the resistance and/or every changing identity being portrayed by the client. Thankfully, Schneider (2008) and others offer important strategies for working with resistance that certainly can be utilized to positive effect with adolescents. These strategies will be discussed in greater detail in a following section. A takeaway message for the time being is that, while challenging at times, it is imperative for therapists working with adolescents from an EI perspective to remain disciplined and nondefensive during the therapy hour. Remembering that resistance serves a survival function and attacks on the therapist by the adolescent are often symptomatic of high anxiety and a sense of powerlessness can hopefully provide the therapist with a degree of insulation and patience that preserve the primary nutrient of a positive therapeutic relationship: presence.

Invoking the Actual

Schneider (2008) refers to invoking the actual when he discusses a range of creative ways a therapist can inspire presence within the context of a therapeutic encounter. The silence, tone of voice, word choice, and specific questions a therapist chooses all have the potential of striking at the heart of a client's struggle and amplifying the experience. Indeed, a therapist's initial utterances to a client can play an important role in setting the stage for an electric and meaningful therapeutic encounter. He encourages the use of the following statements and questions at the beginning of a therapeutic hour: *Take a moment to settle in. What's of concern to you? What really matters to you right now? Where are you at today?* In addition, Schneider (2008) encourages clients to use the present tense, refer to their experiences by using "I" statements, and will often have them comment on their body experiences in order to promote contact with one's deeply felt hurts. The underlying aim of invoking the actual is to draw out the client's inner struggles with the various polarities or his or her existence (e.g., chaos versus obliteration, smallness versus greatness). Once contact is made with these core struggles, the EI therapist should remain present with the client, trust the client's pain will eventually transform, and assist the client in developing that same trust.

Schneider (2008) suggests using several techniques to invoke the actual in clients, including the use of embodied meditation, experimentation in therapy, and experimentation outside of therapy. All can be very effective in facilitating contact with core hurts. In the specific case of adolescents the author has found most success using experimentation in the therapy session. More specifically, many adolescents seem to benefit from role-play and empty chair techniques. As Schneider (2008) notes, role-playing allows the individual to experiment with new interpersonal relationships using "one's imagination, energy, and spirit" (pg. 71). Though role-playing with children and adolescents frequently serves as a method for teaching social skills it can also be used to resolve trauma experiences. Joyce and Sills (2010), in an excellent work on Gestalt skills, describe this application in some detail. They refer to this specific form of role-playing as an "enactment" and delineate two types of these experimentations. They describe the two approaches in the following manner:

> There are two types of enactment or role-playing. One is when the client engages in some communication with his image of real people in his life – either historical or current. This is a particularly useful experiment because it provides direct access in the therapy room to co-created situations outside. The other is when the client embodies disowned or marginalized aspects of him or herself that is not in full awareness. Here the client is able to have a dialogue with these different qualities or parts of himself. It is often used in exploring polarities. (pg. 101)

The author has used a combination of these two approaches when working with adolescents who have experienced traumas ranging from invalidation by a primary caretaker, the loss of a loved one, and bullying episodes. For example, adolescents who are victims of bullying frequently struggle with a range of core existential concerns. The victim's sense of safety may be compromised, leading to chronic and intense concerns about one's emotional and physical integrity. Feelings of marginalization and a profound sense of aloneness are common as well. The young person might also begin to question the meaning of his or her existence when life becomes a daily struggle with fending off assaults on one's being. A truly darker existence is played out often in silence as the adolescent abandons hope of being helped.

Simply instructing the adolescent bully victim to discuss the bullying experiences can fall short of rendering a deeper picture of what has occurred. The adolescent may gloss over the experience and talk in generalities, never truly making contact with the emotional component of the bullying experience. This detached and overgeneralized recall likely serves an avoidant function. In these cases, the author will encourage a two-step role-playing process where the client first plays the role of the bully and the author plays the role of the client. The author seeks guidance from the client on how to respond (as the client). This role-reversal seems more tolerable and "safe" for the client as they assume a teaching (mastery) role while not initially feeling compelled to re-experience the encounter as a victim. At times, however, the author will ask the client "What am I feeling here?" when playing the role of the client as victim. This, too, can provide the client with sufficient distance to elaborate in more detail on the emotional experience of bullying.

When a distinct picture of the bullying interaction has been achieved through this role-play, the author will ask clients who seem ready to reverse roles if they feel ready to do so. However, in assuming the victim role in the bullying scenario the client is gently reminded of their strength, courage, and agency. They are also reminded of potential resources available to them and their problem-solving capacities. In cases where the bullying is no longer occurring, focus shifts more to the client's bravery and resilience in surviving these episodes. To be clear, the author is very careful not to encourage the adoption of an unrealistic or potentially dangerous stance in a bullying encounter. But, as part of assisting a client in developing a safety plan (if necessary), having them role-play encounters in a manner that highlights options for pursuing assistance and minimizing exposure to the aggressor(s) can be a very empowering exercise that reminds clients of their strength and capacities to self-advocate. Role-play and enactment exercises like this can help an adolescent client achieve a greater sense of balance in their struggle to deal with the smallness/greatness polarities of their existence. They are reminded that they are not infinitely small, but have strength, resilience, and presence. The support a concerned therapist and parents demonstrate also can hopefully reduce the sense of aloneness the victim may be feeling.

Vivifying and Confronting Resistances

As previously noted, many adolescents demonstrate resistance in therapy. Schneider (2008) refers to resistances as blockages that serve both protective and destructive functions. The client overtly and/or covertly refuses to engage in the therapeutic encounter and reverts to a protective shell. The therapist working with a resistant client is left to wonder if the client will choose to evolve or remain immobilized in the therapeutic encounter.

There are several strategies and stances a therapist can take when working with a resistant client. Schneider (2008) suggests the following five: (1) *vivifying resistance* – this is a gradual and indirect process of holding a mirror up to a client to show the world they have constructed and what might be necessary to change the world; (2) *verbal and nonverbal feedback* – these consist of efforts to note and tag instances of resistance as well as mirroring of the client's behavioral gestures; (3) *reviewing old territory* – this refers to the process of repetitively noting resistances in the hope of transcending familiar patterns of behavior; (4) *tracing out and enabling* – these are efforts by the clinician to demonstrate to the client how the resistance results in certain consequences that may not be life fulfilling as well as attempts by the clinician to give permission to the client to behave differently; and (5) *confronting resistance* – this is an amplified form of vivification that can alarm and mobilize a client to move beyond a resistant stance when applied with skill and discretion.

All of the approaches suggested by Schneider (2008) for working with resistant clients can certainly work well with adolescents. The author mostly uses a combination of the vivifying, providing feedback, and tracing approaches. Confrontation approaches are used sparingly as they rarely produce the desired results of stimulating an adolescent client's positive engagement. The author painfully recalls an occasion in family therapy years ago where he confronted strong resistance by interpreting the behavior as symptomatic of the client being afraid to make contact with his feelings. While perhaps an accurate interpretation, the adolescent referred to the therapist and interpretation as both a "joke" and retreated further into a shell of defensiveness punctuated with moments of overt hostility and disdain for the therapist. It did not help that the "joke" comment by the adolescent was met with hysterical laughter by the adolescent's younger brother and an "I told you so" look by the adolescent's mother. Therapy limped to a painful conclusion shortly thereafter.

When working with adolescents who are demonstrating resistance from an EI framework, the author suggests the following four-step process. First, like Schneider, the author vivifies the resistance by empathizing with the adolescent and his or her need to adopt a resistant stance. When initially meeting with the adolescent and his/her parents, the author always asks the adolescent how they learned that they would be attending therapy and what were the reasons given for pursuing the appointment. The stories they tell never cease to amaze. Many are provided misinformation or only partial information by their parents about what type of appointment they will be attending. Some are told nothing beyond "get in the car." This will occur even though the author explicitly tells parents during initial phone consultations not to misinform or shield the nature of the appointment. Is it any wonder then why an adolescent may adopt a defensive stance when entering the therapy room for the first time? In these cases, the therapist needs to achieve a balance of connecting with the adolescent's negative experience of starting therapy and the parents' motivations and concerns that led to the referral. The author typically will express appreciation for the adolescent's willingness to attend the session and participation in the initial dialogue. In addition, the author will note the potential discomfort the adolescent might be feeling in an initial attempt to form an alliance and work with the resistance. This noting process also serves a secondary function of modeling patience and highlighting the positive aspects of the adolescent's attendance for parents. Sometimes merely demonstrating some patience and understanding can significantly reduce the adolescent's resistance.

The remaining steps often occur in the context of meeting individually with the client. The second step initially consists of efforts to note and tag additional instances of verbal and nonverbal resistance in a nonaccusatory manner. This is often far from a complicated process. In an effort to shine direct light upon the resistance, the author will once again ask an adolescent how he or she feels about working together. Common responses include "I think this is a waste of time" or "My parents are the ones who should be here." From there the author will direct the discussion to an exploration of what the adolescent wants. Typically, in addition to not having to attend therapy, the adolescent will express a wish for more freedom from meddlesome and unhelpful parents and adults. Here the author poses a question to the adolescent, asking him or her, "Will refusing to give counseling a try get you closer or further away from that freedom?" If possible the author will also gently highlight that, for better or for worse, the parents are concerned about the adolescent and that those worries might be amplified if the therapeutic experiment ends prematurely due to a lack of nonengagement by the adolescent. This dialogue most closely approximates Schneider's (2008) tracing out approach to working with resistance and hopefully increases the adolescent's awareness of the likely unwanted consequences associated with adopting a resistant stance. At times the author openly concedes that the adolescent may be able to successfully sabotage therapy through nonparticipation. But this concession is made in the broader context of assuring the adolescent that parental concerns and restrictions are likely to remain the same or worsen if therapy grinds to a premature halt. When these potential options and outcomes are outlined dispassionately by the author, many clients will grudgingly reach the conclusion that their participation on a time-limited basis may be beneficial.

A third step in working with adolescent resistance is rooted in Weinblatt and Omer's (2008) nonviolent resistance (NVR) parent training model. NVR is designed to reduce oppositional behaviors and escalations of conflict in the home. The model is based upon sociopolitical research on how disadvantaged groups combat oppression (Sharp, 2005). Parents of adolescents who engage in oppositional and aggressive behaviors in the home frequently experience a profound sense of helplessness and vent frustration by acting punitively or aggressively, which in turn exacerbates the power struggle. These parents are drawn into conflict with their children, losing their own control and engaging in precisely the behaviors they wish for their child to cease. A close parallel can be made with the experience of a therapist who encounters a resistant adolescent client. The urge to confront or attempt to control an adolescent who is not cooperating with the norms and expectations of a therapeutic encounter can lead to some very bad choices by a therapist. NVR reminds parents that they are doomed if they try to control an adolescent's oppositional behaviors. One can only resist in a nonviolent manner through one's peaceful presence and modeling of behavioral traits expected of the adolescent (openness, transparency, respect).

A similar, but slightly adjusted, stance can be adopted by a therapist working with a resistant adolescent client. Specifically, consistent with NVR the therapist openly acknowledges his or her powerlessness to control the adolescent. However, rather than utilize certain nonviolent resistance strategies that parents are encouraged to use when their adolescents are engaged in maladaptive behaviors, therapists working with resistant adolescent clients are encouraged to remain open and accepting of the stance while conveying the expectation that the adolescent will participate when he or she is ready. Specifically, the author will openly acknowledge his powerlessness to make the adolescent participate in the therapeutic encounter by simply saying, "We both know that I am powerless to make you talk to me, but I sure hope you might give it a try." In saying this the therapist removes (or at least significantly reduces) the potential for a power struggle to ensue. Sometimes painfully long silences can follow as the adolescent is unsure how to proceed and the author resists the temptation to force participation by pestering the client with additional questions. At times an adolescent might counter with, "Well, my parents are making me be here." In these cases the author empathizes with the adolescent's plight but also reminds the client of his or her agency by stating, "I understand that there may be consequences imposed by your parents for not participating, but let me assure you I have no intention of trying to make you do anything here and you are not trapped. You, not your parents or I, are in control of what happens here." Again, the intent is to reassure the adolescent that the therapist recognizes his or her free will. In the author's experience, these second and third steps (i.e., appealing to the adolescent's urge for freedom and demonstrating respect for the adolescent's agency) frequently will provide the resistant adolescent enough assurance to emerge at least partially emerge from their resistant shell.

Viktor Frankl's (1980) discussion of values serves as the source for the fourth step one can take when working with a resistant adolescent client. He identifies three major sources of values – creative, experiential, and attitudinal. The individual in search of meaning can often find such in creative pursuits (e.g., these can include meaningful work and artistic activities) and enriching and awe-inspiring life experiences (e.g., these can be as simple as marveling at the beauty of a rising sun or the smile on a child's face). Unfortunately, certain unfortunate life circumstances can reduce the individual's ability to find meaning through creative and experiential means. For example, an individual faced with a terminal illness may experience a reduction in mobility and increase in suffering that eventually destroys the individual's ability to pursue meaning through more obvious creative activities. In these cases, Frankl argues that the individual can still find meaning in the attitude he or she chooses to adopt in the face of suffering and death. He describes this attitudinal value beautifully in the following description of the doctor-patient relationship:

> A doctor who is sensitive to the imponderables of a situation will always feel a kind of shame when attending a patient with an incurable disease, or a dying person. For the doctor himself is helpless, incapable of wresting this victim from death. But the patient has become a hero who is meeting his fate and holding his own by accepting it in tranquil suffering. That is, upon a metaphysical plane, a true achievement – while the doctor in the physical world, in his physician's realm, has his hands tied, is a failure. (pg. 116)

So just how does Frankl's discussion of attitudinal values relate to working with a resistant adolescent client? The author will gently remind a client of the choice in attitude that he or she can adopt even under the unfortunate circumstance of having to sit with the author for an hour. A comment such as "Well, I appreciate that this is not where you want to be. Even so, we have this given hour, and how you want to approach the hour remains entirely up to you. When given lemons, can we make some lemonade?" If a client is even remotely open to receiving this message the author often follows up by questioning the adolescent about how they handled adversity and other unwanted commitments in the past. The underlying message remains the same as Frankl's discussion of attitudinal values – the individual faced with even the most dire circumstances can still creatively choose the attitude from which they face those circumstances.

Rediscovering Meaning and Awe

A final major area of treatment focus in EI consists of efforts by the therapist to assist the client to cultivate a sense of intentionality and freedom in their approach to life (Schneider, 2008). An individual who is in closer touch with the limitations he or she has imposed upon him or herself begins to see the world through a very different lens. This clarity and depth of focus leads to more experiences of awe and wonderment. These "awe" moments are described by Schneider as "the humility and wonder, thrill and anxiety, or full living that can emerge from optimal experiential liberation" (pg. 80). Thus, the liberation process involves inward focusing that increases intentionality and outward focusing that increases a sense of awe.

van Deurzen (2015) states the underlying question that addresses the issue of intentionality is "What is this all for?" An individual who struggles to find a meaningful answer to the question may experience life as "gratuitous, absurd, and random." It becomes increasingly difficult for the individual to feel motivated and a sense of connection with the world when, for example, things go badly or one experiences unexpected losses and/or trauma. In these moments of despair, a therapist can assist a client in making sense of their existence. In fact, van Deurzen states *the* essence of existential therapy is "turning hardship into emotional strength and wisdom" (p. 2010). This is done by cultivating a sense of transcendence. She defines transcendence as "that which goes beyond" or "surpasses" something and compares it to the divine. Therapy provides the client a forum in which they can pause and consider developing an enriched philosophy of life and existence. The therapist stimulates this self-evaluation by posing philosophical questions that probe and challenge a client's worldview. Included in these discussions are investigations into clients' spiritual lives. Long considered a taboo topic in therapy, existential therapists identify a client's spiritual experience as a window into that which they hold most near and dear to them. A failure to understand what a client will both live and die for results in an incomplete conceptualization that will ultimately yield a less effective treatment approach. Initiating a dialogue about spirituality is therefore a critical component of an existential treatment approach. That being said, van Deurzen reminds us that at no point in time does the therapist impose his or her values upon the client.

Schneider (2008) does not believe that therapists need to arm themselves with a specific set of tools to assist clients in consolidating what has true meaning. A client that has reached this level of experiential liberation will be sufficiently prepared to search within for these answers. The therapist, by his or her mere consistent presence, will certainly aid the client and reinforce the search process. Like van Deurzen, Schneider frequently invites clients toward the end of therapy to elaborate on "which values they hold dear and how they plan on implementing those values" (pg. 81). Thus, rather than mastering a specific technique, existential therapists seeking to awaken a client's sense of "awe" and intentionality simply need to possess the courage and wherewithal to open a dialogue with clients about their worldview, values, and spirituality. These dialogues often signal the beginning of the latter stages of therapy.

When working with adolescents, the author initiates a dialogue about meaning early in the process. Oftentimes the adolescent is asked, "What has meaning to you?" in the first session. The reactions to this question are striking. The majority of adolescents react with puzzled looks, nervous laughter, or silence followed by efforts to clarify the question. A small percentage seems to search for the "right" answer and the result is a notable lack of passion in their delivery of the answer or difficulty expanding upon their rationale. The categories of "family," "school," "friends," and "sports" are frequently nominated but there is a hollowness and lack of specificity surrounding these choices. It is as if the adolescent believes these aspects of life are supposed to be important, but they are not sure why and are not sure if the answer truly matches their inner experience. Precious few seem to possess a clear sense of what has meaning to them.

It makes sense that most adolescents struggle early in therapy when posed with the question of what has meaning to them. It is rare for an adolescent to have achieved experiential liberation *prior to* entering therapy. A fundamental and deep question about meaning will stump most individuals who have not engaged in considerable self-analysis. Some could argue posing the question at the start of therapy short-circuits the process of facilitating deeper self-awareness in clients through the long and arduous "work" of therapy. It is like giving a history test in school prior to lecturing on the topic. The author, however, believes there are strong rationales for posing the question early *and* often in therapy. First, it serves an important assessment function. Specifically, it can help inform the therapist of the degree of intentionality and self-awareness an adolescent possesses upon entering therapy. Second, the author would argue that posing the question is a specific way to "invoke the actual" in the client. It signals to the client the therapist's intent to utilize the therapeutic hour as a safe place for the client to move toward greater experiential liberation. Finally, and relatedly, it signals to the client the therapist's intent to really get to know the client at a deeper level than most. Several adolescents have responded to the question by informing the author that "I've never been asked that before." What a truly remarkable concession. Here we have a human being on the verge of adulthood surrounded by loving and concerned parents, teachers, coaches, friends, and relatives, none of whom has thought to ask, "What matters to you?" How could this be? There are likely a myriad of reasons – an assumption on the part of those who know the adolescent that the adolescent shares the same values as them, a discomfort with or lack of interest in considering the question, a predisposition to teach and tell rather than listen and ask – for the absence of the question, none of which suggests overt negligence or other malignant factors. Either way, when the therapist asks the question it signals that the therapy experience and relationship being formed is different. A sense of anticipation and excitement is established. The therapist, by asking the question, is saying *I truly want to get to know you.*

Initial questions regarding meaning are not the only questions the author will pose to adolescents in order to stimulate contact with a deeper sense of themselves and their being. Other existential themes are probed. When embarking on this journey with clients the author in more recent times has referred to Spinelli's (2015) discussion of key existential themes and concerns. He offers specific ways to broach these core existential concerns and challenges clinicians to consider their own stance regarding these questions. Several of these core themes and the questions/exercises that he suggests are included in bullets below. It is common practice for the author to pose these questions to adolescents at various stages of therapy (including the early stages) dependent upon the client's concerns and readiness to contemplate these issues.

- *Theme of meaning/meaningless*: Ask the client to complete the following statement "One thing that is truly meaningful to me is . . . "
- *Theme of choice:* Ask the client to complete the following statements "One choice that I believe I have made in my life is . . . " and "Something that has happened in my life that I did not choose is . . . "
- *Theme of freedom:* Ask the client to think of a time when they felt most free in their life and when they felt least free in their lives.
- *Theme of responsibility:* Ask the client to think of something for which he/she feels responsible for and for something they feel no responsibility for.
- *Authenticity and inauthenticity:* Ask the client to think of an example in their own life where they felt the closest to being existentially authentic.
- *Isolation (aloneness) and relation:* Ask the client to think of a life event where they felt isolated or alone. Ask them to share how they experienced missing someone else.
- *Death anxiety:* Ask clients to consider the prospect that they would die within the next 5 years. Then ask how this knowledge would affect their plans, goals, and relationships with others. Also ask how their lives might be different if they learned they were immortal.

Again, it is important to emphasize that these questions are posed not haphazardly but at times when issues in the client's life relate to these core existential themes *and* the client seems stable enough to delve deeper into the root fears and existential anxiety they may be experiencing. For example, more than a handful of adolescents have arrived at a therapy session visibly shaken by the death of a friend or acquaintance due to suicide, accident, and/or disease. In the course of assessing the impact of the loss upon the client and processing the client's reaction to the death the author will frequently note life's fragility and may ask the client to consider questions that speak to the client's own death anxiety. These conversations almost universally seem to have a calming effect upon the adolescent and can also increase the client's sense of intentionality. The broader point to be remembered is that the existential discussion was initiated by the client's report of an event that speaks to a core existential theme as opposed to the clinician introducing the existential concern without cause.

A final comment regarding the process of assisting adolescents in discovering meaning returns our focus to van Deurzen's (2015) discussion of spirituality. To recall, van Deurzen encourages the exploration of a client's spiritual life for the purpose of learning more about values and potential sources of transcendence. While the author certainly will ask adolescents about their spiritual experience, this is done very carefully and with a healthy respect for the client's stage of development. More specifically, the author remains mindful of the fact that the adolescent is (often) still a minor and parents are often engaged in the treatment process. A rupture in the treatment relationship may occur if either the adolescent and/or the parents of the adolescent interpret a dialogue about spirituality negatively. For example, if a therapist asks, "What are your religious beliefs?" and this question is communicated to a parent second-hand by the adolescent, the parent could understandably wonder about the treatment focus and fear perhaps a threat to the family's religious belief system. Thus, the therapist will always pose the question by stating, "How does spirituality fit in your life?" and accompany the specific question by stating that the question is asked only for the purpose of potentially learning more about the client's values and life-sustaining influences. If an adolescent wishes to offer his or her own commentary/critique on their religious experience, the author, of course, listens in an attentive and supportive manner. But, again, great attention is devoted to ensuring that the client does not feel judged and the author's own religious beliefs are not imparted.

Dreamwork

Several prominent existential therapists utilize dreamwork with their clients (Bugental, 1987; May, 1983; Schneider, 2008; Spinelli, 2015). They do not view dreams as random, haphazard, and/or meaningless mental activity that occur during sleep. Rather dreams are thought to reflect essential components of the individual's personality and values. Tensions, fears, and emotional blockages are also capable of being revealed. These core aspects of an individual's experience are often concealed from consciousness because of the smothering presence of reason and defense mechanisms. Dreams analysis, creative experiential exercises, and "play" activities (e.g., sand play for adults in therapy) are frequently utilized by existential therapists in an effort to circumvent an individual's defense systems and reach the core of a human's being.

A review of existential approaches to analyzing client dreams reveals, with one notable exception, relatively little detail about the process. Most references to dream work simply indicate that when dreams are reported by a client the clinician assists the client in discovering the meanings of the dream through the use of questioning. This general description leaves a fair amount to the clinician's imagination when attempting to conduct a dream analysis with an actual client. Thankfully, van Deurzen (2012) provides one of the more comprehensive accounts of dream analysis conducted from an existential framework. She, like most other existential therapists, believes the aim of working with dreams, "is to assist the client in distilling the essential meaning from the reported experience, whether this experience was real or imagined" (pg. 170). The author follows van Deurzen's approach when analyzing the dreams of adolescents. Therefore, a brief review of her methodology is provided for the purpose of highlighting the major components of the procedure.

van Deurzen (2012) states the first step of what she refers to as the structural existential analysis (SEA) of the dream is to have the client carefully describe the dream several times in a row *without* offering an interpretation. The therapist's job during this initial stage is to simply encourage the client to repeatedly tell the story. Once a dream has been shared multiple times and a vivid picture has emerged, van Deurzen continues to detail the "lifeworld" of the dream at the following dimensions of existence: (1) physical, (2) social, (3) personal, and (4) spiritual. One can see the close parallels between van Deurzen's four-tiered system of an individual's experience and Schneider's (2008) six layers of human consciousness (i.e., physiological, environmental, cognitive, psychosexual, interpersonal, and experiential). During this deeper portion of the analysis she emphasizes the importance of the client assigning meaning to the dream. She strongly advises therapists not to offer their own interpretations. Even if a therapist suspects a client's interpretation does not ring true, he or she should remain patient and continue to revisit the dream with the client over the course of several sessions. Thus, van Deurzen maintains unshakeable faith in the client's ability to eventually reach a more accurate account of the dream.

What is perhaps most helpful in van Deurzen's (2012) description of her SEA approach is the detailed list of specific areas of dream focus. This better informs the search process for a clinician conducting existential dream analysis. For example, at the physical level of functioning, she suggests clinicians clarify what material world a client's dream takes place in (e.g., natural or man-made), whether the world is known or unknown to the dreamer, and whether it is real or unreal. As for the social dimension, she notes the importance of clarifying whether the dream's main character is alone or with others, the function the dreamer has in relation to others, and the degrees of friendliness/unfriendliness. Regarding the personal dimension, the therapist is encouraged to learn more about the main character's motivations, intentions, and personality traits. Finally, within the spiritual dimension the therapist asks questions designed to reveal the main character's worldview, values, and assumptions. These are just a small sample of the SEA areas of interest and readers who are inclined to pursue dream analysis with adolescents are strongly encouraged to read the entirety of van Deurzen's (2012) discussion of the topic.

In the author's clinical practice it is fairly rare for an adolescent to introduce a dream in session. When this does occur it often seems due to the fact that the client is distressed by the content of the dream and it happened in the evening prior to the session. More often, the author will ask about a client's dream life after a strong alliance has been established and the core themes/issues that have led to the client's concerns are at least fairly well understood. On these occasions most adolescents will have at least one recurrent, recent, and/or memorable dream that they are eager to share. Those few who do not are encouraged to be mindful of them moving forward and some spontaneously offer to log them as a homework assignment.

Most adolescents are also patient with the retelling process of the dream and extensive question. However, when impatience with the ELA process is detected, the author heeds van Deurzen's (2012) advice and simplifies the dream analysis process to the focus on the following six areas: (1) What has the dreamer learned about his/her mode of being from analyzing the dream? (2) What has the dreamer learned about his/her attitudes, actions, and possible consequences? (3) What lessons can be learned for the future? (4) What are the paradoxes and dilemmas for the future? (5) What changes might be required in everyday life to accommodate what the dream teaches us? (6) What is the existential message that can be taken from the dream? van Deurzen (2012) also suggests encouraging clients to summarize what the dream is telling them in a single sentence. This would seem helpful for all adolescent clients participating in ELA analysis regardless of the degree of depth to the process.

Specific Techniques

As previously discussed, in a prior effort the author suggested four techniques/area of focus that clinicians may consider using when working with adolescents from an existential perspective (Shumaker, 2012). These strategies include promoting client acceptance of unwanted emotions, understanding and channeling one's daimonic, infusing hero metaphors into the dialogue, and the general encouragement of the pursuit of creative activities. Each of these specific strategies is reviewed in detail below. In addition, paradoxical intentions are suggested as a specific technique as well.

Promote Acceptance Through Education

This strategy channels the spirit of modern mindfulness/acceptance approaches to therapy (Hayes et al., 1999; Segal et al., 2004). Or, perhaps more accurately, mindfulness/acceptance approaches to therapy seem to channel several core components of existential therapy – most notably one's acceptance of all emotions. Like traditional cognitive and cognitive-behavioral therapies these approaches target the client's inner experience, including one's expectations and beliefs, cravings, distressing emotions, and bodily experience. However, there are important distinctions between the theoretical orientations which will be discussed in some detail.

Acceptance and commitment therapy (ACT) is predicated upon the belief that therapy is most effective when it is focused on changing one's awareness of their thoughts and feelings as opposed to an emphasis on changing the content of those thoughts (Hayes et al., 1999). This view is based in part upon empirical research that indicates attempts to suppress unwanted thoughts and/or emotions are often counterproductive. Avoidant coping strategies are also not helpful in alleviating a client's emotional distress over the long term, nor is a belief system that one has no control over the experience of threatening events.

Hayes and Duckworth (2006) have identified six core principles of ACT that capture the essence of the approach. First, acceptance remains the heart of the approach. Clients are taught to embrace and experience unwanted emotions without attempts to fight the experience. Second, clients are taught cognitive defusion strategies that alter the undesirable function of thoughts as opposed to the thoughts themselves. There are a variety of specific techniques used here, each designed to decrease the believability and client's attachment to a particular thought. A third principle is being present. This consists of emphasizing the importance of remaining focused on one's present inner experience in a nonjudgmental manner. Self as context is a fourth principle. It reminds clients to always consider themselves and their experience within a broader, relational context for the purpose again of establishing some distance between oneself and one's problems. The fifth principle is an emphasis on having clients identify their core values. By doing so a client will perhaps shift focus from life choices based upon avoidance or social compliance. The sixth and final principle is committed action. This essentially is a follow-up to the discussion of values where the client is encouraged to follow through with actionable steps that reflect core values.

The parallels between existential therapy and ACT become more striking when one considers the aforementioned list of core ACT principles. Perhaps the most obvious parallel is that both ACT and existential therapy do not try to eliminate the experience of negative emotions. In ACT there is acceptance that anxiety, fear, sadness, and anger will be experienced and the individual's relationship with these emotions are examined closely for the purpose of creating distance and less urgency to act upon the negative cognitions that accompany these emotions. By comparison, a core underpinning of existential therapy is the general understanding that humans experience a wide range of emotions *and* eliminating the experience of anxiety and other uncomfortable emotions is not possible or advisable. While cognitive-behavioral strategies that seek to eliminate catastrophic thinking, overestimations of risk, excessively rigid and/or dichotomous thinking, and confusing "wants" with "needs" are undoubtedly helpful (Ollendick & Jarrett, 2009), existential therapists do not believe it is their duty to facilitate the elimination of a client's normative existential anxiety. For example, how can one overestimate the likelihood that they will eventually die? This is a certainty. Pursuing the question further, how can the threat of nonbeing ever be overly dramatized or catastrophized by the individual? The prospect of nonbeing can understandably feel quite terrifying. Existential therapists recognize that we all face the threat of nonbeing and Becker (1973) for one believes that society as a whole has dramatically undersold the potential terrors associated with nonbeing that all humans face because to contemplate them head on would lead to both individual and collective incapacitation. It is normative therefore to experience anxiety pertaining to one's mortality.

Beyond anxiety stemming from a fear of death, existential therapists also acknowledge the presence of fear of life concerns. Consciousness is a fundamental component of humanity. It bestows upon the individual awesome responsibility. We are faced with thousands of decisions on a daily basis in our moment-by-moment experience of ourselves and our world around us. We have freedom of choice, a capacity that can be both exciting and overwhelming. We are also ultimately alone in our thoughts and our experience. Though there are times when the external world and/or our own physical limitations may limit our choices, with few exceptions most of us will never lose our sense of agency at least as it pertains to our internal thoughts and experience. When individuals are forced to make difficult life decisions or experience even normative choice-points of daily existence under duress, the responsibility can weigh heavily and anxiety can result. The tensions that stem from the nature of our human condition are an inevitable by-product of the development of consciousness and appreciation for the responsibility of choice (Rank, 1936). Existential therapists can both affirm a client's normative anxieties while simultaneously identifying and correcting irrational fears. In the author's experience most adolescents seamlessly integrate the existential concept of acceptance with classic cognitive-behavioral strategies of identifying irrational or maladaptive cognitions followed by the development of more accurate and reality-based cognitions.

A second parallel that exists between ACT and existential therapy is that both encourage the client to reflect upon their experience within the broader context of the world that exists beyond their immediate experience. Indeed, the ACT principle of "self as context" that is designed to create space between a client and their distressing cognitions seems quite similar to attempts made by existential therapists to encourage transcendence. As clients develop their metacognitive abilities and self-awareness a logical by-product of the self-analysis can be a reappraisal of what has meaning. When one's values are clarified yet another logical consequence is an evaluation of the extent to which one's stated beliefs and values are being lived on a daily basis. Here too both ACT and existential therapy encourage clients to assume the responsibility for their actions and to live a life that is congruent with the individual's stated values. When working with adolescent clients from an existential perspective a common component of the discussion of the client's values is an analysis of the degree of consistency between the stated value and the client's behavior. For example, the adolescent who identifies "doing good in school" as an important value may be encouraged, or even gently challenged, to consider the extent to which playing the XBOX for several hours on a school night while smoking marijuana reflects the self-proclaimed importance of doing well in school.

Embrace the Daimonic

Rollo May (1969) introduced the concept of the daimonic for consideration by a wide audience of existentially inclined thinkers in *Love & Will.* The roots of the word can be found in the ancient Greek concept of the daimon, a term the Greeks equated to the concept of "Eros." While more modern Christian interpretations essentially associated the word with the devil, Diamond (1996) in an expert analysis of the word's origin notes the initial meaning incorporated a range of emotions that affirmed one's divine life force. This rather complex history notwithstanding, May defines the daimonic as "any natural function which has the power to take over the whole person" (pg. 123). He further emphasizes that this life force can potentially be either creative or destructive. It reflects an essential urge or motivation in the individual to seek affirmation and ensure one's survival. When this drive consumes the individual and, as May puts it, "usurps the total self without regard to the integration of the total self," evil emerges. In this more primitive state of being one utilizes any means necessary, including aggression and cruelty, to satisfy the drive.

While tempting and, in the shorter term, even partially satisfying, simply ignoring or repressing the daimonic is not advised (May, 1969). Chronic repression results in apathy and a risk for periodic explosions of rage. The individual needs to remain aware of daimonic urges and anticipate its emergence to the extent one can. This powerful survival force of nature requires directing and channeling for one to live a life with maximal experiential freedom. Of course it takes time and effort for the individual to truly ascertain the power of these daimonic urges. One can feel its force when in a state of rage or ecstasy, but contact in these extreme emotional states is often associated with harmful consequences. One should endeavor to anticipate and experience it responsibly and with awareness to the extent one can. As May (1969) points out, "the denial of the daimonic is, in effect, a self-castration in love and a self-nullification in will" (pg. 131). When the individual is in harmony with one's daimonic then the most life-affirming and creative experiences have the potential to be achieved.

May's (1969) consideration of the daimonic touches upon a fundamental component of existential thinking. Existential theory allows for the healthy experience of not only anxiety, but also sadness, anger, fear, jealousy, and despair. As previously stated, denial of the existence of these more painful emotions places the individual at risk for experiencing a slow spiral into a sea of apathy and/or for becoming vulnerable to regretful and potentially harmful fits of rage. The assumption held by many in today's society, including several well-intentioned therapists, is that the pursuit of individual happiness is the unquestioned objective for all. While existential therapists are certainly not resistant to their client's experiencing this emotion and will work with clients to improve their quality of life, they believe part of being human is to experience a wide range of emotions that run the gamut from excruciating to blissful. As Frankl reminds us, there is meaning in our suffering. To wit, finding meaning in one's existence and clarifying one's values are more pressing objectives to the existential therapist. Exploring a client's experience of painful and unwanted emotions is a vital component of the therapy process because these emotions are thought to reflect blockages in the client's life. Therefore, when an adolescent presents in therapy with the perhaps more naive expectation that mental health equals an absence of negative emotion, the existential therapists should over time work to gently dissuade the client of this notion.

Of course, it is entirely understandable why many adolescents (and adults) enter therapy harboring the belief that an absence of negative emotions is the measure of good mental health. First, these emotions at best are uncomfortable and at worst excruciating. It is hardly surprising therefore that there is a strong pull in humans to avoid experiencing these emotions. These emotions are important signals that have much to teach us, but many adolescents want to avoid the painful lesson entirely. Second, many adolescents have learned through adults and social media that painful/uncomfortable emotions are to be avoided. If the adolescent harbors ill thoughts toward another while experiencing the emotion of jealousy, for example, he or she may be condemned by his or her parents for experiencing "bad" or "wrong" thoughts. In more extreme cases the individual may even be told that experiencing these thoughts and emotions makes one a "bad" individual. More often though the adolescent's behavior, not his or her thoughts or emotions, is meant to be condemned. But it is not uncommon for the intent to be misconstrued. Third, in a society dominated by smartphones and access to a never-ending supply of provocative distractions, there seems to be very little tolerance for boredom, frustration, or loneliness. Sitting with these unpleasant emotions and working through them in a constructive manner (e.g., through creative pursuits, using one's imagination, exercise) seems to be a foreign concept for many of the adolescents the author sees in his clinical practice. The therapist has an opportunity in these instances to impress upon the client his or her capacity to use these emotions to clarify priorities, live life authentically, and seek love and connection as opposed to rendering oneself incapacitated and/or without direction or a sense of responsibility. Chessick (1996) offers an excellent illustration of an existential approach to treating adolescent depression where the client's experience of depressive symptomatology was used as a springboard for a sophisticated and in-depth discussion of the client's values. This represents the type of depth therapy that arguably many confused, frustrated, and/or disenfranchised adolescents would greatly benefit from (and unconsciously crave) but fail to experience in a mental health field dominated by managed care and the search for the perfect technique. Ultimately, reminding adolescents of their "creative will" and potential inspiration that can be drawn from even the darkest of emotions can have very positive effects.

Embrace Hero Metaphors

Existential theorists and therapists have a deep appreciation for the power of the hero metaphor. Otto Rank (1989) in *Art and Artist* drew a close parallel between the motivations of heroes and poets, the former expressing his vitality and will in social settings, the latter who does the same in an artistic/creative format. He writes, "Ultimately this activity, whether social as with the hero, or artistic as with the poet, is a magical attempt not only to evidence but to attain to the immortality-belief by actualizing their thought, their wish, or their word" (pg. 289). Of course, both the hero and poet are destined to fail in their quest for personal immortality. However, that does not prevent them from achieving ideological immortality. The sacrifices both make in their heroic deeds and artistic devotion are what reverberates in the memory of those who follow. The broader point, however, remains that through the ages humans have struggled to come to terms with death's inevitability. The manner in which one lives provides important clues into how the individuals resolve this particular existential given.

Becker (1973) also wrote extensively about how humans cope with the inevitability of their death. He states humans are predisposed to develop the narcissistic belief that all others are expendable except oneself. Other theorists and philosophers have noted this tendency as well. For example, Aristotle observed that most acts of courage in life are undertaken under the false belief that the man to either side of you will be felled by the arrow. The individual defends against death by courting it himself and exercising control over the preservation and annihilation of others. If an individual can convince him or herself that his or her "special" or "heroic" status will spare them in battle, the individual will be emboldened to act in a heroic manner. Further, engaging in acts of heroism and living to receive the adulation certainly can serve as a powerful affirmation of one's divine nature. As Becker (1973) writes, "it is still a mythical hero system in which people serve in order to earn a feeling of primary value, of cosmic specialness, of ultimate usefulness to creation, of unshakable meaning." This is where a connection between heroism and therapy can be drawn.

Specially, the author has previously noted that great strength, courage, and comfort can be drawn from the belief that one's life has meaning and a special, unique quality (Shumaker, 2012). At the risk of stating the obvious, life is hard. The existential givens humans face are formidable and omnipresent. Not only does death loom and we each carry the burden of choice, but we are also fundamentally alone. The brief individual journeys we each make in life can feel overwhelming, pointless, directionless, and isolating on at least some occasions for all. Faced with these considerable burdens of existence, life has the potential to feel more secure and intentional if we believe in our specialness and heroic status. A therapist is in a unique position to encourage the transformation of a client's self-narrative from one mired in a sea of pain and isolation to one that celebrates the client's courage and uniqueness. The use of hero metaphors by the therapist can stimulate this process.

Given these beneficial effects, it is not surprising that May (1977), Tillich (1952), and Rank (1936) freely use heroic terminology in both their theory and therapeutic dialogue with clients. Clients who can embrace an identity that includes meaning and uniqueness as opposed to meaninglessness and despair improve their prognosis. The therapist can infuse the therapeutic dialogue with references to the client's courage and heroism in order to stimulate a self-narrative that reflects the same. Specific examples of this approach abound in existential literature. To begin, May (1977) encouraged clients in the throes of depression to have both the "courage" and "patience" to endure the "valleys" of truly dark emotional experience in their "journey" back to the peak emotional experiences of joy, ecstasy, and enlightenment. More recently, Ellerman (1999) recommended that clinicians "replace [a client's] destructive fictions with new life affirming deceptions." Yalom (1980) also argues that a primary purpose of existential therapy is to provide clients with a sense of purpose by means of fictional interpretations for the ultimate objective of sparking a dormant will. What could be a more effective means of doing so than for a therapist to convey to a client that he or she is a hero in the therapist's eyes?

Of course, there should be reasonable limits on the extent to which an existential therapist encourages the development of a client's heroic self-narrative. At all times it is the therapist's primary responsibility to act in accordance with a realistic assessment of a client's capacities and degrees of freedom. A good therapist is always encouraging and believes in a client's capacities at times when the client is in a state of despair, but at no point should the therapist foster unrealistic expectations or distort reality. Still the practice of championing a client's divine and heroic qualities can be defended as a necessary means through which a demoralized and/or immobilized client can increase self-esteem, gain a sense of mastery, and envision hope for a brighter future (Ellerman, 1999).

When working with adolescents, especially those in a state of despair and those with low self-esteem, the author's fundamental interpersonal stance is that of a benign guide in support of a young jedi (i.e., the client) who has only just embarked on a perilous but what will ultimately be a successful quest for future peak experiences. The benign guide imparts wisdom as necessary but perhaps his or her most critical function is the unshakeable belief he or she imparts in the wounded adolescent's capacity to heal and ultimately thrive. Knowing someone understands and believes in you can provide immeasurable comfort and hope. When anxious and depressed adolescents have their struggles framed in heroic terms this can serve as a starting point for the road to recovery and sustain the adolescent's long and painful journey toward the same. The therapist's efforts to cultivate a heroic self-narrative need to be authentic. That is, if the therapist truly does not experience the client in these terms, then this technique will come across as likely forced and inauthentic. Of course, in these circumstances it should not be used. But in the author's experience one can seamlessly see the heroism in all adolescent clients if their presence in the therapeutic setting is considered in context. Specifically, as previously stated, life is hard. Adolescence is particularly hard for many. It is a time of great physiological change, immense academic and social pressures, and confusion about one's identity and place in the world. Presenting oneself to an adult stranger in therapy, especially when the adolescent does not feel choice in the matter, is yet another challenge that can understandably be viewed as an unwanted threat. The decision to cross the threshold from the waiting room to the therapist's office represents an act of courage by the adolescent. The author endeavors to remain acutely aware of the adolescent's experience in this respect from virtually the moment the adolescent enters the therapy room. This empathic attunement fosters a strong sense of admiration and patience for the courage the adolescent has demonstrated by agreeing to meet. In essence, the client is already viewed as a hero in the author's eyes before a single word is spoken.

Encourage Creativity and Intentionality

Existential theorists have long championed the belief that creative pursuits are a healthy way for individuals to work through core existential fears of nonbeing and meaninglessness (Rank, 1936; May, 1977; Tillich, 1952; Yalom, 1980). In the prior section on the use of hero metaphors in therapy, for example, Rank's (1989) parallel between the hero and the poet underscored his view that creative pursuits represent another attempt by humans to achieve immortality. For some it may not be inherently obvious how a creative pursuit might relate to the human struggle for immortality. Another quote from Rank (1989) can help to explain the relationship. He writes, "the fundamental idea is that for all created things there is needed not only a creator, but a piece of life, life itself, which is somehow withdrawn from its proper destiny of death and fixed in an intransient existence" (pg. 293). Herein lies the crux of the relationship between creative pursuits and immorality. The artist makes a sacrifice when he or she engages in a creative act. The act itself siphons a piece of the artist's life force. Upon completion of the creative project the individual is spent. However, the creation – whether it be a painting, poem, play or in more modern times a screenplay, new video game, or blog – is a permanent embodiment of the artist's life force. Thus, while a sacrifice has been made by the artist, it is certainly not in vain. The resulting artistic creation preserves the memory of the creator and radiates the individual's life force for future generations to experience.

Existentialists certainly concede the obvious. Creative pursuits, like acts of heroism, are doomed for failure if they are undertaken in an effort to achieve biological immortality. At best, they perhaps provide the individual a means to assert their specialness in the face of their biological limitations and eventual death. Still, existentialists are in complete agreement that using one's will in creative ventures is a much healthier means of tackling life's anxieties than a retreat into passivity and nonparticipation. In society today, however, it seems like there is a tendency to content oneself with being a consumer. Others perhaps mistake the lure of engaging in anonymous and vicious criticism via social media forums as a form of creativity. This begs the question of what causes certain individuals to create and others to consume. van Deurzen (2015) offers a compelling answer to this question. In drawing a parallel between schizophrenia and artists, she writes, "what the two have in common is an extraordinary openness to the dilemmas of the human condition, coupled with a capacity to make unexpected links and observations" (pg. 31). She further notes this capacity can make it difficult for these individuals to fit in society where hypocrisy and a façade of normalcy exist while pain and suffering are endured by many. Artists, as opposed to those who experience psychosis, are somehow able to "process and channel these insights in some constructive manner." Thus, it is the ability to convert one's sensitivity to the existential givens of life into a life-affirming creative exercise that separates individuals. Though speculative, perhaps the presence of a certain combination and/or number of protective factors that were introduced in Chapter 3 will predict an individual's ability to harness existential anxiety and channel this life force into creative pursuits.

When working with adolescents from an existential perspective in therapy, any creative effort, however seemingly small, should therefore be strongly encouraged. Clinicians should remain vigilant and open to recognizing nontraditional forms of creativity in their clients. Beyond classic arts (e.g., painting, drawing, poetry, writing, acting, and other performing arts) many adolescents demonstrate their creative side through their style of dress, pursuit of nontraditional sports, journaling, cartooning, photography, and blogging. It pays for the therapist to closely assess the adolescent's video-gaming interests even if these interests are primarily consumer oriented and pursued instead of more classically creative pursuits. For within the experience of playing these video games there are often small ways that adolescents are shaping their identity and asserting their uniqueness. The clinician who fails to embrace the opportunity to connect with adolescents through these mediums misses critical opportunities to reinforce the client's courage to create and connect with others. Celebration of any small efforts on the part of a client to express creativity will hopefully encourage the client's involvement in more of these creative activities.

Paradoxical Intentions

On certain occasions when conducting therapy with adolescents it may make sense to use the paradoxical intention technique. Frankl (1986) identified this intervention strategy as one of the core treatment techniques involved in Logotherapy. In the simplest sense paradoxical intention is the act of prescribing the symptom to the client. Frankl utilized the approach frequently when treating anxious clients, especially those experiencing debilitating anticipatory anxiety and/or obsessive compulsive symptomatology. In *The Doctor and the Soul* he describes treating a physician who struggled with a fear of sweating in public. The physician developed intense anticipatory anxiety about experiencing a recurrence of the symptom. Unfortunately, this anxiety certainly did not help prevent a recurrence of the sweating when new situations occurred. Instead, Frankl believe it likely worsened the condition. Fear in this case may have intensified the physiological symptom which resulted in additional instances of unwanted perspiration leading to increased anxiety about future recurrence of the problem. A vicious cycle was in full effect. Frankl was determined to break the cycle and therefore instructed the client to, "in the event that his anticipatory anxiety should recur, to resolve deliberately to show those whom he was with at the time how much he could really sweat" (p. 223). This instruction struck at the heart of the client's root fear – to be exposed for sweating. The client ultimately responded very well to this instruction and followed through in real world settings, reminding himself that he should sweat "at least ten quarts" upon making contact with another. Within a week's time the client reported he was free of the phobia.

Frankl (1986) conceded that not all clients respond so quickly and completely to the paradoxical intention technique. At the heart of the intervention is a mandate for the client to adopt a fundamentally different attitudinal stance toward their symptom. That which is most feared needs to become that which is most embraced and sought out. Not all clients are ready or capable of making this attitudinal change.

Frankl was quite aware of this fact, noting that "this procedure must make use of the specific human capacity for self-detachment inherent in a sense of humor" (pg. 224). Some clients are simply not capable of laughing at their worst fears. In these cases the use of a paradoxical intention could possibly produce disastrous results but more likely would be rejected by the client out of hand. From a behavioral perspective, the technique is essentially a way to encourage an exposure task in the client. The client is told to continue to seek out the situations that are most feared as opposed to slipping into an avoidant pattern. They are instructed to act "as if" they were someone entirely different then themselves. Again, this requires both cognitive flexibility and courage. While the technique has the potential to be an extremely powerful intervention, adolescents who are in the throes of a phobia may find the approach overwhelming or even insensitive to their current functioning. For these reasons the author uses paradoxical intention sparingly with adolescents only after a thorough assessment of the client's readiness to engage in an exposure task has been conducted and sufficient rapport and support outside of the therapy setting is in place. Those considering using the technique would be wise to consider adopting a similar approach.

Conclusions

This chapter has explored several treatment techniques and focal areas that commonly occur in existential therapy. While existential therapists have traditionally resisted having their therapeutic approach reduced to a manualized set of procedures and techniques, there seems benefit to providing "guideposts" as Schneider (2008) suggests to practicing the approach. It is in this spirit that the author included descriptions of several core and specific aspects of the EI approach he incorporates into his work with adolescents. As previously stated, what has been introduced in this chapter is not meant to represent the totality of existential techniques and approaches to working with clients. However, at the very least, it hopefully provides the reader with a greater appreciation for the subtleties and complexities of engaging adolescents within this framework. Not to be forgotten, the chapter has hopefully also impressed upon the reader the potentially incredible benefits of incorporating an existential approach into one's treatment plan when working with adolescents.

References

Barrett-Lennard, G. T. (1993). The phases and focus of empathy. *Psychology and Psychotherapy: Theory, Research and Practice, 66*(1), 3–14.

Becker, E. (1973). *The denial of death*. New York, NY, US: Free Press.

Beutler, L. E., Forrester, B., Gallagher-Thompson, D., Thompson, L., & Tomlins, J. B. (2012). Common, specific, and treatment fit variables in psychotherapy outcome. *Journal Of Psychotherapy Integration, 22*(3), 255–281. doi:10.1037/a0029695

Bugental, J. T. (1987). *The art of the psychotherapist*. New York, NY, US: W W Norton & Co.

Chessick, R. D. (1996). Heidegger's "authenticity" in the psychotherapy of adolescents. *American Journal Of Psychotherapy, 50*(2), 208–216.

Craig, P. E. (1986). Sanctuary and presence: An existential view of the therapist's contribution. *The Humanistic Psychologist, 14*(1), 22–28. doi:10.1080/08873267.1986.9976749

Diamond, S. A. (1996). *Anger, madness, and the daimonic: The psychological genesis of violence, evil, and creativity*. Albany, NY, US: State University of New York Press.

Edgette, J. S. (2006). *Adolescent therapy that really works: Helping kids who never asked for help in the first place*. New York, NY, US: W W Norton & Co.

Ellerman, C. P. (1999). Pragmatic existential therapy. *Journal Of Contemporary Psychotherapy, 29*(1), 49–64. doi:10.1023/A:1022957209378

Frankl, V. (1980). *The doctor and the soul: From psychotherapy to logotherapy*. New York: Random House.

Frankl, V. E. (1986). Logotherapy and the challenge of suffering. *Review Of Existential Psychology & Psychiatry, Spec Issue 20*(1–3), 63–67.

Hayes, S. C., Strosahl, K. D., & Wilson, K. G. (1999). *Acceptance and commitment therapy: An experiential approach to behavior change*. New York, NY, US: Guilford Press.

Hayes, S. C., & Duckworth, M. P. (2006). Acceptance and Commitment Therapy and Traditional Cognitive Behavior Therapy Approaches to Pain. *Cognitive And Behavioral Practice, 13*(3), 185–187. doi:10.1016/j.cbpra.2006.04.002

Joyce, P., & Sills, C. (2010). *Skills in gestalt counselling and psychotherapy*. London: Sage.

May, R. (1969). *Existential psychology*. New York, NY, US: Crown Publishing Group/Random House.

May, R. (1977). *The meaning of anxiety*., Rev. *ed*. New York, NY, US: W W Norton & Co.

May, R. (1983). Socrates and God. *Contemporary Psychology, 28*(5), 412–413. doi:10.1037/022069

Ollendick, T. H., & Jarrett, M. A. (2009). Empirically supported treatments for adolescent depression. In C. A. Essau, (Ed.), *Treatments for adolescent depression: Theory and practice* (pp. 57–80). New York, NY, US: Oxford University Press. doi:10.1093/med:psych/9780199226504.003.0003

Rank, O. (1936). *Will therapy. An analysis of the therapeutic process in terms of relationship*. Oxford, England: Knopf.

Rank, O. (1989). *Art and artist: creative urge and personality development*. New York: Norton.

Schneider, K. J., Galvin, J., & Serlin, I. (2009). Rollo May on existential psychotherapy. *Journal Of Humanistic Psychology*, *49*(4), 419–434. doi:10.1177/0022167809340241

Schneider, K. J. (2008). *Existential-integrative psychotherapy: Guideposts to the core of practice*. New York, NY, US: Routledge/Taylor & Francis Group.

Segal, Z. V., Teasdale, J. D., & Williams, J. G. (2004). Mindfulness-Based Cognitive Therapy: Theoretical Rationale and Empirical Status. In S. C. Hayes, V. M. Follette, M. M. Linehan, (Eds.), *Mindfulness and acceptance: Expanding the cognitive-behavioral tradition* (pp. 45–65). New York, NY, US: Guilford Press.

Sharp, G. (2005). Waging nonviolent struggle. Boston: Extending Horizons Books.

Shea, S.C. (1998). *Psychiatric Interviewing: The Art of Understanding*. 2nd. ed. Philadelphia: W.B. Saunders.

Shumaker, D. (2012). An existential–integrative treatment of anxious and depressed adolescents. *Journal Of Humanistic Psychology*, *52*(4), 375–400. doi:10.1177/0022167811422947

Spinelli, E. (2015). Experiencing change: A phenomenological exploration. *Existential Analysis*, *26*(1), 4–20.

Tillich, P. (1952). Anxiety, religion, and medicine. *Pastoral Psychology*, *3*11–17. doi:10.1007/BF01769082

van Deurzen, E. (2012). Reasons for living: Existential therapy and spirituality. In L. Barnett, G. Madison, (Eds.), *Existential therapy: Legacy, vibrancy and dialogue* (pp. 171–182). New York, NY, US: Routledge/Taylor & Francis Group.

van Deurzen, E. (2015). Structural existential analysis (SEA): A phenomenological method for therapeutic work. *Journal Of Contemporary Psychotherapy*, *45*(1), 59–68. doi:10.1007/s10879-014-9282-z

Wampold, B. E. (2012). Humanism as a common factor in psychotherapy. *Psychotherapy*, *49*(4), 445–449. doi:10.1037/a0027113

Weinblatt, U., & Omer, H. (2008). Nonviolent resistance: A treatment for parents of children with acute behavior problems. *Journal Of Marital And Family Therapy*, *34*(1), 75–92. doi:10.1111/j.1752-0606.2008.00054.x

Yalom, I. D. (1980). *Existential psychotherapy*. New York, NY, US: Basic Books.

CHAPTER 5

EI Approaches to Treating Anxiety in Adolescents

Introduction

A chapter that explores the use of EI in the treatment of adolescents experiencing anxiety is perhaps the most inherently obvious addition to this book. Anxiety is thought to be a normative and universal human experience when viewed from an existential perspective. The "givens" of one's existence never lurk far from our consciousness. Their presence is felt most often through anxiety. This particular emotion strikes at the heart of existential thinking. Still there are other sources of anxiety that respond well to cognitive, cognitive-behavioral, and psychodynamic forms of treatment. Successfully distinguishing the sources of an adolescent's anxiety and developing a treatment plan that incorporates EI thinking and clinical stances is a challenge for even the most skilled clinicians. This chapter seeks to clarify some of those challenges and provide recommendations for when EI can and should be integrated.

Clinical Description, Incidence, and Prevalence

DSM-5 anxiety disorders cover a wide range of psychopathology and behavioral concerns that share a common core emotional component of anxiety (American Psychiatric Association, 2013). The most common specific diagnoses include generalized anxiety disorder (GAD), panic disorder (PD) with or without agoraphobia, social anxiety disorder, separation anxiety disorder, and specific phobia. Obsessive compulsive disorder (OCD) is

D. Shumaker, *Existential-Integrative Approaches to Treating Adolescents*, DOI 10.1057/978-1-349-95211-3_5

no longer included under the general umbrella of anxiety disorders, reflecting a growing appreciation for the distinct etiology of this particular behavioral disturbance. While there is still considerable variation among the remaining specific anxiety disorders, there are several important commonalities. Craske and colleagues (2009) identify five common factors, including (1) self-reported symptoms of fear and anxiety, (2) heightened anxiety responding to cues that signal a threat, (3) elevated stress reactivity to aversive stimuli, (4) attentional biases to threat stimuli and threat-based appraisals of ambiguous stimuli, and (5) elevated amygdala responses to threat-based stimuli. In short, individuals experiencing any of these disorders are more distressed, vigilant, and preoccupied with threat management than most. This combination of chronic fear, intense subjective and physiological distress, and hypersensitivity to real and imagined threats can lead to avoidant and escape behaviors that frequently perpetuate and even exacerbate the concern. Even in cases where the threats can be avoided, the individual frequently suffers. Social connections, school/career options, self-confidence, and self-concept are frequently negatively affected, resulting in mood disturbances and even suicidality.

Unfortunately, this manner of disturbance is quite common during adolescence. Meta-analytic studies have estimated the worldwide prevalence of mental health disorders in children and adolescents at approximately 13% (Polanczyk et al., 2015; Roberts et al., 1998; Verhulst & Koot, 1995), affecting over 200 million youth. Anxiety disorders are the most prevalent class of mental health disorders impacting this age group (Kessler et al., 2001). Specifically, Polanczyk and colleagues (2015) believe the prevalence estimate is 6.5% for youth between the ages of 5 and 19 years old. This would mean that approximately 117 million children and adolescents worldwide are suffering from an anxiety disorder at any given time. The one-year incidence rate of anxiety disorders in youth between ages 11 and 17 years is approximately 2.8% (Roberts et al., 2009). Thus, by all estimates anxiety disorders are a serious health concern that impact hundreds of thousands of adolescents to a debilitating degree.

Common Conceptualizations/Etiological Overview

Considerable research has been devoted to better understanding the etiology of anxiety disorders in youth. A wide range of factors have been explored. While it is beyond the scope of this chapter to provide an in-depth overview of these efforts, some general trends and findings are reported here. The discussion is divided into biological, familial, and cognitive/social learning theory influences on the development of anxiety disorders.

To begin, research on the heritability of anxiety disorders supports a nature-nurture, developmental vulnerability model. For certain there is a strong heritability component to the development of anxiety disorders. For example, Turner and colleagues (1987) found that children of parents who have an anxiety disorder were seven times more likely to develop an anxiety disorder than those children of parents who do not have an anxiety disorder. The exact mechanisms of transmission are less clear. Some estimates suggest genes account for 30% of the variance in child anxiety, with shared environments (i.e., familial influences) accounting for 20% of the variance and the remaining 50% due to nonshared environmental factors (Gregory & Eley, 2007). Thus, the development of anxiety in youth is complex and multifactorial.

In regard to potential biological influences there is a strong association between temperament and the development of anxiety disorders (Degnan et al., 2010). Behavioral Inhibition (BI) is a temperament typology characterized by negative emotionality and reactivity to novel stimuli in infancy, vigilance and withdrawal to novelty in toddlerhood, and extreme social withdrawal later in childhood. Approximately 15% of children demonstrate this temperament (Degnan & Fox, 2007). The physiological experience of these individuals is fundamentally different from those who display different temperaments. Specifically, BI is associated with increased cortisol levels, increased amygdala reactions to novel stimuli, heightened startle responses, and more vigilant attention styles (Perez-Edgar & Fox, 2005). Parents of these youth may also possess a BI temperament and/or suffer from anxiety disorders, fostering an environment where behavioral avoidance is supported and modeling elevated fear based responses to novel stimuli occurs. Thus, there is likely a strong biological-environmental interaction that not only perpetuates problematic behavioral responses to feared stimuli, but may also exacerbate the concern.

Early attachment experiences also play an important role in the development of anxiety disorders. Insecurely attached children are at greater risk for developing an anxiety disorder (Bohlin et al., 2000). It has been hypothesized that primary attachment figures who are less consistently supportive and available elicit chronic vigilance and distress in the child. These children also may experience disruptions in the learning process pertaining to emotional regulation, resulting in a long-term sensitivity to emotional stimuli and increasing the likelihood of maladaptive coping (Esbjorn et al., 2012). Over time the trauma of inconsistent parental attunement leads to fears of abandonment that can extend beyond the primary attachment relationship (Shamir-Essakow et al., 2005). The relationship between temperament, specifically BI, and attachment in the formation of anxiety disorders has been studied as well. Manassis and Bradley (1994) introduced a model of anxiety development in which temperament and attachment are equally influential risk factors. Their model also argues that when both risk factors are in evidence the child is at the greatest risk for developing an anxiety disorder. Clearly, early developmental factors are major influences on whether a youth will experience an anxiety disorder at some point in time.

Drake and Ginsburg (2012) have extensively reviewed the familial risk factors in the development of anxiety disorders in childhood. They identify two broad sources of familial influence, parenting behaviors and family environment. Regarding the former, they isolate controlling behaviors, warmth, criticism/rejection, anxious modeling behaviors, specific parental cognitions, and parental anxiety as subcategories of influence. Each of these specific factors represents potential sources of risk. For example, they found that parental overcontrol explain as much of 18% of the variance in child anxiety (McLeod et al., 2007). Overcontrol is associated with overprotective and restrictive parenting behaviors. Children who experience this manner of parenting have less autonomy and opportunities to master new skills through varied life experiences. This can undermine the child's sense of self-efficacy and skill development, resulting in increased anxiety. Regarding the other subcategories of parenting behaviors, there is limited evidence indicating lower parental warmth and higher parental criticism increase the risk for child anxiety. There is more evidence, however, supporting the belief that parental negative evaluations of a child and anxious modeling can increase the risk for the same.

Regarding family environment factors that relate to the development of anxiety, Drake and Ginsburg (2012) argue both low and very high family cohesion levels are risk factors for the development of child anxiety. Families low in cohesion see estrangement among family members and a lack of emotional connection. This lack of warmth can create insecurity for the child and lead to anxiety. At the other end of the spectrum, high cohesion reflects enmeshment. Similar to the case of overcontrolling parenting behaviors, high cohesion leads to overprotection and security concerns that undermine a child's sense of agency resulting in anxiety as well. The review also suggests that families who are either low or high in adaptability, which refers to the degree of flexibility a family establishes regarding familial roles and power structure, increase the risk of child anxiety. Similarly high familial, interparental, and sibling conflict all increase the risk of a child developing an anxiety disorder.

The final major area of study pertaining to the etiology of anxiety in children and adolescents is learning theory. Mineka and Zinbarg (2006) have closely examined the ways in which learning theory can explain the development and maintenance of anxiety in this age group. While they propose a general model of anxiety disorders from a cognitive framework that includes prior and post-conditioning experiences, perceptions of controllability and other cognitive features, and contextual aspects of fear-inducing situation(s), the strength of their analysis is the ability of the model to account for idiosyncratic features of the various DSM anxiety disorders. For example, in the case of Specific Phobia, they account for individuals who may not have come into direct contact with the feared stimuli through a discussion of vicarious conditioning. They cite extensive empirical evidence in support of a learning theory account of the development of anxiety disorders in children. In the more specific case of GAD, the authors highlight the influence of perceived controllability and worry in the disorder's development. Indeed, it seems that worry is a cardinal component of GAD (Borkovec, 1994).

Given the abundance of research on the etiology of anxiety it is hardly surprising that developmental models have been proposed. The most cited ones include a model of psychopathological anxiety by Vasey and Dadds (2001) and a more specific model of GAD by Rapee (2001). Both incorporate genetic, biological, temperament, cognitive, parental, and other familial influences. More recently, Kertz and Woodruff-Borden (2011) have proposed a developmental model of pathological levels of worry. This model builds upon the prior efforts by Vasey and Dadds (2001) and Rapee (2001). It, too, incorporates biological factors (genetics, temperament), parental factors (parental anxiety, parental anxiety modeling, parenting behaviors), affective responses (emotion regulation, avoidance), and cognitive factors (problem orientation, intolerance of uncertainty, beliefs about worry, and information processing) in the development of pathological levels of worry. Readers are encouraged to explore the model in greater depth as it inevitably will lead to a deeper appreciation for the complex etiology of anxiety in adolescents.

Evidence-Based Practice Approaches

Silverman et al. (2008) conducted an exhaustive review of evidence-based approaches for treating anxiety disorders in children and adolescents. Their review followed an initial effort by Ollendick and King (1998) 10 years earlier that did the same. These efforts provide the basis for this brief summary on the state of evidence-based practice pertaining to adolescents diagnosed with anxiety disorders. To begin, Silverman and colleagues were able to identify 32 group design studies rated according to Nathan and Gorman's (2002) six-tier classification system of methodological rigor. Studies that are considered the most rigorous (Type 1) are randomized, include comparison groups, incorporate blinded and state-of-the-art assessment methods, and have adequate sample size with clearly described statistical methodology. Type 2 studies include most of the major components that comprise a Type 1 study minus a single component. At the other end of the continuum are case studies, essays, and opinion papers. Twenty-two studies that were reviewed were considered Type 1, seven were Type 2, and the remaining three were Type 3. Thus, the state of research methodology on adolescent anxiety disorder treatment seems fairly robust.

After rating studies on their research methodology, Silverman and Hollon (2008) used Chambless and Hollon (1998) criteria to determine the specific classification of a treatment approach. The classifications subcategories are well-established treatments, probably efficacious, possibly efficacious treatments, and experimental treatments. There are a number of criteria that need to be met for a treatment to be considered well-established, including at least two independent group designs conducted independently that include a comparison group, treatment manuals, valid assessment measures, and appropriate data analyses. A treatment is considered probably efficacious if there is a single study in existence that meets the aforementioned standards. Based upon this classification system, no psychosocial treatments of anxiety disorders for children and adolescents were considered well-established but five treatments met criteria for being a probably efficacious treatment. The five treatments include the following: (1) Individual Cognitive Behavior Therapy (ICBT) (Barrett et al., 1996; Kendall, 1994), Group Cognitive Behavior Therapy (GCBT) (Barrett, 1998; Gaston et al., 2006), GCBT with parents (Barrett, 1998; Spence et al., 2006), GCBT for social phobia (SOP) (Gallagher et al., 2004), and

Social Effectiveness Training for Children for SOP (Beidel et al., 2000). Eleven treatments met criteria for being a possibly efficacious treatment. A short description of ICBT and GCBT follows for the reader's benefit.

Kendall (1994) conducted the first randomized controlled study of ICBT with 47 youth between the ages of 9 and 13 years old who were diagnosed with an anxiety disorder. The main treatment components included the following: (1) cognitive analyses designed to help the client identify and clarify distorted cognitions and attributions; (2) planning strategies to help the client cope with anxiety; (3) regular evaluation of progress; (4) in vivo exposure of feared stimuli; (5) relaxation training; and (6) contingent reinforcement instructions. Anxious youth who receive this treatment package routinely demonstrate statistically and clinically significant superior outcomes to those who remained in a waitlist control condition. There is also considerable longitudinal, follow-up research suggesting long-term maintenance of the initial gains made in therapy.

GCBT utilizes the basis cognitive and behavioral treatment strategies that comprise ICBT in a group setting typically with therapists, parents, and children present (Barrett, 1998). The sessions follow a regimented script with typically the first half of a session being devoted to a youth's skill enhancement and the second half to enhancing a parent's component to assist the child in managing his or her emotions and problem solving. Psychoeducation, cognitive restructuring, and exposure therapy remain core components of this intervention (Paulus et al., 2015). Common core group processes such as peer modeling, feedback, reinforcement of gains made, and emotional support are typically emphasized in the course of treatment. Children and adolescents who participate in this form of treatment routinely experience clinically significant benefits that are maintained over time (Barrett, 1998; Silverman et al., 1999). When ICBT and GCBT have been directly compared, both forms of treatment have been effective with perhaps a slightly greater positive impact of ICBT (Manassis et al., 2002).

While ICBT and GCBT remain the "gold" standard of evidence-based practice currently, there is growing support for psychodynamic approaches in the treatment of anxiety disorders (Slavin-Mulford & Hilsenroth, 2012). For example, Leichsenring and Salzer (2014) have recently proposed a Unified Psychodynamic Protocol for Anxiety Disorders (UPP-ANXIETY) that implements the principles of psychodynamic therapy that seem most effective for treating anxiety. It is important to note that the treatment has not been studied with adolescents, but it represents a promising alternative and/or adjunctive treatment option.

In conclusion, there is considerable evidence supporting the utility of utilizing CBT in both individual and group formats when treating adolescents diagnosed with an anxiety disorder. Psychoeducation, cognitive restructuring, exposure therapy, and relaxation training seem to be the most critical elements of these approaches. Research on psychodynamic approaches in treating anxiety is in early stages but initial results support future research.

EI Conceptualization

The EI formulation of anxiety is complex and multifactorial. For the most part it is based upon the following three major underpinnings: (1) human awareness of the existential "givens" of life (e.g., death, freedom, isolation, meaninglessness, capacity for awe); (2) the omnipresent horizons of constriction (smallness) and expansion (greatness); and (3) trauma (Schneider, 2008; Yalom, 1980). Each of these components is explored at some length below.

The first major underpinning – the human awareness of existential "givens" of life – has been contemplated by several pioneers in the field including Rank, Tillich, and May. Rank argued that Freud's conceptualization of neurosis as resulting primarily from the psychosexual crises was an insufficient explanation of the condition (Rank, 1936/1978a; 1936/1978b). Instead, he believed that a child's relationship with his or her mother had a considerably greater impact upon one's overall development and, more specifically, the individual's experience of anxiety (Kramer, 1995a; Rank, 1924/1994). His ability to see the importance of attachment formation at a time when intra-individual explanations of human psychological development dominated the field suggests a genius matched by few. Indeed, empirical research supports his contention that a primary caregiver's empathic attunement and consistent attentiveness is a much greater developmental influence than psychosexual crises.

Rank also held a deep appreciation for the impact that one's subjective experience of consciousness can have upon the individual (Rank, 1936/1978b). This heightened self-awareness of oneself and one's surroundings endowed humans with an expanded range of freedom and choices for how to conduct themselves. For certain consciousness is the foundation upon which agency and intentionality rest. It represents an incredible advantage for our species that has led to great advances in science and culture but also domination and exploitation of other inhabitants of earth. On an individual basis, however, the experience of consciousness and, more specifically, the responsibility that comes with having the power to make informed choices on matters pertaining to our conduct can be overwhelming at times. Rank, as much an anyone, appreciated the tension this creates in the individual and believed that anxiety stemming from the freedom of choice and the responsibilities that come with this freedom was a "given" of our existence. Awareness of the other existential "givens" of life, such as one's eventual death, was another by-product of consciousness. In more extreme cases, the awareness of these "givens" can again be so overwhelming that it leads the individual to engage in a failed attempt to avoid both life and death by refusing to live life to the fullest. For example, certain individuals who demonstrate agoraphobic behaviors may be experiencing a struggle managing their awareness of one, some, or all of these "givens." Their avoidance of feared situations and, in extreme cases, refusal to leave the confines of their home may be a failed attempt to avoid both life and death through flight. Kramer (1995b) refers to this approach as "bribing" life itself. The individual falsely believes if they "hurl a Big No at living" they will somehow cheat death.

Rank (1936/1978b), in part, conceptualized human anxiety as the residue of two opposing polarities – *a fear of life and a fear of death* – that are constantly pulling for a resolution that may at best be only partially forthcoming. He did not believe there was a final solution in existence that could eradicate these anxieties, nor did he think it was advisable to even try. They were a "given" of life and human consciousness. Having conceded this, he believed the most constructive manner through which the individual could contend with these anxieties was through self-nurturing and cultivating one's *creative will,* a spontaneous, life-affirming product of human consciousness that could potentially divert psychic energy from neurotic symptom formation (Rank, 1936/1978b). Rank was particularly in favor of individuals pursuing creative arts but he conceded that even this form of expression represented an imperfect solution to the ultimate anxieties of one's existence. At its core this form of creativity represents an attempt by the individual to achieve immortality and express one's uniqueness and freedom. In the act of creating the human expends a part of his or her life force onto the object of their creation. The creation may capture the individual's life force, but the creator is drained and part of their life energy has passed from them. This is the death component of creation. Regarding guilt, an act of creation involves changing the world around us on a permanent basis in an effort to boldly assert one's uniqueness and immortality. The artistic effort therefore represents a futile effort to deny (even if for a fleeting moment) biological limitations and the fundamental dependence one has upon nature (Rank, 1932/1989). The flip side of creating is that something in the world is changed in the act of creation and, to put it more provocatively, destroyed. Thus, even a healthy creative pursuit can generate feelings of guilt due to a recognition of both the motivations behind the act and the impact the effort may have upon the world.

As for the impact of a positive therapeutic relationship, Rank (1936/1978b) believed it helps for one to contemplate the dilemma of living and suffering with the support of another. The experience of being heard and unconditionally accepted by another was thought to lead to increased self-acceptance and reductions of anxiety and guilt. Client acts of will in therapy were not to be interpreted as resistance. Kramer (1995b) argues that Rank viewed the therapist's role as more of an "assistant I" or collaborator. The purpose of therapy was to help clients increase self-awareness and make contact with their anxieties regarding the existential "givens" of their existence. In turn, this collaborative examination process would "[allow] clients to own unacknowledged parts of their suffering, letting the pain sit in their laps, rather than displacing or projecting it onto others" (Kramer 1995b, pg. 72). The client-therapist relationship, as opposed to offering refined psychoanalytic interpretations, was the key mechanism for positive change. The mergence and brief union of client and therapist was seen as a healthy microcosmic experience of one's life journey and primary desire to achieve the inherently unachievable perfect balance of connectedness with another in conjunction with one's maintenance of a sense of autonomy and freedom (Kramer, 1995b).

Tillich (1952) conceptualized existential anxiety, neurosis, and healthy personality formation similarly to Rank. Drawing heavily from the works of Nietzsche (1878/1996; 1886/1990) and Kierkegaard (1843/1954a; 1849/1954b), Tillich separated existential anxiety into three domains: (1) fate and death, (2) meaninglessness and emptiness, and (3) guilt and condemnation. Quite clearly this classification system closely resembles the existential "givens" proposed by Yalom (1980). Like his predecessors, Tillich believed awareness of life's finitude and the contemplation of nonbeing form the basis of anxiety. The fears that stem from these sources of anxiety (e.g., fear of death, meaninglessness, condemnation) were seen by Tillich as universal to all. Like Rank, he also discriminated normative existential anxiety from pathological anxiety, the latter of which was thought to result from an overuse of avoidance, defense mechanisms, and unrealistic self-affirmation. He believed the individual who suffers from a neurosis likely was, first, more sensitive to the threat of nonbeing than most individuals and, second, futilely attempting to protect him or herself from death by building a metaphorical "castle of certitude" against the threat. The "castle" remained perpetually vulnerable because it was based upon an unrealistic appraisal of life and death. Here there are obvious parallels between Tillich's discussion of unrealistic formulations of reality with classic cognitive-behavioral references to "dysfunctional," "maladaptive," and "irrational" thinking (Beck & Mahoney, 1979; Ellis & Harper, 1975). Helplessness, a lack of intentionality, and maladjustment were thought to occur when the individual experienced heightened existential anxiety and ultimately struggled to channel this energy force into meaningful pursuits. These individuals also frequently struggled to maintain an adequate buffer between their daily life experience and the awareness of impending death and nonbeing (Weems et al., 2004). At the most extreme limits of intensity and chronicity existential anxiety could morph into psychosis (Becker, 1973).

While the matter has been broached by others, Tillich (1952) provided one of the best explanations of the difference between fear and anxiety. Fear, he wrote, "has a definite object... which can be faced, analyzed, attacked, endured," while "anxiety has no object, or rather, in a paradoxical phrase, its object is the negation of every object" (Tillich, 1952, pg. 36). He suggested a strong working relationship between fear and anxiety, arguing that individuals strive (often unconsciously) to convert anxiety into fear because, at the very least, fear can be met with courage. If one is faced with the existential given that there may be no inherent meaning to our existence, for example, the anxiety that stems from this awareness is channeled into a fear of not realizing one's potential. This fear, while still a potentially great source of discomfort to the individual, can be more easily contemplated and addressed if one possesses the courage to pursue a life of intentionality and hard work. In the end, however, Tillich conceded that anxiety stemming from the threat of nonbeing cannot be eliminated because death is unavoidable. Thus, like Rank, he believed humans will never completely rid themselves of existential anxiety.

Tillich (1952) further believed there were healthier alternatives to living with the ultimate threats to our existence than that which the neurotic pursues. However, the road to doing so required courage. First, he argued individuals need to summon the strength to contemplate the existential givens of our existence on a deeper level. When one does so it will almost inevitably lead to a state of despair. Tillich defined despair simply as one without hope. This rock bottom emotional state was felt when awareness of nonbeing was contemplated head on. At that moment the terror and absolute nature of nonbeing overwhelms the individual. But even in these awful moments of despair, Tillich pointed out that the individual still was alive as evidenced by his or her feeling despair and contemplating nonbeing. In essence the experience of feeling despair affirmed one's being. To feel, one had to be. Thus the despair that results from contemplated one's nonbeing was seen as a crucial component of one's humanity, just as critical to one's emotional development as feelings of joy, happiness, and contentment. Tillich's views on the root causes of anxiety and other negative emotions stand in stark contrast to classic cognitive behavioral theory which argues that anxiety results from maladaptive or irrational cognitions derived from inaccurate cognitive schemas (Beck and Mahoney, 1979; Ellis, 1973).

Once true despair has been felt and endured, Tillich (1952) believed an individual's next mandate was to summon the courage to be. He defined this act as "the self-affirmation of being in spite of the fact of nonbeing... the act of the individual self in taking the anxiety of nonbeing upon itself by affirming itself as a part of an embracing whole or in its individual selfhood" (Tillich, 1952, pg. 155). A boxing metaphor describing this process is the ability of the fighter to pick him- or herself up off the canvas after being knocked out, and drawing more strength in the process of doing so. When individuals are able to do so Tillich believed they could begin to approach life with vitality and "life power." They had braved the storm of despair, chosen to persevere and lean into life as opposed to away from it and, in turn, approach their remaining days on earth with a healthier balance of self-affirmation in the face of nonbeing. Within an EI framework they are demonstrating Schneider's (2008) experiential liberation state of being, possessing the having the courage to live with intentionality, create beyond oneself without losing oneself, and accept responsibility for the choices one makes. Yet again a close parallel is drawn between Tillich's operational definition of an individual who possesses the courage to be and Rank's belief in the therapeutic effects of artistic creativity. Both theorists saw courage and advanced self-awareness and self-development in an individual's creative endeavors.

The final existential theorist and therapist reviewed here, Rollo May, also wrote extensively about existential anxiety and the "givens" of human existence. In a manner similar to Rank and Tillich, he defined anxiety as "the apprehension cued off by a threat to some value that the individual holds essential to his existence as a personality" (May, 1977, pg. 205). The "threats" could take many forms, including physical (e.g., threat of death), psychological (e.g., the loss of freedom, meaninglessness), or the potential loss of a cherished value (e.g., patriotism, love of another). Thus, anxiety served as a signal, alerting the individual to the presence of a threat to one's being and/or values. May also noted the differences between anxiety and fear. Like Tillich he believed the crucial distinguishing factor was that fear could be objectified while anxiety could not because it impacts an individual's most basic sense of security and reaches at the heart of the individual's personality. Further, he also thought anxiety was normative and that when, "the goal in all life is a total absence of anxiety, the judgment becomes delusive and even dangerous" (May, 1977, pg. 375). As for what exactly could be dangerous about an effort to eliminate one's anxiety entirely, May argued that the emotion plays a crucial role in motivating humans to adopt a philosophy of life that values urgency over complacency, creativity over indifference, and a sense of zest for life over cynicism. Further, within the therapeutic setting he argued that a client's experience of anxiety was a key motivating emotion that enhanced the likelihood of a positive outcome being realized (Schneider, Galvin, & Serlin, 2009).

May (1977) classified anxiety into two basic categories, "normal" and "neurotic," the former which can be equated with existential anxiety and the latter more resembling a cognitive and cognitive-behavioral interpretation of the emotion. Specifically, he believed normal anxiety comprised the following four parts: (1) it is proportionate to the objective threat; (2) it does not involve repression; (3) it does not require neurotic defense mechanisms for management; and (4) it can be confronted constructively. By contrast, neurotic anxiety is disproportionate, involves repression, and is managed by avoidant and other less healthy defense mechanisms. Like Rank and Tillich, May (1977) believed psychotherapy held great potential to assist an individual in managing normal anxiety and reducing or even eliminating neurotic anxiety. A therapist could expand a client's awareness more generally through careful attentiveness, empathic support, and poignant questioning. Existential therapy could unlock a client's limited self-awareness and assist the individual in seeing the values that are threatened and the conflicts between a client's stated goals and how he or she is actually living. When these critical discrepancies between stated goals and behavior were illuminated, what followed was re-education. At this point the therapist begins to assist the client in restructuring their life goals, clarifying their choice of values, and developing a realistic and responsible plan for obtaining these goals.

Like Rank, May placed a higher value on the power of the therapeutic relationship to promote positive change in comparison to the delivery of sophisticated psychoanalytic interpretations of a client's behaviors. Still, therapy was work and clients routinely made contact with darker, more uncomfortable feelings in the process of gaining increased self-awareness. May spoke at length about the need for both clients and therapists to take risks in therapy. These risks often would bring the individual in contact with feelings historically characterized as negative that May referred to as the *daimonic*. He defined this term as "any natural function that has the power to take over the whole person" and believed that it could either be creative, destructive, or both (May, 1969/2007). Thus, for therapy to be successful a client needed to have the courage to take risks and faith in a therapist to keep them safe when they chose to do so. Therapists supported this risk by allowing clients the freedom to experience their choices and assume responsibility for their actions (Pitchford, 2009).

The author has previously summarized some of the critical commonalities that emerge among Rank, Tillich, and May's conceptualization of anxiety (Shumaker, 2012). They bear mentioning here as this section nears its end. The five main areas of agreement include the following: (1) anxiety is seen as an natural, objectless source of tension that is based upon an individual's awareness of impending nonbeing, a sense of meaninglessness, and feelings of isolation and guilt; (2) anxiety can be both normative and pathological; (3) fear is seen as objectless anxiety converted into object form and allows for individuals to summon courage to face the challenges of life in a positive, self-affirming manner; (4) creative pursuits, an appreciation for all that is beautiful, and a sense of connection are positive means through which individuals affirm their inherent uniqueness in the face of biological limitations and finite being; and (5) a positive therapeutic relationship can help an individual mediate existential anxiety by increasing awareness, clarifying goals, and momentarily promoting a sense of understanding and connection. Yalom's (1980) classification of the existential "givens" into four components – the human consciousness of mortality, meaninglessness, freedom, and isolation – is rooted in the efforts of Nietzsche, Kierkegaard, Rank, Tillich, May, and other philosophers, theologians, and existential theorists. It is the human struggle with these givens that forms the basis of existential anxiety.

As previously mentioned, however, EI also conceptualizes anxiety (and other core emotions) as a struggle between polarities of human consciousness (Schneider, 2008). Individuals have the capacity to both expand and constrict when faced with contemplating themselves and their inherent potencies. The former is associated with a sense of "advancing, enlarging, dispersing, ascending, filling, accelerating" while the latter is associated with "the perception of retreating, restricting, isolating, falling, emptying, slowing" (Schneider, 2008, pg. 39). Neither process is inherently desirable or undesirable. At times, it can be adaptive to contemplate the expansion or constriction of one's potencies. However, contact with the extreme ends of these experiences certainly can be associated with a sense of dread. In the case of expansion Schneider argues there can be a dread of exploding or chaos. As for constriction there can be a fear of obliteration. Schneider believes two specific polarities – chaos and obliteration, greatness and smallness – literally "haunt" humans throughout their existence. How an individual manages these eventualities will play a large role in determining their mental health and adjustment. Herein lies an alternative to experiencing debilitating feelings of expansion and constriction. Schneider refers to the ability to more adaptively manage the tension created by these polarities as "centering." He defines this process as the individual's ability to direct one's expansive and constrictive experience through self-awareness. A client's enhanced ability to center therefore is a correlate of experiential liberation and can represent a positive outcome of an EI treatment.

Schneider (2008) believes anxiety disorders are rooted mainly in a hyper-constrictive approach to managing the polarities of chaos versus obliteration and greatness versus smallness. Specifically, anxiety is viewed as a symptom of the individual's contemplation of his or her potency. These individuals are acutely aware of and burdened by the freedom that consciousness and the ability to make choices entails. They are overwhelmed with the responsibility that comes with being free to make choices. This phenomenon is what Rank refers to as the fear of life. The innumerable decisions one is forced to make on a daily basis and the implications of making a mistake can weigh very heavily upon these individuals as their subjective experience is one of feeling out of control. Faced with the constant possibility of making grievous errors and losing control the individual feels precariously close to insanity and a permanent descent into the chaos of a cluttered and excessively troubled mind. The most common response is to either attempt to deny or limit one's exposure to life and life's choices by adopting a hyper-constrictive stance. However, Schneider also believes that some individuals manage their anxiety by behaving in foolish, unpredictable, and spontaneous ways. In either case, these types of responses are maladaptive and do not ameliorate the anxiety over the long term. The sufferer remains anxious and often leads a limited life characterized by avoidance, withdrawal, and excessive worry.

The third and final developmental pathway through which pathological anxiety occurs in the individual is prior trauma experiences (Schneider, 2008). As previously discussed in Chapter 1, Schneider identified three forms of trauma – acute, chronic, and implicit – that can impact an individual's experience of the aforementioned polarities of one's existence. He argued that acute traumas are immediate and involve a threat to one's very existence. These experiences therefore raise the specter of one's diminishment or even dissolution. A dread of the hyper-constrictive polarities ensues. The individual overcompensates in these moments by attempting to expand and assert their greatness in the face of possible annihilation. Crying, fighting, and defying may be examples of this process. In the case of chronic trauma, however, Schneider believes the opposite polarities are feared as the individual experiences time after time a negation of the efforts to combat assaults upon one's integrity. Now the individual attempts to render oneself as small as possible in a frequently futile attempt to minimize or eliminate the threats to one's existence. Ultimately, trauma experiences can increase an individual's risk for developing a host of anxiety disorders for multiple reasons, most notably the immediate threat to one's being and integrity. EI is designed to increase the client's awareness of how trauma has impacted the relation the individual has with the polarities of his or her existence. Through increased self-awareness the hope is for the client to develop an approach to living that is more centered and less vulnerable to pronounced pendulum swings of overcompensation between the dreaded polarities.

EI Case Example

Carrie[1] was referred to counseling in the summer prior to her freshman year in high school by her parents after experiencing debilitating anxiety and panic attacks. She had begun to avoid seeing friends and had recently quit her summer job waitressing due to a fear of experiencing additional panic episodes. She recalled the initial panic experience occurred roughly six months prior in the context of an otherwise normal school day. Shortness of breath, a sense of choking, a rapid heartbeat, and a fear of passing out and/or dying were the most prominent symptoms she described. There were one or two additional attacks during the remaining months of the school year, but as the summer progressed they were occurring more frequently (approximately 2–3 per week). She was a willing participant in counseling, having requested the prior winter to see someone after the initial panic attack and in the context of an overall increase in anxiety pertaining to school and family concerns. She presented as a bright, earnest, but distressed individual who frequently teared up in our initial intake session in which her mother attended. She was extremely worried about not only her own capacity to return to school but also her parents' welfare. We agreed weekly individual counseling was the most appropriate modality and frequency of meetings. It is also important to note that she had previously consulted with her primary care physician about the panic symptomatology and there were no medical explanations that might otherwise account for these symptoms.

Carrie lived at home with her parents. She was the youngest of three siblings. Her two older sisters were in their twenties, one away at college and the other working and recently married. Carrie's mother had run a successful business for many years but in the prior year the business had suffered financially. Her father had been unemployed over the prior two years, having been laid off from a day laborer's job. Carrie was close to both parents and witnessed a lot of her mother's business struggles and her father's anxiety as he often looked for work online from home. She recalled experiencing a lot of concern about her parents, their financial struggles, and the future of her mother's business in the year prior to our initial meeting. To make matters worse, her father had experienced what Carrie and her mother referred to as a "minor nervous breakdown" approximately a year earlier. It hardly seemed "minor" to the therapist. Though Carrie was somewhat shielded from the extent of her father's disturbance she was fully aware he had required multiple psychiatric hospitalizations over the span of a several months. She had visited him several times during these hospitalizations. The experience of seeing her father in these facilities was terrifying. Her father was her hero and had been a bedrock of stability for the entirety of her existence prior to his apparently sudden decline. She now described him as "fragile" and "weak." He was improving and no longer was attending a partial day treatment program, but seemed remote, subdued, and, for lack of a better term, simply "not himself" anymore. He would go for long walks alone and appeared indifferent to the ever growing prospect of having to file for bankruptcy. Carrie did not know how to be around her father, felt uncomfortable as a result when they were together, and simply avoided him. When asked whether she would want to participate in separate family counseling with her parents to address the relationship concerns, Carrie said she was not comfortable with the prospect and that her father seemed consumed in his own recovery. She also expressed significant guilt regarding her own mental health struggles, believing that the family's focus should remain on her father and his recovery.

Academically Carrie had always excelled at school but it had not come easy to her. She had witnessed her older siblings do quite well academically with what she perceived as relatively little effort, while she often worked several hours on weekday nights completing her homework. Her sisters, teachers, parents, and fellow students had collectively conveyed to her that her initial years of high school were going to be much harder and yet also the most critical years in her academic career. Not surprisingly, she felt overwhelmed with the prospect of starting school. Carrie was also a gifted athlete. She was hoping to make the varsity cross country team as an underclassman (and ultimately succeeded in doing so) and stood a realistic chance of potentially obtaining an athletic scholarship in this sport. Her anxiety and panic concerns had not directly affected her performance on the club teams she had been running for throughout the spring and summer months. But, when she was not actually running, she worried immensely about her performance and set very high standards for herself. Socially, she was well liked and had two close female friends. She attracted the romantic interest of many of her peers but had not dated, stating the boys in her school were immature and she simply did not have the time. She was vague regarding her longer-term goals, offering more general statements about going to a "good college" on a scholarship, getting a "good job," and perhaps traveling or settling down with someone and raising children.

Based upon this history the therapist conceptualized Carrie as a high functioning individual with multiple strengths (e.g., her intelligence, motivation to feel better, support system, generally positive premorbid history, and absence of mental health concerns) who was experiencing acute anxiety concerns and panic attacks in the context of a highly distressing family disturbance (i.e., her father's significant mental health concerns and the family's financial concerns) and ongoing chronic stressors to perform at a high level academically and in her extracurricular activities. The immediate causal factors contributing to the emergence of her panic symptoms were unclear and likely multifold (e.g., she was at an age where many individuals experience their first attacks, there was a family history of anxiety disorders, she had been under intense stress and had experienced a lack of consistent sleep in the days prior to her initial attack). Further, the destabilizing effect of seeing a primary caretaker become so vulnerable so quickly appeared to have activated many existential concerns that perhaps had been less prominent in her thinking prior to this family crisis. Specifically, Carrie seemed to be awakened to both her father and her own mortality and physical vulnerabilities vis-à-vis his hospitalizations and her panic symptoms, she was struggling with the burdens of responsibility that her more advanced age had thrust upon her, and she was also struck with pangs of intense guilt. On the surface, the guilt seemed limited to the impact her anxiety and mental health concerns were having on her parents but, at a deeper level, also seemed to reflect deeper self-doubt and uncertainty about her choices and capacities.

Given this conceptualization, the author chose to integrate evidence-based approaches for the treatment of panic attacks and generalized anxiety in adolescents with an EI approach that encouraged Carrie to achieve a more comfortable relationship with some of the core existential concerns she was contemplating. To begin, given the acute distress Carrie's panic attacks were causing, her growing tendency to restrict her activities and avoid situations where an attack either had occurred or she thought might occur, and the real potential for her to struggle with a fear of further attacks upon resuming school, it seemed imperative to first address this specific symptom through cognitive-behavioral treatment strategies. Pincus and colleagues' (2010) Panic-Control Treatment for Adolescents (PCT-A) served as the guiding force for this area of focus. PCT-A is based upon an 11-session adult treatment for PD developed by Craske, Antony, and Barlow (2006) that has proven effective in reducing PD symptoms. The major components of this treatment initially included a psychoeducational component designed to teach Carrie about the physiological experiences of panic, breathing retraining, cognitive restructuring to reduce her tendency to overestimate the likelihood of a panic attack occurring and to reduce catastrophic misinterpretations of her panic symptoms, and some limited interoceptive exposure training. It is important to note that the author did not precisely follow the recommended session sequence suggested by Pincus et al. (2010) given that Carrie had other concerns she wished to focus on in sessions and parent involvement in treatment was not possible. However, these aforementioned areas of focus dominated the first four to five sessions of our individual work together. Once Carrie had established a better understanding of panic attacks and developed a "tool kit" to help her cope when panic symptoms occurred, she and the author began to have her perform exposure tasks outside of sessions for the purpose of reversing the trend of avoidance and habituating to feared situations. Specifically, she resumed socializing with friends and picking up shifts waitressing with positive results. A particularly reinforcing moment during this stage of treatment came when she was able to work through an episode of shortness of breath during a 4-hour waitressing shift through self-talk and breathing exercises. She proudly entered the session following this experience exclaiming, "I think I've got this panic thing under control!"

With these gains in hand and rapport well-established, Carrie seemed to intuitively sense she was ready for movement toward increased experiential liberation. The author probed minimally to facilitate to her reaching a deeper level of self-awareness, on one occasion noting the tears that formed when she spoke of her father going for his solitary, shaky walks, on another occasion marveling at how hard it must be for her carry the weight of the world on her shoulders. These observations or, perhaps more precisely put, *invitations*, borne out of attempts to remain present and invoke the actual, provided Carrie the opportunity to address some of the existential concerns she had been experiencing in a safe environment. She began to speak at length about her fear of losing not just her father but both of her parents. She confessed that she *really* had felt like she was going to die when she experienced her first panic attack and that it was such a devastatingly horrible feeling for her like none other she had felt before that she had been close to asking her mother to admit her to the same psychiatric hospital her father had been in. It is fascinating how clients' stories are like onions in the way in which, as they hopefully grow more comfortable with the therapists and themselves, they can access deeper and deeper layers of hurt and detail. Of course, during the PCT-A work Carrie had described in broader terms her belief that she might be choking during the initial panic attack, but it was only later, when more trust had formed and time had elapsed in the treatment experience that the depth of her horror really came to light.

As Carrie faced head on two of the ultimate anxieties that all humans face – a fear of death, a fear of freedom and responsibility – she seemed to benefit greatly from being asked to contemplate what had meaning to her. She quickly identified her family and friends as having the ultimate meaning to her. After further consideration she also found it important to be a "good person" which she defined as someone who is caring, thoughtful, loyal, generous, and kind. She seemed to appreciate the author's authentic and purposefully matter-of-fact observation that, "Well, you've got all of those in spades" comment. Many adolescents, like Carrie, report they do not often hear such unflinching endorsements of their character and being. In Carrie's case, her parents were generally supportive and certainly loving, but they also placed high expectations on her and openly expressed disappointment and doubts about her capacities and motivations at times. This "tough love" approach seemed to the author to have been a tragic miscalculation of how to best motivate their daughter. Hence the "got all of those in spades" effort to infuse some self-confidence and ease her guilt. Over time Carrie began to relax some of her self-imposed academic achievement and athletic expectations, transcending the collective anxieties of her parents, teachers, and coaches in the process. She also responded well to the therapist's inquiry about what she felt passionate about in life. Aside from running she struggled to identify another source of passion. After contemplating the question for a week she was able to recall that she had once loved playing the piano when she was in middle school prior to when the demands by her teacher and parents to practice harder had made it first unenjoyable and then untenable. With minimal encouragement by the therapist she embraced the idea of resuming playing "just for the fun of it." And she did, finding it another positive, creative outlet that channeled her stress and anxiety into a creative pursuit. By the holiday season of her sophomore year she had been panic free for several weeks and was excelling academically while her general worries were less. Roughly a year after her initial panic attack (and her father's last psychiatric hospitalization) she and the author mutually agreed the therapeutic work was done. Ultimately, the overall treatment duration was approximately 8 months.

Note

1. The cases depicted in the book are composite representations of multiple client experiences where names, gender, and other potentially identifiable aspects of the case experience have been changed to protect client confidentiality.

References

American Psychiatric Association. (2013). *Diagnostic and statistical manual of mental disorders (5th ed.)*. Arlington, VA: American Psychiatric Publishing.

Barrett, P. M., Dadds, M. R., & Rapee, R. M. (1996). Family treatment of childhood anxiety: A controlled trial. *Journal Of Consulting And Clinical Psychology, 64*(2), 333–342. doi:10.1037/0022-006X.64.2.333

Barrett, P. M. (1998). Evaluation of cognitive-behavioral group treatments for childhood anxiety disorders. *Journal Of Clinical Child Psychology, 27*(4), 459–468. doi:10.1207/s15374424jccp2704_10

Beck, A. T., & Mahoney, M. J. (1979). Schools of "thought." *American Psychologist, 34*(1), 93–98. doi:10.1037/0003-066X.34.1.93.b

Becker, E. (1973). *The denial of death.* New York, NY, US: Free Press.

Beidel, D. C., Turner, S. M., & Morris, T. L. (2000). Behavioral treatment of childhood social phobia. *Journal Of Consulting And Clinical Psychology, 68*(6), 1072–1080. doi:10.1037/0022-006X.68.6.1072

Bohlin, G., Hagekull, B., & Rydell, A. (2000). Attachment and social functioning: A longitudinal study from infancy to middle childhood. *Social Development, 9*(1), 24–39. doi:10.1111/1467-9507.00109

Borkovec, T. D. (1994). The nature, functions, and origins of worry. In G. L. Davey, F. Tallis, (Eds.), *Worrying: Perspectives on theory, assessment and treatment* (pp. 5–33). Oxford, England: John Wiley & Sons.

Chambless, D. L., & Hollon, S. D. (1998). Defining empirically supported therapies. *Journal Of Consulting And Clinical Psychology, 66*(1), 7–18. doi:10.1037/0022-006X.66.1.7

Craske, M. G., Antony, M. M., & Barlow, D. H. (2006). *Mastering your fears and phobias: Therapist guide.*, 2nd *ed.* New York, NY, US: Oxford University Press.

Craske, M. G., Rauch, S. L., Ursano, R., Prenoveau, J., Pine, D. S., & Zinbarg, R. E. (2009). What is an anxiety disorder?. *Depression And Anxiety, 26*(12), 1066–1085. doi:10.1002/da.20633

Degnan, K. A., & Fox, N. A. (2007). Behavioral inhibition and anxiety disorders: Multiple levels of a resilience process. *Development And Psychopathology, 19*(3), 729–746. doi:10.1017/S0954579407000363

Degnan, K. A., Almas, A. N., & Fox, N. A. (2010). Temperament and the environment in the etiology of childhood anxiety. *Journal Of Child Psychology And Psychiatry, 51*(4), 497–517. doi:10.1111/j.1469-7610.2010.02228.x

Drake, K. L., & Ginsburg, G. S. (2012). Family factors in the development, treatment, and prevention of childhood anxiety disorders. *Clinical Child And Family Psychology Review, 15*(2), 144–162. doi:10.1007/s10567-011-0109-0

Ellis, A., & Harper, R. A. (1975). *A new guide to rational living.* Oxford, England: Prentice-Hall.

Ellis, A. (1973). Are cognitive behavior therapy and rational therapy synonymous?. *Rational Living*, *8*(2), 8–11.

Esbjørn, B. H., Bender, P. K., Reinholdt-Dunne, M. L., Munck, L. A., & Ollendick, T. H. (2012). The development of anxiety disorders: Considering the contributions of attachment and emotion regulation. *Clinical Child And Family Psychology Review*, *15*(2), 129–143. doi:10.1007/s10567-011-0105-4

Gallagher, H. M., Rabian, B. A., & McCloskey, M. S. (2004). A brief group cognitive-behavioral intervention for social phobia in childhood. *Journal of Anxiety Disorders*, *18*(4), 459–479.

Gaston, J. E., Abbott, M. J., Rapee, R. M., & Neary, S. A. (2006). Do empirically supported treatments generalize to private practice?. A benchmark study of a cognitive-behavioural group treatment programme for social phobia. *British Journal Of Clinical Psychology*, *45*(1), 33–48. doi:10.1348/014466505X35146

Gregory, A. M., & Eley, T. C. (2007). Genetic influences on anxiety in children: What we've learned and where we're heading. *Clinical Child And Family Psychology Review*, *10*(3), 199–212. doi:10.1007/s10567-007-0022-8

Kendall, P. C. (1994). Treating anxiety disorders in children: Results of a randomized clinical trial. *Journal Of Consulting And Clinical Psychology*, *62*(1), 100–110. doi:10.1037/0022-006X.62.1.100

Kertz, S. J., & Woodruff-Borden, J. (2011). The developmental psychopathology of worry. *Clinical Child And Family Psychology Review*, *14*(2), 174–197. doi:10.1007/s10567-011-0086-3

Kessler, R. C., Keller, M. B., & Wittchen, H. (2001). The epidemiology of generalized anxiety disorder. *Psychiatric Clinics Of North America*, *24*(1), 19–39. doi:10.1016/S0193-953X(05)70204-5

Kierkegaard, S. (1843/1954a). *Fear and trembling*. Princeton, NJ: Princeton University Press. (Original work published 1843)

Kierkegaard, S. (1849/1954b). *The sickness unto death*. Princeton, NJ: Princeton University Press. (Original work published 1849)

Kramer, R. (1995a). The "bad mother" Freud has never seen: Otto Rank and the birth of object- relations theory. *Journal of the American Academy of Psychoanalysis*, *23*, 293–321

Kramer, R. (1995b). The birth of client-centered therapy: Carl Rogers, Otto Rank, and "The Beyond." *Journal of Humanistic Psychology*, *35*, 54–110.

Leichsenring, F., & Salzer, S. (2014). A unified protocol for the transdiagnostic psychodynamic treatment of anxiety disorders: An evidence-based approach. *Psychotherapy*, *51*(2), 224–245. doi:10.1037/a0033815

Manassis, K., & Bradley, S. J. (1994). The development of childhood anxiety disorders: Toward an integrated model. *Journal Of Applied Developmental Psychology*, *15*(3), 345–366. doi:10.1016/0193-3973(94)90037-X

Manassis, K., Mendlowitz, S. L., Scapillato, D., Avery, D., Fiksenbaum, L., Freire, M., &...Owens, M. (2002). Group and individual cognitive-behavioral therapy for childhood anxiety disorders. A randomized trial. *Journal Of The American Academy Of Child & Adolescent Psychiatry, 41*(12), 1423–1430. doi:10.1097/00004583-200212000-00013

May, R. (1969). *Existential psychology.* New York, NY, US: Crown Publishing Group/Random House.

May, R. (1977). *The meaning of anxiety.*, Rev. *ed.* New York, NY, US: W W Norton & Co.

May, R. (2007). *Love and will.* New York, NY: Norton. (Original work published 1969).

McLeod, B. D., Wood, J. J., & Weisz, J. R. (2007). Examining the association between parenting and childhood anxiety: A meta-analysis. *Clinical Psychology Review, 27*(2), 155–172. doi:10.1016/j.cpr.2006.09.002

Mineka, S., & Zinbarg, R. (2006). A contemporary learning theory perspective on the etiology of anxiety disorders: It's not what you thought it was. *American Psychologist, 61*(1), 10–26. doi:10.1037/0003-066X.61.1.10

Nathan, P. E., & Gorman, J. M. (2002). *A guide to treatments that work.*, 2nd *ed.* New York, NY, US: Oxford University Press.

Nietzsche, F. (1878/1996). *Human, All too human.* Lincoln: University of Nebraska Press. (Original work published in 1878).

Nietzsche, F. (1886/1990). *Beyond good and evil.* London, England: Penguin Books. (Original work published in 1886).

Ollendick, T. H., & King, N. J. (1998). Empirically supported treatments for children with phobic and anxiety disorders: Current status. *Journal Of Clinical Child Psychology, 27*(2), 156–167. doi:10.1207/s15374424jccp2702_3

Paulus, D. J., Hayes-Skelton, S. A., & Norton, P. J. (2015). There's no 'I' in GCBT: Identifying predictors of group-level outcome in transdiagnostic group cognitive-behavioral therapy for anxiety. *Group Dynamics: Theory, Research, And Practice, 19*(2), 63–76. doi:10.1037/gdn0000023

Pérez-Edgar, K., & Fox, N. A. (2005). Temperament and Anxiety Disorders. *Child And Adolescent Psychiatric Clinics Of North America, 14*(4), 681–706. doi:10.1016/j.chc.2005.05.008

Pincus, D. B., May, J. E., Whitton, S. W., Mattis, S. G., & Barlow, D. H. (2010). Cognitive- behavioral treatment of panic disorder in adolescence. *Journal Of Clinical Child And Adolescent Psychology, 39*(5), 638–649. doi:10.1080/15374416.2010.501288

Pitchford, D. B. (2009). The existentialism of Rollo May: An influence on trauma treatment. *Journal Of Humanistic Psychology, 49*(4), 441–461. doi:10.1177/0022167808327679

Polanczyk, G. V., Salum, G. A., Sugaya, L. S., Caye, A., & Rohde, L. A. (2015). Annual research review: A meta-analysis of the worldwide prevalence of mental disorders in children and adolescents. *Journal Of Child Psychology And Psychiatry, 56*(3), 345–365. doi:10.1111/jcpp.12381

Rank, O. (1924). The Trauma of Birth in Its Importance for Psychoanalytic Therapy. *Psychoanalytic Review*, *11*241–245.

Rank, O. (1932). *Art and artist.* Oxford, England: Knopf.

Rank, O. (1936/1978a). *Truth and reality: A life history of the human will* (J. Taft, Trans.). New York, NY: Norton. (Original work published 1936).

Rank, O. (1936/1978b). *Will therapy: An analysis of the therapeutic process in terms of relationship* (J. Taft, Trans.). New York, NY: Norton. (Original work published 1936).

Rapee, R. M. (2001). The development of generalized anxiety. In M. W. Vasey, M. R. Dadds, (Eds.), *The developmental psychopathology of anxiety* (pp. 481–503). New York, NY, US: Oxford University Press. doi:10.1093/med:psych/9780195123630.003.0021

Roberts, R. E., Attkisson, C. C., & Rosenblatt, A. (1998). Prevalence of psychopathology among children and adolescents. *American Journal of Psychiatry*, *155*(6), 715–725.

Roberts, R. E., Roberts, C. R., & Chan, W. (2009). One-year incidence of psychiatric disorders and associated risk factors among adolescents in the community. *Journal Of Child Psychology And Psychiatry*, *50*(4), 405–415. doi:10.1111/j.1469-7610.2008.01969.x

Schneider, K. J. (2008). *Existential-integrative psychotherapy: Guideposts to the core of practice.* New York, NY, US: Routledge/Taylor & Francis Group.

Schneider, K. J., Galvin, J., & Serlin, I. (2009). Rollo May on existential psychotherapy. *Journal Of Humanistic Psychology*, *49*(4), 419–434. doi:10.1177/0022167809340241

Shamir-Essakow, G., Ungerer, J. A., & Rapee, R. M. (2005). Attachment, Behavioral Inhibition, and Anxiety in Preschool Children. *Journal Of Abnormal Child Psychology*, *33*(2), 131–143. doi:10.1007/s10802-005-1822-2

Shumaker, D. (2012). An existential–integrative treatment of anxious and depressed adolescents. *Journal Of Humanistic Psychology*, *52*(4), 375–400. doi:10.1177/0022167811422947

Silverman, W. K., Kurtines, W. M., Ginsburg, G. S., Weems, C. F., Lumpkin, P. W., & Carmichael, D. H. (1999). Treating anxiety disorders in children with group cognitive- behavioral therapy: A randomized clinical trial. *Journal Of Consulting And Clinical Psychology*, *67*(6), 995–1003. doi:10.1037/0022-006X.67.6.995

Silverman, W. K., Pina, A. A., & Viswesvaran, C. (2008). Evidence-based psychosocial treatments for phobic and anxiety disorders in children and adolescents. *Journal Of Clinical Child And Adolescent Psychology*, *37*(1), 105–130. doi:10.1080/15374410701817907

Slavin-Mulford, J., & Hilsenroth, M. J. (2012). Evidence-based psychodynamic treatments for anxiety disorders: A review. In R. A. Levy, J. S. Ablon,

H. Kächele, (Eds.), *Psychodynamic psychotherapy research: Evidence-based practice and practice-based evidence* (pp. 117–137). Totowa, NJ, US: Humana Press. doi:10.1007/978-1-60761-792-1_7

Spence, S. H., Holmes, J. M., March, S., & Lipp, O. V. (2006). The feasibility and outcome of clinic plus Internet delivery of cognitive-behavior therapy for childhood anxiety. *Journal Of Consulting And Clinical Psychology, 74*(3), 614–621. doi:10.1037/0022-006X.74.3.614

Tillich, P. (1952). Anxiety, religion, and medicine. *Pastoral Psychology, 3*11–17. doi:10.1007/BF01769082

Turner, S. M., Beidel, D. C., & Costello, A. (1987). Psychopathology in the offspring of anxiety disorders patients. *Journal Of Consulting And Clinical Psychology, 55*(2), 229–235. doi:10.1037/0022-006X.55.2.229

Vasey, M. W., & Dadds, M. R. (2001). *The developmental psychopathology of anxiety.* New York, NY, US: Oxford University Press. doi:10.1093/med:psych/9780195123630.001.0001

Verhulst, F. C., & Koot, H. M. (1995). *The epidemiology of child and adolescent psychopathology.* New York, NY, US: Oxford University Press.

Weems, C. F., Costa, N. M., Dehon, C., & Berman, S. L. (2004). Paul Tillich's theory of existential anxiety: A preliminary conceptual and empirical examination. *Anxiety, Stress & Coping: An International Journal, 17*(4), 383–399. doi:10.1080/10615800412331318616

Yalom, I. D. (1980). *Existential psychotherapy.* New York, NY, US: Basic Books.

CHAPTER 6

EI Approaches to Treating Depression in Adolescents

Introduction

Rollo May's (1969) famous quote "Depression is the inability to construct a future" encapsulates the EI conceptualization of this mood disturbance. A sense of hopelessness, apathy, numbness, and/or deeply felt psychic pain can dramatically impact an individual's subjective inner experience and ability to see a life beyond. In extreme forms this mood disturbance can lead to social and emotional withdrawal, incapacitation, self-harm behaviors, suicidal ideation, and, most tragically, suicide. An adolescent who presents in therapy in the throes of a depressive episode can generate sleepless nights for even the most seasoned clinician, as their client's sense of patience and faith that better days may be ahead is sorely tested by a lack of life experience that supports such a seemingly preposterous claim. For the adolescent, the subjective emotional experience of a depressive episode can represent a qualitatively different type of pain and/or psychic deadness than that heretofore ever felt. It can simply feel *intolerable*. To further complicate matters, many adolescents are at risk for acting impulsively on a "good" day. Under the strain of a depressive episode, the judgment and impulsivity can be even more compromised, leading to rash decisions and high-risk behaviors that can result in dire consequences. To help weather the storm of a depressive episode requires the presence of a skilled and present therapist who can instill a sense of hope, courage, and patience in his or her young client. It is an awesome responsibility that can test the therapist's own ability to remain faithful to the process even when change

D. Shumaker, *Existential-Integrative Approaches to Treating Adolescents*, DOI 10.1057/978-1-349-95211-3_6

does not seem forthcoming. This chapter explores EI approaches to treating adolescents suffering from depression in the hope of helping clinicians and their young clients navigate the haze of a depressive episode in the belief that, despite all evidence to the contrary, better days remain.

Clinical Description, Incidence, and Prevalence

The transition from the DMS-IV-TR to the DSM-5 brought significant changes in the classification of specific mood disorders. The main diagnoses in the DSM-5 framework now include major depressive disorder, persistent depressive disorder (formerly referred to as dysthymic disorder), disruptive mood dysregulation disorder, premenstrual dysphoric disorder, and substance/medication-induced depressive disorder. The bipolar depressive disorders are now classified in their own section of the DSM-5. The etiology, clinical features, and treatment of bipolar disorders were deemed sufficiently different from the unipolar experience of depression to merit this distinction. In general, the main clinical features common to all depressive disorders include the subjective experience of sadness, irritability, and/or emptiness, as well as cognitive changes (e.g., loss of concentration, guilty thoughts) and physiological/somatic changes (e.g., disturbances of sleep and appetite). The intensity, range, and length of specific symptomatology are for the most part the major distinguishing factors among the specific diagnoses. It is important to note that this chapter's focus will be on the treatment of DSM-5 depressive disorders only. Bipolar disorders are not included in the discussion because the author concurs with the growing consensus in the field that its etiology and treatment is quite distinct from depressive disorders. Readers interested in learning more about potential existential applications in the treatment and conceptualization of bipolar disorder are encouraged to review Havens and Ghaemi's (2005) article entitled "Existential Despair and Bipolar Disorder: The Therapeutic Alliance as a Mood Stabilizer."

Considerable research has been conducted on the incidence and prevalence of depressive disorders (Lakdawalla et al., 2007). Similar to anxiety disorders, clinically significant depression is unfortunately a common experience during adolescence. Approximately 5–25% of the individuals will experience depression at some point in their lives (Gotlib & Hammen, 2002). The mean age of onset appears to be 15 years old and the average duration of an episode lasts approximately 6 months (Lewinsohn et al., 1994). There is strong evidence suggesting that the incidence of depression increases as individuals transition from childhood into adolescence. For example, Hankin and colleagues (1998) conducted a 10-year longitudinal study on the development of depression from childhood through early adulthood and found that while approximately 2% of 13 year olds are depressed the rate jumps to 17% in 18 year olds. Further, there are indications that the age of initial onset may be decreasing. Specifically, Abela and Hankin (2008) found that approximately 9% of youth experience an initial major depressive episode prior to the age of 14 years.

Beyond these general findings, epidemiological research indicates females seem to experience higher rates of depression than males, especially during adolescence (Costello et al., 2003). There is also a high degree of comorbidity between depressive and anxiety disorders in youth. Community-based samples of adolescents suggest that approximately 25–50% of adolescents who carry a primary diagnosis of depression will meet diagnostic criteria for an anxiety disorder (Costello et al., 2003). Most disturbingly, the risk of suicide increases dramatically when an adolescent is diagnosed with a depressive disorder. In general, as much as 15% of individuals diagnosed with depression will go on to commit suicide (Gotlib and Hammen, 2002). In 2010, 4,600 youth between the ages of 15 and 24 years old living in the USA committed suicide (McIntosh & Drapeau, 2012). A sense of hopelessness and prior self-injury behaviors, common to many adolescents who are depressed, seem to be strong risk factors for suicide attempts (Taliaferro and Muehlenkamp, 2014). Beyond the obvious risk of self-harm and suicide, depressive disorders exact a high cost in terms of loss of productivity at school, work, and in extracurricular activities. Core depressive symptoms such as social withdrawal, concentration difficulties, and a loss of interest and energy can all contribute to the lack of engagement and productivity.

Common Conceptualizations/Etiological Overview

Similar to the study of anxiety disorders in youth, there has been considerable research conducted on the etiology of depression. The range of risk and protective factors are expansive and, as one might expect, the causes of depression in adolescence appear multifactorial and complex. Brent and Maalouf (2009) reviewed several of the more common areas of focus in the research literature and a brief summary of their analysis – augmented in sections with additional research findings – is included here.

The authors identified the following 12 domains of risk: (1) developmental epidemiology; (2) neurocognitive risk factors; (3) positive affect and reward; (4) emotion regulation; (5) parental depression and genetics; (6) family interaction; (7) early experiences; (8) life events; (9) sleep; (10) peer relationships; (11) school and activities; and (12) health risk behaviors.

Regarding the developmental epidemiology risk factor, Brent and Maalouf (2009) argue changing demands upon the individual that occur during adolescence may impose risk. For example, decreased adult supervision and support, a natural occurrence during adolescence may promote healthy individuation in some but increase the risk for depressive symptomatology in others (Nelson and Barry, 2005). Neurocognitive risk factors include a cognitive bias toward negative emotion (Perez-Edgar et al., 2006), while positive affect and reward risk factors pertain to a decreased ability to respond positively to rewards (Hardin et al., 2007) and/or access positive affect (Silk et al., 2007). Studies pertaining to emotional regulation have found depressed adolescents produce higher cortisol secretions as compared to peers (Forbes et al., 2006), suggesting an increased sensitivity to stress. Further, depressed youth are more likely to demonstrate deficits in their emotional regulation strategies (Wilkinson & Goodyer, 2006). For example, they may find it more difficult to distract themselves or reflect upon positive memories when their mood is low.

Brent and Maalouf (2009) also found considerable evidence that family functioning exerts a strong influence on the experience of depression during adolescence. To begin, there appears to be a heritability factor. The offspring of parents who experienced depression are at increased risk. The risk increases as a function of the extent of the familial loading for depression, the recurrence of the disorder in parents, and when there is an earlier age of onset of the parental depression (Weissman et al., 2006). Family interaction styles are another source of risk. Specifically, both parental discord and high levels of expressed emotions increase the risk for a child to develop depression during adolescence (Emslie et al., 1998). Early parent care, which may include abuse, deprivation, and prenatal risk factors, is third source of familial risk (Felitti et al., 1998). The specific factors of rejection and control are critical parenting behaviors that impact risk (Rapee, 1997). McLeod and colleagues (2007) found that, while both factors are associated with depression, parental rejection has a significantly stronger association than excessive parental control. Thus, parents who engage in aversive behaviors and lack warmth are most likely to witness the development of depressive symptoms in their children.

Moving beyond the specific familial factors identified by Brent and Maalouf (2009), as one might expect the quality of the parent-child attachment relationship also seems to play an important role in the development of depressive symptoms during adolescence. Specifically, clinically depressed adolescents are more likely to demonstrate less secure attachments to their parents than nondepressed peers (Armsden et al., 1990; Brumariu and Kerns, 2010), with disorganized attachment most often identified as the specific attachment style that increases risk for depression. More recently, Freed and colleagues (2016) found a strong relationship between emotional clarity (the ability to recognize, discriminate, and understand one's emotions), family functioning, and adolescent depression. Specifically, emotional clarity may mediate the relation between low family functioning and adolescent depression whereby low emotional clarity in the context of low family functioning increases the risk for depression. Clearly, family factors can influence the adolescent experience of depressive symptoms through a variety of pathways.

Broader social factors, such as adverse life events and peer relationships, can also increase the risk for depression during adolescence (Brent and Maalouf, 2009). In the specific case of peer relationships, it appears that many depressed youth may actually spend *more* time with their friends than nondepressed counterparts but that this relatively greater amount of contact is associated with increased negative affect (Silk et al., 2007). As for sleep, youth who are depressed report more subjective sleep problems, frequently sleep less, and have greater difficulty falling asleep (Forbes et al., 2008). School engagement and underachievement is another domain of risk with the long-term occupational and educational prognosis of untreated depression being quite poor (Lewinsohn et al., 1998). Finally, depressed adolescents are more likely to engage in health risk behaviors such as substance abuse, overeating, low physical activity, and/or unprotected sex with each of these factors potentially prolonging or precipitating a depressive episode (Brooks et al., 2002).

Epkins and Heckler (2011) also reviewed risk factors for adolescent depression to provide a basis for their "Cumulative Interpersonal Risk Model" of youth social anxiety and depression. While there is significant overlap between their review and Brent & Maalouf's (2009), they focus in more detail on temperament, parent-child attachment, and peer-related interpersonal relationship problem risk factors. Of note, they cite considerable research indicating that youth who demonstrate a high neuroticism/negative affectivity (NE/A) temperament are at increased risk for depression (Anderson & Hope, 2008). Further, deficits in effort control (EC), which is defined as "the ability to inhibit a dominant response and/ or to activate a subdominant response" (Rothbart and Bates, 2006, pg. 129), also increases risk for depression. Finally, elevated levels of behavioral inhibition (BI) have been associated with depression in youth (Bardone et al., 1996). Thus, there is likely a combination of temperament factors that can potentially play a role in the development of depression during adolescence.

Epkins and Heckler (2011) also highlight social skill development as an important influence upon the development of depressive symptoms. Considerable research indicates that youth who demonstrate social skill deficits are more likely to be diagnosed with depression (Rudolph et al., 2008). It may be that social skill deficits are frequently accompanied by negative cognitive schemas about oneself and one's capacity to effectively engage socially. Thus, a negative self-evaluation and lack of confidence could contribute to depressive symptomatology beyond the actual skill deficit. Relatedly, peer rejection has been associated with depression (Newcomb et al., 1993). (Kistner et al., 2006) argues that a youth's negative perception of their social acceptance is both a causal factor and consequence of depressive symptoms. Epkins and Hecker (2011) argue that both low acceptance and rejection are likely influences in the development of adolescent depression. Finally, as one might expect, peer victimization (i.e., being the target of peers' aggressive behaviors), loneliness, and an absence of friendships, are all associated with depression.

In an effort to deepen our understanding of how biological and psychological factors interact across multiple levels of functioning in the development of youth depression, Cicchetti and Toth (1998) constructed a developmental psychopathology model of the disorder. Their model is based upon an organizational framework of development where four basic systems – cognitive (e.g., social cognition, attributional style), biological (e.g., genetics, brain structure anomalies), socioemotional (e.g., affect regulation, guilt), and representational (e.g., internal representational models, self-schemas) – interact constantly throughout each stage of a child's development. Difficulties in any one of these areas can impact the other areas, retard growth, and increase the risk for depression. Or, as they put it more simply, "early incompetence tends to promote later incompetence" (pg. 225). Given the broad array of formative influences, it is hardly surprising that their model posits multiple potential developmental pathways that can result in depressive formations in adolescence. Another hallmark of the model is that it adopts a transactional perspective on the develop of depression whereby multiple exchanges between caregivers, environmental influences, and the youth in question will exacerbate or decrease the likelihood of depression emerging. Finally, the model's ecological perspective is also reflected in its inclusion of ontogenic, microsystem, exosystem, and microsystem factors in the emergence of depression. At the ontogenic stage of development they maintain that four influences: (1) homeostatic and physiological regulation, (2) affect regulation and attention modulation, (3) secure attachment development, and (4) self-system development – greatly influence the course and trajectory of future depressive experiences. Their model similarly isolates specific microsystem, exosystem, and microsystem influences in the development of youth depression. In conclusion, Cichhetti and Toth's (1998) model of youth depression does an impressive job of capturing the complex nature and wide range of developmental influences upon adolescent depression. Clinicians working with depressed youth are well served to familiarize themselves with their framework.

Empirically Supported Treatments/Evidence-Based Practice Approaches

Considerable research has been conducted examining the efficacy of psychosocial treatments for adolescent depression. In general, there are strong indications that both cognitive-behavioral therapy (CBT) and interpersonal therapy (IPT) approaches are effective treatments for this disorder in adolescents. More specifically, David-Ferdon and Kaslow (2008) conducted a review of psychosocial treatments for adolescents using the Task Force on Promotion and Dissemination of Psychological Procedures criteria and found these general approaches reached the threshold to be considered two "well-established" modalities. Further, they found three "probably efficacious" specific treatment approaches for adolescent depression. Each of the general modalities will be considered briefly here.

The Adolescents Coping with Depression (CWD-A) program is a "probably efficacious" treatment (Lewinsohn et al., 1990) that falls under the general umbrella of CBT treatment approaches. The treatment program consists of the following five general components: (1) relaxation training, (2) cognitive restructuring, (3) pleasant activity scheduling,

(4) communication and social skills training, and (5) conflict-resolution strategies and training. In most forms the length of treatment is approximately 15–16 sessions with sessions lasting anywhere between 45 minutes to up to 2 hours. Further, some versions of the treatment include a separate parent meeting component where information regarding the general treatment progress, skills being taught, and rationale for their usage is provided. The underlying theoretical rationale for this approach is the belief that depressive symptoms arise when the individual is involved in a relative lack of positive experiences, especially mastery experiences and positive social interactions (Lewinsohn et al., 1989). Viewed in this framework, mood is believed to be a function of a ratio of one's positive and negative life experiences. Key components to an effective intervention, therefore, must include training in skills that the individual can utilize to more effectively handle the demands of everyday living as well as adjustments to the attributions the individual makes when events occur. There is a strong educational component to this approach and a heavy reliance upon homework and self-monitoring of one's mood and cognitions outside of sessions. While multiple studies have demonstrated the efficacy of CWD-A, one of the more notable ones examined CWD-A in comparison to Health Maintenance Organization (HMO) care. Specifically, Clarke and colleagues (2001) found that adolescents who received CWD-A plus whatever normal HMO services they were receiving at an HMO clinic showed significantly greater improvements in overall functioning and depressive symptoms than their peers who received the HMO services only. Further these comparatively different gains were maintained at 12-, 18-, and 24-month follow-up intervals.

As previously stated, the second well-established modality is IPT. Mufson and Sills's (2006) Interpersonal Psychotherapy for depressed adolescents (IPT-A) is considered to be a probably efficacious specific treatment that falls within the general approach. The treatment is based upon Harry Stack Sullivan's interpersonal theory of human development which argues that personality develops within the context of interpersonal relationships. The approach also has roots in Adolf Meyer's theory that psychopathology results from difficulties adapting to relationships and the environment as well as Bowlby's attachment theory which posits a strong link between attachment loss and depression. Thus, the core aim of the approach is "to treat depression by addressing the patient's interpersonal interactions and how they affect his or her depressive symptoms" (Mufson and Sills, 2006, pg. 432).

The main goals of IPT-A are to simply reduce depressive symptoms and improve interpersonal functioning. To achieve these ends IPT-A first identifies a specific problem area, then selects effective problem-solving and communication techniques designed to help the problem area, and finally encourages a client to practice these techniques both in and outside of sessions. Mufson and Sills (2006) also emphasize their approach encourages adolescents to take greater ownership of identifying effective problem-solving strategies that suit their personality. Further, there is a focus on promoting an adolescent's independence and ability to negotiate relationships where there remain interdependency needs (e.g., working with parents). Parents are incorporated at various stages of treatment, initially for the purpose of educating them on the etiology of depression. The disorder is conceptualized as a medical condition that is treatable with the hope that parents will reduce blaming tendencies when the adolescent struggles academically and/or socially.

The typical course of an IPT-A intervention is 12 sessions (Mufson and Sills, 2006). The initial phase lasts four sessions and the chief tasks are to explain the nature of depression to both the client and parents and introduce the principles behind the intervention. The therapist also assesses the nature of the problem and develops a treatment contract with the client and parents. In the middle phases of treatment (sessions 5–9) the target problem is further defined and strategies are identified and implemented to treat the area of concern. The therapist will use exploratory techniques such as interviewing, supportive acknowledgment, and the encouragement of the client expressing affect. Communication techniques are also common. For example, problematic interactions that occur outside of the session are dissected and role-played in session followed by an analysis of what changes should be made in the future when similar situations arise. Specific interpersonal problem areas that are the focus of these intervention strategies are grief situations, interpersonal role disputes, role transitions, and interpersonal deficits. The final phase of therapy is referred to as the termination phase and consists of roughly sessions 9–12. Progress toward the goals of treatment is reviewed and the therapist and clients discuss what specific strategies seemed to be most helpful. As one can see, IPT-A offers clinicians a strong alternative/adjunct treatment approach to treating adolescent depression from a strictly CBT modality.

Despite the promise and proven efficacy of CBT and IPT approaches to treating adolescent depression there is still considerable room for improvement. Curry (2014) has identified four specific areas where future psychotherapy research should focus in order to improve client outcomes. First, he believes studies need to adopt a long-term perspective and track client outcomes over a longer period of time in order to better prevent relapse. Second, studies should begin to examine what exactly are the necessary treatment components and learning processes that lead to success over the long term. Third, research should focus on when it is appropriate for clinicians to address comorbid conditions in the treatment of a depressive episode. Finally, Curry argues that there should be a focus on whether more simple models of treatment should be pursued in favor of increasingly more sophisticated – and lengthy – models that incorporate "third-wave" approaches into the treatment protocol.

Beyond these recommendations, Probst (2008) also raises the issue of the portability of these empirically supported treatments (EST). She believes that most adolescents who are referred to therapy in an outpatient setting will not receive either CBT or IPT in part due to the difficulty in transporting these treatments which were developed and tested in a laboratory setting to a real-world setting. She outlines a host of client, therapist, contextual, and treatment delivery variables that can impact the portability of a CBT or IPT manualized treatment. She believes that future research needs to focus at the outset on how one's treatment will translate into a real-world setting.

EI Conceptualization

EI conceptualizes depression as a hyper-constrictive pattern where the individual's root fears are based in a dread of ultimate expansion (Schneider, 2008). Schneider identifies the more specific concerns of asserting oneself, being stimulated, demonstrating ambition, standing out, and contemplating the vast possibilities that are part of our human experience of consciousness and freedom as the core aspects of a depressive experience. From this it seems safe to assume that Schneider believes both polarity continuums – chaos and obliteration, greatness and smallness – can be involved in a depressive experience. The EI conceptualization of depression is therefore similar to the manner in which it conceptualizes anxiety. In both cases the individual is aware of the acute "givens" of our existence, including one's potential for unbounded expansion and rootlessness, which tap into the expansive dreads. However, as Schneider (2008) also notes, fears of obliteration, smallness, and nothingness certainly also can play a role in the development of both anxiety and depression. Thus, not only "greatness" concerns but "smallness" concerns can trigger this emotional reaction. This is not surprising given the array of existential givens that affect the individual. The overwhelming anxiety that one can feel can naturally lead to despair. As Tillich (1952) reminds us, despair can be interpreted as a logical outgrowth of intense, chronic, and/or overwhelming anxiety concerning the existential root fears of emptiness, nonbeing, condemnation, and/or potential meaninglessness

Beyond Schneider's (2008) basic conceptualization of the emotional experience within the EI framework there has been considerable attention devoted to understanding depression from a more general existential perspective. Some of the more prominent conceptualizations are reviewed here. To begin, Frankl (1986) argued that depressive symptoms were rooted in existential anxiety and guilt feelings. This anxiety is transformed into what he referred to as "melancholia" when the individual senses his or her psychophysical insufficiency to meet the standards associated with becoming a responsible adult. As he writes, this sense of insufficiency "is experienced in uniquely human fashion as tension between what the person is and what he ought to be. The melancholic exaggerates the degree to which he as a person falls short of his ideal" (Frankl, 1986, pg. 202). Thus, the gap between reality and the ideal is perceived to be such a huge abyss that the individual experiences a crisis of conscience with no resolution in sight. In certain cases the depressive episode is borne out of a sense of insufficiency about one's ability to preserve one's life. Here the underlying existential concern is a fear of death. For others who feel grossly inadequate in their ability to act in a morally righteous manner their depression includes a strong guilt component.

Regardless of the specific triggering existential concern, Frankl believed all existential depressive episodes included a profound sense of hopelessness about not only one's abilities but also the future in general. The individual is blinded to his or her own inherent values as a human being. A nihilistic attitude may follow. To treat these clients Frankl believed one must remind the individual of their capacity to develop creative, experiential, and attitudinal values that are more focused on meaning rather than the pursuit of happiness per se. By cultivating one's sense of intentionality and meaning an improvement in mood and happiness was thought to naturally occur.

Emmy van Deurzen (2015) conceptualizes depression as the lowest of emotions with strong associations with a sense of disengagement and disappointment in life. She argues that humans need "passion, dedication, persistence, and courage" as well as a willingness to suffer in in order to live in a "soulful" manner (pg. 91). In essence, depression is a sign and symptom of an individual's withdrawal from life. The individual may be estranged from both his or her body and the world in general. Further, the depressed person often operates under the belief that others fare better than him or herself, that life has dealt one an unfair hand. At the root of the depression is what Rollo May has referred to as a neurotic anxiety formation where the individual has attempted to avoid life (and death) by not letting new experiences and others into their inner world. The paradox, as both May and van Deurzen see it, is that by avoiding life, "we begin to atrophy…[and] we may become deadened all together" (van Deurzen, 2015, pg. 92). If an individual complains of depression this signals the individual has given up and abandoned the fight for survival. They may experience a release and even a level of relaxation upon this surrender, but over time these initially positive feelings will give way to "bitterness, despondency, dejection, and despairing." In treatment, she argues the initial task of the therapist is to certainly validate the client's suffering but also to help the client let go or "move on" from prior trauma before embarking on the task of rediscovering what one is passionate about. The "moving on" process of course takes courage on the client's part, a feat that is not lost upon van Deurzen. As she writes, "existential courage is to know that it is with fear and trepidation that the battle is begun and that is because of our challenges and our failures that we learn to become who we are capable of being. The pleasure of leaving our disconsolate negativity behind is its own reward" (pg. 93).

Another cogent analysis of depressive episodes from an existential framework is offered by Bugental (1987). He refers to depressive symptoms as "dispiritedness." His conceptualization of this emotional state is similar to the authors already reviewed. For him, the essence of a vital life is the individual's ability to live with intentionality and in a manner consistent with their self-concept. When there is incongruence between how we live our life and our sense of self, or when there is a lack of purpose and direction, he argues, "anxiety is aroused, a backlog of intentionality work accumulates, and there is a deadening of vitality" (pg. 232). This can lead to dispiritedness, a "condition of blocked intentionality," which includes a blend of anxiety and dysphoria. The intensity of one's dispiritedness is quite often a function of how close one is to satisfying an impulse or objective before it becomes blocked. For example, if one had hoped to secure acceptance at a college to pursue further studies but ends up receiving a rejection letter, then an even more intense sense of dejection, anxiety, and/or sadness may follow if the individual believed he or she to be on the cusp of obtaining a lifelong goal that had tremendous meaning. Thus, there is a strong relation between expectancy and depressive symptoms.

Bugental (1987) also notes that it can be important for the individual's mental health functioning to recognize and relinquish what he refers to as "wants" as opposed to willed intentions. He writes, "it is hard for many of us – having lived in a time of rising expectations – to let go of possibilities, even though holding on to them may prevent desired actualities. Yet let go we must" (pg. 233). This can be immensely difficult. As he points out, actualizing one's goals and wants breathes life into us while relinquishing the same is often equated with death. A period of mourning may follow a significant relinquishment. Finally, Bugental also notes that both anger and a sense of inertia are common correlates of the more general state of being dispirited. The anger can be in response to being blocked and forced to relinquish goals. Inertia can signal an absence of goals or sense of direction that occurs again when goals are blocked. He believes inertia has the potential, however, to serve a useful purpose. Specifically, it can provide space and time for the individual to construct new purposes and to grieve the loss of old purposes.

A therapist can serve a critical function in helping a client work through his or her dispiritedness. Bugental (1987) offers a three-phase treatment approach. The first phase involves efforts by the clinician to promote a sense of presence in the client about their dispiritedness. He states many clients will attempt to detach themselves from their blockages and emotional state of dysphoria through a more casual and even humorous self-report. The therapists job, when such detachment is detected, is to note it and repeatedly bring this layer of resistance to the client's awareness when he or she is utilizing this defense mechanism. The second phase, which he refers to as "Dealing with Secondary Reactions," is a logical outgrowth of a client letting go of their sense of detachment and becoming more attuned to their emotional experience of being dispirited. He argues other emotions and processes, such as blaming tendencies, guilt, and rationalizations may come to the fore. Like detachment, the therapist needs to note these patterns for the client in an attempt to reduce a client's reliance upon them. By doing so, he believes a clinician can help free clients of emotional blockages that prevent them from healing and re-establishing a sense of intentionality and spiritedness. The third and final phase of treatment is treating the client's "Primary Intentionality Blocking." Here, when the client has owned their dispiritedness, the goal is to have them accept it and then work through it without distraction or attempt to minimize/avoid. Core existential fears will often emerge in the client at this stage of treatment such as fears of death, meaninglessness, or ultimate aloneness. Yet Bugental believes that the emergence of these fears signal the client's readiness to engage in deeper psychotherapeutic work that can ultimately lead to a more intentioned and spirited life approach.

Turning toward more recent conceptualizations of the disorder, there has been limited peer-review research conducted on existential causes and treatments of depression. That which has been conducted seems to support the general premise of a strong link between existential concerns and depression. To begin, Mascaro and Rosen (2008) investigated the relationship between a sense of meaning and depression and found evidence to support Frankl's basic premise that an increased sense of meaning reduces the risk for a depressive experience. Specifically, the authors administered three validated measures of meaning and three validated measures of depression to 574 college students and assessed their progress over a two-month period. The authors found that baseline levels of meaning predicted changes in depressive symptoms in these individuals. Specifically, lower levels of meaning are associated with a vulnerability to increases in depressive symptoms over time. Conversely, increases in meaning can be associated with decreases in depressive symptoms. The authors also concluded that what has meaning can vary considerably among individuals, with spirituality, interpersonal relations, self-transcendence, altruism, vocational, and artistic activities all potentially serving as important pathways for the individual to live a life with a sense of intentionality and purpose.

Graham and colleagues (2010) put forth an Existential Model of Perfectionism and Depressive Symptoms (EMPDS) that they investigated in a sample of 240 college students. The model is based upon prior research investigating perfectionism and depression. These efforts identify perfectionistic concerns (PCs; i.e., negative reactions to failures, concerns over other's criticisms and expectations, and doubts about one's abilities) and perfectionistic strivings (PSs; i.e., rigid and unrelenting, self-imposed performance expectations) as two critical factors that relate to depression. The study authors hypothesized that high PC is a risk factor for depressive symptoms. These individuals tend to catastrophize even relatively minor concerns, have difficulty accepting past experiences that were felt to be uncomfortable or dissatisfying, and may be predisposed to view life negatively. Further, the combination of higher self-criticalness and a need to please others makes life more difficult for the individual and can even impede growth. The model asserts that, over time, life may seem meaninglessness and unsatisfying to high PC individuals because of these catastrophizing tendencies and difficulties accepting painful past experiences. Overall, the study results supported this model. Interestingly (and somewhat surprisingly) the study authors recommended both cognitive-behavioral and third-wave (mindfulness and acceptance) approaches to treating individuals with high PC tendencies who exhibit depressive symptoms but did not specifically recommend an existential approach. It would seem that the study authors did not deem the existential concerns of high PC individuals as potentially benefitting from an EI or other existential treatment approach even though their model of depression includes "existential" in the title and there is a general recognition that existential concerns are a core component of the depressive experience of high PC individuals.

More recently Stalsett and colleagues (2012) conducted a matched comparison treatment study examining the efficacy of their "VITA" existential therapeutic approach in the treatment of depression in adults with comorbid Cluster C personality disorders. By way of review, Cluster C personality disorders encompass what is considered to be more anxious and fearful personality disorders and are the most common cluster typology. Many individuals with this personality profile often do not benefit from psychotherapeutic treatment when they are depressed. The authors found that this subset of individuals (i.e., individuals with comorbid depression and Cluster C diagnoses who fail to respond to CBT and other "first line" treatments) commonly reported existential concerns pertaining to meaninglessness, death, loneliness, guilt, and shame. Based upon this observation they developed VITA therapy (the word "VITA" means life in Latin) which they describe generally as "an existential short-term dynamic group-oriented therapy focusing on the interweaving of affect, object relations, narrative, and existential issues" (pg. 580). The treatment was administered in an inpatient setting and included multiple therapeutic modalities including individual, group, and art therapies. Fifty patients received the VITA treatment and were compared to 50 patients who received treatment as usual which mainly encompassed individual therapy and normal process groups offered at the psychiatric facility.

The VITA treatment consisted of four main components: (1) existential, religious and spiritual concerns; (2) narrative construction of one's life stories; (3) dynamic-relational issues (e.g., exploration of one's identity, attachment relation, defense mechanisms); and (4) affective capacity (e.g., mindfulness and affect consciousness) (Stalsett et al., 2012). Beyond the shift in content focus, VITA therapy differed from the treatment as usual approach in its use of diary writing, meditation, and peer evaluations of an individual's monthly progress. The typical course of treatment was approximately 12 weeks. The authors found that the VITA treatment participants experienced "remarkable improvement" relative to their initial level of functioning. Their level of improvement was greater than that experienced by individuals who received the treatment as usual. Further, a year after treatment those who participated in VITA continued to make gains in functioning while the treatment as usual participants had maintained their gains but failed to continue to improve. The authors concluded that the treatment appears to a be a "viable and effective" treatment for treatment-resistant depression with comorbid Cluster C personality disorders. They speculate that the therapy's emphasis on identifying and relieving a client's blocked affect through a dynamic, insight-oriented existential approach was likely the key change ingredient.

Smith and Rhodes (2015) offer a final study of depression from an existential perspective that is explored here. In an effort to better understand what the actual experience of depression is like for an individual the authors adopted a qualitative research approach consisting of structured interviews of seven adult participants who had been diagnosed with depression. Sample questions included in the interview process were the following: (1) Can you described what it is like being depressed?; and (2) Can you describe the actual events you have on a daily basis? The authors found that the participants shared a common experience of loss and emptiness. The described this as a "major depletion" of these individuals that affected the relational, corporeal, and temporal aspects of their being. More specifically, the participants reported feeling alone (relational), being empty (corporeal), and sensing a loss of one's life (temporal) such that one's sense as past, present, and future had vanished and/or been worthless. All sense of hope for these individuals was gone making suicide a very real proposition. In addition, the study authors identified a sense of feeling shaken or overwhelmed with negative emotional experiences as another aspect of a depressive episode. In these instances the individual could also suffer from "frenzied" thinking approaching that of a manic or even psychotic process. Many also experienced waves of self-doubt that could cause the individual to not only distrust themselves but also their ability to judge (and trust) others. Not surprisingly, Smith and Rhodes (2015) conclude that the depressive episodes described by the study participants include a strong existential component. They advise clinicians to adopt a phenomenological perspective when inquiring about a client's depressive experience and to focus closely on a client's experience of emptiness, extreme emotions, thought process, and self-doubt.

In summary, existential theorists, researchers, and therapists generally conceptualize depression as an activation of the core polarities of our existence and/or existential concerns that is often preceded by a perceived failure, loss, and/or trauma. Further this threat can lead to feelings of insufficiency/inadequacy (Frankl) and/or a lack of intentionality (van Deurzen, Frankl, and Bugental) that results in a disengagement from life and sense of hopelessness about one's future. Individuals especially high in perfectionistic tendencies and/or who demonstrate pre-existing personality concerns appear to be especially vulnerable to a depressive experience that activates existential concerns. In additional to core EI treatment approaches, Bugental offers a three-phase treatment approach to treating adult depression, Frankl believes Logotherapy can be quite helpful, and van Deurzen, May, and Rank encourage some variation of a grieving and "moving on" process whereby the client redirects focus onto new goals and creative endeavors. Finally, in more recent times Stalsett and colleagues (2012) have proposed VITA therapy as a viable existential approach to treating inpatient clients suffering from major depression.

EI Case Example

Roman,[1] age 15 years, was referred by his primary care physician in the spring of his sophomore year in high school after his mother had found him in the family bathroom acting "peculiarly" a week earlier. Specifically, an hour after an argument she had found him sitting on the rim of the bathtub with a pen knife and belt on the counter near him. She had called Roman's primary care physician the morning following the bathroom encounter seeking a phone consultation. On the basis of what was disclosed over the phone the physician had requested that Roman and both parents meet with him in person. During this meeting Roman admitted to feeling profoundly depressed and contemplating taking his life on several occasions in prior weeks. He further disclosed he had been engaging in cutting behaviors for the prior 6 months, using the pen knife to inflict a series of superficial cuts on both wrists on approximately 10–15 different occasions. These wounds had seemingly gone undetected by his parents. He denied the belt had any lethal significance, stating it had merely been in the bathroom by coincidence. He denied any prior suicide attempts. The primary care physician deemed him safe to return home under the conditions that Roman hand over his pen knife to his parents, start seeing a counselor, and start taking an anti-depressant medication. Roman had reluctantly agreed to these conditions.

Roman attended the initial session with both parents four days after his visit with his physician. He arrived wearing blue-jeans, a dark t-shirt with his favorite metal band emblazoned on it, and sneakers. He wore his blonde hair well below his shoulders and grudgingly took off his headphones which were blasting music when he followed his parents into the therapy room. From there he was subdued but minimally forthcoming during the first meeting. He glared at his parents at different times when they were sharing their concerns and therapy goals, and tended to provide one or two-word answers to questions.

Over the course of the first session the therapist learned that Roman was one of two children. He had an older brother who was ten years older than him and who lived out of state with his girlfriend and had little contact with him or his parents. His father worked full-time in a construction business that was struggling. Roman's father was of medium stature, like his son, but spoke in a serious and authoritative manner. He expressed frustration with Roman for failing to do better in school, for arguing with Roman's mother, and for refusing to try-out for the high school's football team. Roman's mother mostly deferred to her ex-husband in the session. She was an obese woman who spoke infrequently in a barely audible voice with little eye contact. She was out of work and on disability for reasons that were unclear. She expressed relatively more concern about Roman's emotional state and cutting behaviors, but generally seemed overwhelmed and passive. Money was very tight in the family and the financial strain and limited resources seemed to weigh heavily on the entire family. At one point in the initial session Roman noted that he was tired of living in a town with a "bunch of rich-bitch snobs" who dismissed him because of his clothes and the fact that he lived in one of the town's only apartment complexes. Both parents reported generally cooperative co-parenting and no overt conflict was observed despite the father clearly dominating the conversation.

Roman had been diagnosed (by his primary care physician and a former school psychologist) with ADHD when he was 11 years old and had been taking stimulant medications intermittently over the previous three years. At the time of the initial consultation he had not taken ADHD medication for over six months. He stated it did not help him and his prescription had run out anyway. He held little hope that the Prozac his physician had just prescribed would help with his depressive symptomatology but he had resigned himself to take it as prescribed. Roman had seen two therapists previously – one for a period of three months when he was first diagnosed with ADHD, a second when he was in eighth grade for approximately 6 months when his father was concerned about his "attitude" and underachievement at school. Roman and his parents agreed both therapy experiences had been dismal failures. Specifically, they stated the therapists were ineffective and the behaviors had not improved. When asked how he felt about the prospect of commencing therapy again, Roman provided his longest answer of the first session, stating, "No offense. But I think this is a waste of time."

During the initial intake session Roman was also administered the Beck Depression Inventory – II (BDI-II) to assess his depressive symptomatology (Beck et al., 1996). He scored in the severely depressed range. Further the author utilized Jobes' (2006) Suicide Status Form – III (Initial Session) (SSF-III) for suicide assessment and crisis management purposes. Confirming his self-report, on both the BDI-II and SSS-III Roman denied any current or recent (within the past week) suicidal ideation, intent, plan, or attempt. Roman's self-harm behaviors were assessed in accordance with the practice recommendations put forth by Ougrin and colleagues (2012). He denied that he engaged in self-harm behaviors with suicidal intent. Rather he stated cutting helped him cope with both anger and depression. He also acknowledged at other times it served as a form of self-punishment. At the end of the initial session a safety plan was agreed to by all parties and Roman committed to attending weekly individual sessions with the understanding that his parents would be regularly apprised of his general progress and that family "check-ins" would occur as necessary to monitor his safety plan.

Over the course of the next several individual sessions a deeper and even more concerning picture emerged about Roman's struggles. During the first individual session, Roman initially remained minimally cooperative and sullen. The author stayed patient, empathized with Roman's basic mistrust of the therapy process, offered no guarantees but the hope of success, and conceded his powerlessness to "make" Roman talk. Roman seemed to respect this stance and gradually began to engage on a deeper level. Once some rapport and trust had been established, Roman acknowledged in a later session the belt his mother had found him with in the bathroom held more significance than he had previously admitted. He had brought it into the bathroom and was contemplating using it to hang himself later that evening from a tree branch near the apartment complex when his mother had interrupted. More disturbingly, he had apparently experimented with this suicide methodology approximately three months earlier – going so far as to actually tighten the belt around his neck after an argument with his father and a rejection from a girl at school. Thankfully he stopped before hanging himself when he became "scared." Roman first became tearful then openly cried when discussing this incident but seemed relieved and unburdened following doing so. He reluctantly agreed to disclose this information to his parents in a family session for future crisis management and safety planning purposes. The disclosure, while not an abject disaster, seemed to fall flat in positively mobilizing his parents to intensify their support. His mother reacted by crying silently and his father, while surprised and initially hissing, "Jesus, Roman," adopted more of a "the past is the past" attitude.

Roman also disclosed over time that he habitually consumed alcohol and smoked marijuana. He had a small network of close friends who he drank and smoked with, usually on weekends when he would meet them at various locations. The drinking episodes could be to excess at times, as he recalled both "passing out" and a loss of memory at times about his activities while drinking multiple alcoholic beverages in a single sitting. However, he also reported that in recent months he had occasionally smoked by himself prior to going to sleep on evenings when he felt depressed or anxious. He was convinced that marijuana was the most effective remedy for his depressive symptoms, stating, "It helps me to relax and forget about things." He initially fiercely blocked any attempts by the therapist to have him reconsider his stance regarding these substances, but grudgingly accepted that his prescriber and parents should be made aware of his usage. His parents again had a curious reaction to this disclosure, stating essentially, "Boys will be boys," but also (perhaps accurately) attributing his struggling school performance to the negative effects of substance use. The author experienced a sense of collective inertia on both Roman and his parents' parts to address his substance use behaviors that would hinder progress for the remainder of the treatment.

As for his mood and outlook, Roman stated that he had felt sad and/or irritable on most days for over a year. In addition to the low mood and suicidal ideation, he had experienced sleep and appetite disruptions, concentration and energy deficits, and feelings of guilt over an extended period of time. While he was not overtly bullied, he felt like an "outsider" at school who was marginalized and/or overlooked. He did not feel particularly "good" at anything, believing his maximum scholastic efforts would at best allow him to be an "average" student and feeling that he was too small, slow, and untalented to excel at sports. He had a guitar and had once taken lessons before they became too costly. Unfortunately, he had lost interest in playing after he was forced to stop lessons and he had ultimately reached the conclusion he "sucked" anyways. His other strong interest in sketching had also faded in recent months. On an even more personal level, he felt unattractive and self-conscious about his appearance. He struggled to elicit the positive attention of girls he was interested in and, when he did, he became tongue tied or made crude remarks. His two closer male friendships met his most basic companionship needs, but these relationships could also take on a predatory quality as the banter between him and his friends often became cruel and demeaning.

Closer to home Roman felt pressured by his father to achieve at level he felt incapable of reaching. A combination of both guilt and anger festered inside of him at what he sensed was his father's perception of him as a major disappointment. Roman expressed more positive sentiments regarding his mother, but here, too, he felt as if she had failed to stick up for him when his father was being overly critical. He could not understand his mother's passivity. Most notably he was convinced she knew more about his suicide attempt months earlier and substance use than she had led on but had chosen to avoid discussing her suspicions with him directly. Understandably, this left him feeling confused, alone, and misunderstood. When asked to describe his future hopes and dreams in one of his first individual sessions nothing came to his mind. He sat in silence, first contemplative, then seemingly self-conscious and even embarrassed, as he giggled and eventually replied, "Shit Dr. S., I'm just getting through today."

Based upon this brief synopsis of his history one can ascertain that Roman could potentially be classified with at least three separate DSM-5 disorders, including major depression, ADHD (by history at least), and a substance abuse disorder. His depressive episode seemed precipitated by a host of individual vulnerabilities and environmental factors that were complicated by pre-existing attention and impulse control concerns. Tragically, but not atypically when other options were not forthcoming, he was treating his symptoms in part through cutting, substance use, and the development of a nihilistic attitude. From a learning theory perspective Roman was lacking positive and life-enhancing interpersonal connections and activities, had developed a notably negative self-concept through a lack of positive reinforcement and affirmation of his being (e.g., "I am ugly"; "I am no good"), and demonstrated a hostile attribution bias (e.g., "Others will always have it better than me"; "Others are inherently untrustworthy") based in large part due to early learning experiences. From an attachment theory and family systems perspective he exhibited limited closeness to his parents and expressed mixed feelings about these individuals which left him feeling confused, alone, and insecure in himself and his future. From an interpersonal theory perspective he experienced difficulties connecting with others, in part due to distrust and in part due to a more subtle social skills deficit. This lack of intimate and supportive peer connections reinforced his sense of loneliness and unworthiness. All of these conceptualizations could at least partially explain the depth of pain felt by this otherwise healthy and talented young man approaching his sixteenth year of existence. They highlight critical aspects of his depressive episode that required attention in therapy. But might there be more to Roman's story?

The author believed an existential conceptualization of Roman's depressive episode and suicidal behaviors provided more depth and understanding from which to connect with Roman and treat him. From an existential perspective one could immediately see Roman was conscious of but struggling with several of the existential givens of human existence. Specifically, he openly questioned the meaning of life and his existence, more quietly experienced profound guilt for not performing to what he believed was his potential, struggled with an acute awareness of his fundamental "aloneness" in this world, and feared the responsibilities of adulthood. He had contemplated his death and made at least one suicidal gesture, but at the same time the prospect of nonbeing mortified him and had left him feeling ambivalent about taking his own life. His response to the acute existential anxiety and self-perceived inability to handle the responsibilities of life was to a disengage and "check-out" from life when he could. But he was left to suffer alone and bristle at the injustice of his personal circumstances. He had a strong will but struggled to cultivate a sense of intentionality that directed him toward meaningful life pursuits. This was a hard existence on good days and close to intolerable on bad ones. He cycled through periods of rage and morbidly painful subjective sadness, self-destructive efforts to numb his pain, followed by guilt and self-loathing, which would give way in the light of a new day to irritability and ever increasing resentment and dysphoria.

Given the complex history and potential for multiple comorbid disorders impacting Roman's functioning it seemed that rigid adherence to an EST designed to address only a single disorder might potentially become problematic. Static diagnostic categories also fail to encapsulate client factors that need to be considered in treatment planning, most notably in this case the client's readiness for change. Roman was initially a reluctant participant in therapy who had experienced two prior treatment failures. He had close to no motivation change his substance abuse patterns, had felt his ADHD diagnosis was a "crock of shit" for years, and was still struggling to come to terms with prospect that his depressive symptoms could potentially benefit from outside assistance. In all probability Roman would have bristled at a therapy approach that was more directive and regimented. He was tired of being instructed or told what to do. He appeared to be in desperate need of some space, time, and freedom to be understood and listened to.

That Roman eventually shared any of his inner turmoil was quite remarkable given his initial opinion about the prospect of therapy helping. One sensed however a strong resiliency and survival instinct that was dimming but holding on for dear life. By initially utilizing three of the core EI counseling techniques (i.e., remaining present, invoking the actual, and vivifying and confronting resistances) over the course of several individual counseling sessions the therapist seemed to help Roman relax and start to enjoy telling his story. Roman also responded well to two very basic existential premises shared at strategic points by the therapist. First, when Roman expressed despair and doubt about the prospects for things to get better, the therapist shared May's advice that those in the throes of depressive episode essentially need to respond with courage, patience, and faith because, despite all evidence to the contrary, the sun will rise again one day. This wisdom was not imparted in a Pollyannish manner and great care was taken to share the thought when the therapist believed Roman had reached a point of trust in the therapist and understanding about his depressive experience that he would be minimally open to hearing the message. Second, Roman also was captivated by Frankl's life story[2] and the argument that there could be meaning in suffering. He appreciated another simply recognizing the obstacles he had overcome in life and the notion that one could prevail in the most dire of life circumstances. He beamed when his therapist cultivated a hero narrative by marveling at Roman's resilience, will, and agency. In addition, the notion that humans will experience "peaks" and "valleys" throughout the course of life and that one could not be had without the other seemed to further resonate with Roman.

Bolstered with an initial framework for understanding his depressive episode, Roman became a strong and thoughtful voice in the treatment process and plan. The therapist needed to remain judicious in selecting what aspects of the treatment experience were negotiable and non-negotiable. Through careful and collaborative planning during the first several treatment sessions the therapist and Roman agreed that basic crisis stabilization and safety planning was the main priority, reducing Roman's alcohol and marijuana usage would be a longer-term goal, and fostering an improved self-concept, sense of intentionality, and sense of engagement and hope would also serve as the primary therapeutic objectives. While improving family communication was also a goal, Roman held very little hope that his parents were constitutionally capable of productively engaging in this process. Frankly this seemed a bridge too far to take on in a therapy format in which individual work with Roman would predominate. The therapist recommended two very good family therapists for the family to pursue to improve communication. Similar to a prior substance abuse assessment recommendation that went unheeded, the family did not follow through with this recommendation.

With rapport and a clear set of treatment goals established, the treatment consisted of several components. Routine safety/self-harm monitoring and the encouragement of better self-care and coping was a primary focus. Roman's diet, sleeping, and exercise habits were primary targets of the self-care focus. He began to monitor his sleep, cut down on his caffeine and sugar intake, and lift some weights. In addition, four out of five of the CWD-DA approach treatment components were incorporated. Specifically, cognitive restructuring that focused on his negative schemas regarding how he viewed himself and others was a focus. The therapist also encouraged him to schedule more pleasant activities by himself and with his parents. This included resuming his guitar playing for fun, rekindling his cartoon sketching, catching a movie with his father with some regularity, and attending a few local concerts with his friends. Communication and conflict resolution strategies were also a focus at times when Roman would report strain in his relations with his parents, teachers, and friends. Role-playing was the primary methodology utilized when working in this area of functioning.

The chief ongoing existential treatment approaches were the continued emphasis on patience and courage, the reintroduction of a creative element in Roman's life (both guitar and art), and frank discussions about several of the existential concerns Roman faced. Regarding the latter area of focus, as previously mentioned Roman struggled to find meaning in his life. The therapist empathized with Roman's struggle and normalized the experience, but did not attempt to rescue Roman from it by offering potential meanings or a solution to the question. Rather the therapist patiently expressed faith in Roman's ability to work through the question at his own pace. Questions like, "What makes life worth living for?" and "What is worth dying for?" were posed and contemplated at various points in time. By the end of therapy Roman had developed several life-affirming and meaningful interests and goals. These included the aforementioned creative interests of guitar playing and sketching, but also a strong interest in graduating from high school and going to college with an eye toward eventually joining a helping profession himself.

Roman also did some very important healing work in regard to his suicide attempt. He was terrified that he possessed the capacity to come so close to ending his life. The core existential fear of life and fear of death concerns had reaching a boiling point for him in the moment he faced whether to continue on with the attempt or not. Again, the therapist resisted the urge to offer Roman false reassurance (e.g., "I'm sure you would never do such a thing"; "I'm sure your mom would have helped you") or an overly simplistic explanation of what he had experienced. Rather, after agreeing that the moment sounded "Scary as heck" the therapist humbly noted that we all as humans face the crippling force of these existential givens and that the responsibility that comes with our freedom and consciousness can feel incredibly heavy at times. The therapist continued to reiterate his faith in Roman's ability to pursue and find life-sustaining meaning, but conceded that a life of blocked intentionality was possible if Roman continued to adopt a nihilistic attitude and numbed his pain. Finally, the therapist expressed gratitude and "awe" that Roman was sharing his memory of this moment of horror with him as well as a deep sense of relief and joy that such a wonderful being and life had lived to fight another day.

Roman would not engage in any more self-harm or suicide attempts during the course of treatment. Therapy ended after a prolonged period of stabilization shortly after the holidays midway through Roman's junior year. At the time Roman had not experienced suicidal ideation in several months and had not engaged in cutting behaviors in almost a year. He still smoked marijuana occasionally with friends but had stopped drinking alcohol. His mood and outlook had improved considerably. The therapist would have liked to continue working with Roman a bit longer to solidify gains made, but Roman felt ready to stop and the therapist wanted to respect his autonomy in this regard.

Notes

1. The cases depicted in the book are composite representations of multiple client experiences where names, gender, and other potentially identifiable aspects of the case experience have been changed to protect client confidentiality.
2. The author frequently shares Frankl's survival story with his adolescent clients struggling to find meaning.

References

Abela, J. Z., & Hankin, B. L. (2008). *Handbook of depression in children and adolescents.* New York, NY, US: Guilford Press.

Anderson, E., & Hope, D. A. (2008). A review of the tripartite model for understanding the link between anxiety and depression in youth. *Clinical Psychology Review*, *28*(2), 275–287. doi:10.1016/j.cpr.2007.05.004

Armsden, G. C., McCauley, E., Greenberg, M. T., Burke, P. M., & Mitchell, J. R. (1990). Parent and peer attachment in early adolescent depression. *Journal Of Abnormal Child Psychology*, *18*(6), 683–697. doi:10.1007/BF01342754

Bardone, A. M., Moffitt, T., Caspi, A., & Dicson, N. (1996). Adult mental health and social outcomes of adolescent girls with depression and conduct disorder. *Development And Psychopathology*, *8*(4), 811–829. doi:10.1017/S0954579400007446

Beck, A.T., Steer, R.A., & Brown, G.K. (1996). Manual for the Beck Depression Inventory-II. San Antonio, TX: Psychological Corporation.

Brent, D. A., & Maalouf, F. T. (2009). Pediatric depression: Is there evidence to improve evidence-based treatments?. *Journal Of Child Psychology And Psychiatry*, *50*(1–2), 143–152. doi:10.1111/j.1469-7610.2008.02037.x

Brooks, T. L., Harris, S. K., Thrall, J. S., & Woods, E. R. (2002). Association of adolescent risk behaviors with mental health symptoms in high school students.

Journal Of Adolescent Health, *31*(3), 240–246. doi:10.1016/S1054-139X(02)00385-3

Brumariu, L. E., & Kerns, K. A. (2010). Parent-child attachment and internalizing symptoms in childhood and adolescence: A review of empirical findings and future directions. *Development And Psychopathology*, *22*(1), 177–203. doi:10.1017/S0954579409990344

Bugental, J. T. (1987). *The art of the psychotherapist*. New York, NY, US: W W Norton & Co.

Cicchetti, D., & Toth, S. L. (1998). The development of depression in children and adolescents. *American Psychologist*, *53*(2), 221–241. doi:10.1037/0003-066X.53.2.221

Clarke, G. N., Hornbrook, M., Lynch, F., Polen, M., Gale, J., Beardslee, W., . . . & Seeley, J. (2001). A randomized trial of a group cognitive intervention for preventing depression in adolescent offspring of depressed parents. *Archives of general psychiatry*, *58*(12), 1127–1134.

Costello, E. J., Mustillo, S., Erkanli, A., Keeler, G., & Angold, A. (2003). Prevalence and Development of Psychiatric Disorders in Childhood and Adolescence. *Archives Of General Psychiatry*, *60*(8), 837–844. doi:10.1001/archpsyc.60.8.837

Curry, J. F. (2014). Future directions in research on psychotherapy for adolescent depression. *Journal Of Clinical Child And Adolescent Psychology*, *43*(3), 510–526. doi:10.1080/15374416.2014.904233

David-Ferdon, C., & Kaslow, N. J. (2008). Evidence-based psychosocial treatments for child and adolescent depression. *Journal Of Clinical Child And Adolescent Psychology*, *37*(1), 62–104. doi:10.1080/15374410701817865

Emslie, G. J., Rush, A. J., Weinberg, W. A., Kowatch, R. A., Carmody, T., & Mayes, T. L. (1998). Fluoxetine in child and adolescent depression: acute and maintenance treatment. *Depression and anxiety*, *7*(1), 32–39.

Epkins, C. C., & Heckler, D. R. (2011). Integrating etiological models of social anxiety and depression in youth: Evidence for a cumulative interpersonal risk model. *Clinical Child And Family Psychology Review*, *14*(4), 329–376. doi:10.1007/s10567-011-0101-8

Felitti, V. J., Anda, R. F., Nordenberg, D., Williamson, D. F., Spitz, A. M., Edwards, V., & . . . Marks, J. S. (1998). Relationship of childhood abuse and household dysfunction to many of the leading causes of death in adults: The Adverse Childhood Experiences (ACE) Study. *American Journal Of Preventive Medicine*, *14*(4), 245–258. doi:10.1016/S0749-3797(98)00017-8

Forbes, E. E., Williamson, D. E., Ryan, N. D., Birmaher, B., Axelson, D. A., & Dahl, R. E. (2006). Peri-Sleep-Onset Cortisol Levels in Children and Adolescents with Affective Disorders. *Biological Psychiatry*, *59*(1), 24–30. doi:10.1016/j.biopsych.2005.06.002

Forbes, E. E., Bertocci, M. A., Gregory, A. M., Ryan, N. D., Axelson, D. A., Birmaher, B., & Dahl, R. E. (2008). Objective sleep in pediatric anxiety disorders and major depressive disorder. *Journal Of The American Academy Of Child & Adolescent Psychiatry*, *47*(2), 148–155. doi:10.1097/chi.0b013e31815cd9bc

Frankl, V. E. (1986). Logotherapy and the challenge of suffering. *Review Of Existential Psychology & Psychiatry, Spec Issue 20*(1–3), 63–67.

Freed, R. D., Rubenstein, L. M., Daryanani, I., Olino, T. M., & Alloy, L. B. (2016). The relationship between family functioning and adolescent depressive symptoms: The role of emotional clarity. *Journal Of Youth And Adolescence*, *45*(3), 505–519. doi:10.1007/s10964-016-0429-y

Gotlib, I. H., & Hammen, C. L. (2002). *Handbook of depression*. New York, NY, US: Guilford Press.

Graham, A. R., Sherry, S. B., Stewart, S. H., Sherry, D. L., McGrath, D. S., Fossum, K. M., & Allen, S. L. (2010). The existential model of perfectionism and depressive symptoms: A short-term, four-wave longitudinal study. *Journal Of Counseling Psychology*, *57*(4), 423–438. doi:10.1037/a0020667

Hankin, B. L., Abramson, L. Y., Moffitt, T. E., Silva, P. A., McGee, R., & Angell, K. E. (1998). Development of depression from preadolescence to young adulthood: Emerging gender differences in a 10-year longitudinal study. *Journal Of Abnormal Psychology*, *107*(1), 128–140. doi:10.1037/0021-843X.107.1.128

Hardin, M. G., Schroth, E., Pine, D. S., & Ernst, M. (2007). Incentive-related modulation of cognitive control in healthy, anxious, and depressed adolescents: Development and psychopathology related differences. *Journal Of Child Psychology And Psychiatry*, *48*(5), 446–454. doi:10.1111/j.1469-7610.2006.01722.x

Havens, L. L., & Ghaemi, S. N. (2005). Existential Despair and Bipolar Disorder: The Therapeutic Alliance as a Mood Stabilizer. *American Journal Of Psychotherapy*, *59*(2), 137–147.

Jobes, D. A. (2006). *Managing suicidal risk: A collaborative approach*. New York, NY, US: Guilford Press.

Kistner, J. A., David-Ferdon, C. F., Repper, K. K., & Joiner, T. J. (2006). Bias and Accuracy of Children's Perceptions of Peer Acceptance: Prospective Associations with Depressive Symptoms. *Journal Of Abnormal Child Psychology*, *34*(3), 349–361. doi:10.1007/s10802-006-9028-9

Lakdawalla, Z., Hankin, B. L., & Mermelstein, R. (2007). Cognitive theories of depression in children and adolescents: A conceptual and quantitative review. *Clinical Child And Family Psychology Review*, *10*(1), 1–24. doi:10.1007/s10567-006-0013-1

Lewinsohn, P. M., Clarke, G. N., & Hoberman, H. M. (1989). The Coping With Depression Course: Review and future directions. *Canadian Journal Of*

Behavioural Science /Revue Canadienne Des Sciences Du Comportement, 21(4), 470–493. doi:10.1037/h0079846

Lewinsohn, P. M., Clarke, G. N., Hops, H., & Andrews, J. A. (1990). Cognitive-behavioral treatment for depressed adolescents. *Behavior Therapy, 21*(4), 385–401. doi:10.1016/S0005-7894(05)80353-3

Lewinsohn, P. M., Clarke, G. N., Seeley, J. R., & Rohde, P. (1994). Major depression in community adolescents: age at onset, episode duration, and time to recurrence. *Journal of the American Academy of Child & Adolescent Psychiatry, 33*(6), 809–818.

Lewinsohn, P. M., Rohde, P., & Seely, J. R. (1998). Major depressive disorder in older adolescents: Prevalence, risk factors, and clinical implications. *Clinical Psychology Review, 18*(7), 765–794. doi:10.1016/S0272-7358(98)00010-5

Mascaro, N., & Rosen, D. H. (2008). Assessment of existential meaning and its longitudinal relations with depressive symptoms. *Journal Of Social And Clinical Psychology, 27*(6), 576–599. doi:10.1521/jscp.2008.27.6.576

May, R. (1969). *Existential psychology.* New York, NY, US: Crown Publishing Group/Random House.

McIntosh, J. L., & Drapeau, C. W. (2012). USA suicide 2010: Official final data. *Washington, DC: American Association of Suicidology.*

McLeod, B. D., Weisz, J. R., & Wood, J. J. (2007). Examining the association between parenting and childhood depression: A meta-analysis. *Clinical Psychology Review, 27*(8), 986–1003. doi:10.1016/j.cpr.2007.03.001

Mufson, L., & Sills, R. (2006). Interpersonal Psychotherapy for depressed adolescents (IPT-A): An overview. *Nordic Journal Of Psychiatry, 60*(6), 431–437. doi:10.1080/08039480601022397

Nelson, L. J., & Barry, C. M. (2005). Distinguishing Features of Emerging Adulthood: The Role of Self-Classification as an Adult. *Journal Of Adolescent Research, 20*(2), 242–262. doi:10.1177/0743558404273074

Newcomb, A. F., Bukowski, W. M., & Pattee, L. (1993). Children's peer relations: A meta- analytic review of popular, rejected, neglected, controversial, and average sociometric status. *Psychological Bulletin, 113*(1), 99–128. doi:10.1037/0033-2909.113.1.99

Ougrin, D., Tranah, T., Leigh, E., Taylor, L., & Asarnow, J. R. (2012). Self-harm in adolescents. In M. E. Garralda, J. Raynaud (Eds.), *Brain, mind, and developmental psychopathology in childhood* (pp. 219–239). Lanham, MD, US: Jason Aronson.

Pérez-Edgar, K., Fox, N. A., Cohn, J. F., & Kovacs, M. (2006). Behavioral and Electrophysiological Markers of Selective Attention in Children of Parents with a History of Depression. *Biological Psychiatry, 60*(10), 1131–1138. doi:10.1016/j.biopsych.2006.02.036

Probst, B. (2008). Issues in portability of evidence-based treatment for adolescent depression. *Child & Adolescent Social Work Journal, 25*(2), 111–123. doi:10.1007/s10560-008-0115-3

Rapee, R. M. (1997). Potential role of childrearing practices in the development of anxiety and depression. *Clinical Psychology Review, 17*(1), 47–67. doi:10.1016/S0272-7358(96)00040-2

Rothbart, M. K., & Bates, J. E. (2006). Temperament. In N. Eisenberg, W. Damon, R. M. Lerner (Eds.), *Handbook of child psychology: Social, emotional, and personality development, Vol. 3*, 6th *ed.* (pp. 99–166). Hoboken, NJ, US: John Wiley & Sons Inc.

Rudolph, K. D., Flynn, M., & Abaied, J. L. (2008). A developmental perspective on interpersonal theories of youth depression. In J. Z. Abela, B. L. Hankin (Eds.), *Handbook of depression in children and adolescents* (pp. 79–102). New York, NY, US: Guilford Press.

Schneider, K. J. (2008). *Existential-integrative psychotherapy: Guideposts to the core of practice.* New York, NY, US: Routledge/Taylor & Francis Group.

Silk, J. S., Vanderbilt-Adriance, E., Shaw, D. S., Forbes, E. E., Whalen, D. J., Ryan, N. D., & Dahl, R. E. (2007). Resilience among children and adolescents at risk for depression: Mediation and moderation across social and neurobiological context. *Development And Psychopathology, 19*(3), 841–865. doi:10.1017/S0954579407000417

Smith, J. A., & Rhodes, J. E. (2015). Being depleted and being shaken: An interpretative phenomenological analysis of the experiential features of a first episode of depression. *Psychology And Psychotherapy: Theory, Research And Practice, 88*(2), 197–209. doi:10.1111/papt.12034

Stålsett, G., Gude, T., Rønnestad, M. H., & Monsen, J. T. (2012). Existential dynamic therapy ("VITA") for treatment-resistant depression with Cluster C disorder: Matched comparison to treatment as usual. *Psychotherapy Research, 22*(5), 579–591. doi:10.1080/10503307.2012.692214

Taliaferro, L. A., & Muehlenkamp, J. J. (2014). Risk and protective factors that distinguish adolescents who attempt suicide from those who only consider suicide in the past year. *Suicide And Life-Threatening Behavior, 44*(1), 6–22. doi:10.1111/sltb.12046

Tillich, P. (1952). Anxiety, religion, and medicine. *Pastoral Psychology, 3*11–17. doi:10.1007/BF01769082

van Deurzen, E. (2015). Structural existential analysis (SEA): A phenomenological method for therapeutic work. *Journal Of Contemporary Psychotherapy, 45*(1), 59–68. doi:10.1007/s10879-014-9282-z

Weissman, M. M., Wickramaratne, P., Nomura, Y., Warner, V., Pilowsky, D., & Verdeli, H. (2006). Offspring of Depressed Parents: 20 Years Later. *The*

American Journal Of Psychiatry, 163(6), 1001–1008. doi:10.1176/appi.ajp.163.6.1001

Wilkinson, P. O., & Goodyer, I. M. (2006). Attention difficulties and mood-related ruminative response style in adolescents with unipolar depression. *Journal of Child Psychology and Psychiatry, 47*(12), 1284–1291.

CHAPTER 7

EI Approaches to Treating Substance Abuse Disorders in Adolescents

Introduction

While it is not uncommon for alcohol or illicit substance use to be the primary presenting concern when an adolescent is referred for treatment, the author frequently learns of substance use patterns that would reach diagnostic criteria for an abuse or even dependency disorder only after treatment has commenced. As was foreshadowed in the previous chapter on treating depression in adolescents from an EI perspective, many youth will present in therapy with comorbid substance use disorders that contribute to, are the result of, or run parallel to other mental health concerns. The adolescent is quite often not concerned about his or her usage patterns and will offer colorful and impassioned defenses of the virtues of substance use at the slightest hint of a challenge on the part of the therapist. Many parents in these cases are often simply not aware of the extent of their child's usage patterns and therefore do not raise it as a referral concern. For certain a good proportion of these parents will react with appropriate levels of alarm and urgency upon becoming aware of the usage patterns. Unfortunately, many parents do not. This subset often fails to see a connection between the anxiety, depression, impulse control, and/or underachievement concerns that cause them to seek out treatment and their child's substance use behaviors. Almost universally these parents will acknowledge that they enjoy a drink themselves, or used to smoke marijuana in high school, or that they do not want to rob their child of crucial social connections by prohibiting the youth from associating in

D. Shumaker, *Existential-Integrative Approaches to Treating Adolescents*, DOI 10.1057/978-1-349-95211-3_7

unsupervised settings with peers who consume alcohol or use illicit substances on a routine basis. Some of these same individuals will even go so far as to concurrently note their own struggles with addiction and/or a family history of addiction, but this knowledge does not seem to induce action. Instead these parents choose to ignore, minimize, tacitly approve of, or openly acknowledge substance use as a rite of passage during adolescence. Incredibly, the author has also worked with adolescents who state their own parents and/or friend's parents will drink or smoke with them. Sometimes it is the context of the adolescent hosting a party at their home and sometimes it is done privately with a parent for various reasons.

It can be maddening for a therapist to work with a family where the parents refuse to adjust or eliminate their own substance use and remove alcohol from the home when their adolescent clearly struggles with addictive tendencies. The adolescent sees only hypocrisy and fuel to resist making hard changes in their own substance use behaviors when a parent is not practicing what they preach. It is hardly surprising therefore that substance abuse disorders in adolescence are incredibly common and quite challenging to treat. It is unfortunately often the case that only after a critical incident has occurred (e.g., a car accident, expulsion for being under the influence of drugs at school, overdose) that these families may be mobilized to reexamine the adolescent's substance use behaviors in a more critical light. Tragically, the call to action often occurs far too late as it becomes evident that the adolescent has been abusing substances for a much longer period of time and to a much greater degree than the parents would have ever dared to imagine. A quick "fix" will not be forthcoming in these cases as the dependency needs are strong, tolerance has occurred, and even potentially uncomfortable withdrawal experiences become a very real concern.

This chapter elaborates on some of the challenges and methods of working with adolescents who present with substance abuse concerns from an EI perspective. The author and a colleague have recently outlined an EI approach designed to treat adolescent clients who present with substance abuse problems and this effort is referred to often in this chapter (Karavalaki and Shumaker, 2016). It also seems important to note at the outset that the author never attempts to treat an adolescent in an outpatient setting who is exhibiting clear signs of high dependency or is engaged in high-risk behaviors that require more intensive levels of support. There are, however, a large population of adolescents that are at least minimally functioning (e.g., they attend school and are passing their classes, play sports, have meaningful social relationships) who may meet DSM diagnostic criteria for a substance abuse disorder but can also effectively be treated on an outpatient basis. Sometimes, of course, the depth of an adolescent's substance abuse problems is not fully apparent at the time treatment is initiated. Knowing this the author routinely requires families where significant substance use concerns are evident to pursue an outside diagnostic consultation with a colleague who works in a larger agency where multiple levels of care are available. This is done for not only risk management purposes but also to make an initial contact between the client and the agency in the case a higher level of care is needed at some point during the course of the author's work with the adolescent. Of course, having an outside diagnostic consultation also can help reduce tension between the author and a client if the client and/or the parents tend to minimize the level of substance use concerns. The author has the weight of an additional expert opinion to help support whatever level of focus and intervention strategies seem appropriate. Having said this, there is always risk whenever an adolescent chooses to consume alcohol, use illicit substances, or abuse prescribed or over-the-counter medications. Tragedy remains one bad choice away. A therapist can certainly benefit from the counsel of an expert to not only make sure the treatment modality is clinically defensible, but to also share the burden of worry that comes with trying to help a young person who is playing with fire.

Clinical Description, Incidence, and Prevalence

Adolescent substance abuse has been defined in various ways. In more general terms, Hawkins and colleagues (1992) have referred to it as the frequent maladaptive pattern of alcohol or other drug use during teenage years that is associated with negative consequences with self or others. The transition from the DSM-IV-TR to DSM-5 brought with substantial changes to the manner in which substance abuse concerns are classified. The overall category is now referred to as "Substance-Related and Addictive Disorders." Chief among these changes is that, as opposed to the DSM-IV-TR, the DSM-5 combines the categories of abuse and dependence into a single class of disorders. This overarching diagnosis discriminates between mild, moderate, and severe levels of problematic usage patterns. Specific substances (e.g., alcohol, stimulants) are listed as separate disorders. Relatively more diagnostic criteria need to be met as well for an individual to be diagnosed with a "Mild" substance abuse disorder. Specifically, as opposed to the DSM-IV-TR where only one of eleven specific diagnostic criteria needed to be met, the DMS-5 now requires two to three criteria to be met. Examples of the 11 specific criteria include taking the substance in larger amounts than one meant to, wanting to decrease usage patterns but not being able to do so, and the experience of cravings or urges to use the substance.

The reasons behind the shift in diagnostic approach between the DMS-IV-TR and DSM-5 in regard to substance use disorders are complex and it is beyond the scope of this effort to go into detail about the history in this regard. In brief, it was previously thought that substance abuse disorders were a milder prequel to the development of a more serious dependency disorder. While there is some truth to that conceptualization, in reality there were often cases where an individual who only met the criteria for a substance abuse disorder was actually quite severely impaired. Thus, the distinction between abuse and dependency seemed blurred at times. The DSM-5 classification system seems to provide a degree of flexibility that can better encapsulate the specific symptoms an individual demonstrates in relation to substance use patterns.

Regarding the "Addictive Disorders" piece of the overall diagnostic category, the DSM-5 recognizes pathological gambling as a behavioral addiction that is sufficiently similar in its etiology, expression, and physiology to substances abuse disorders to merit classification under the same general umbrella. There is a hope that inclusion of pathological gambling with other substance abuse disorders will also mobilize resources for individuals suffering with this problem on par with substance abuse services. Internet Gaming Disorder is also included in the DSM-5 as a potential future diagnostic category that merits future research. While gambling, internet gaming, and other behavioral addictions (e.g., pornography) are serious concerns that impact many adolescents, the focus of the current chapter is on the conceptualization and treatment of maladaptive substance use.

Substance abuse disorders are among the most common psychiatric diagnoses among adolescents and adults of any age, gender, racial, and/or ethnic background. In 2014 approximately 1.3 million adolescents in the USA between the ages of 12 to 17 years old met diagnostic criteria for a substance abuse disorder (Center for Behavioral Statistics and Quality, 2015). Put differently, approximately 1 in 20 adolescents (or 5%) are engaged in clinically significant problematic substance use behaviors at any given point in time. Alcohol and marijuana are the most popular substances abused by adolescents. By 12th grade as much as 80% of adolescents have used alcohol at some point and nearly 50% have used marijuana (Tarter, 2002). In terms of consistent usage, approximately 1 in 9 adolescents regularly use alcohol, 1 in 16 have binged in the past month, and 1% intensively and chronically consume alcohol. Marijuana usage patterns are similar to that of alcohol. Approximately 10% of adolescents use marijuana on a frequent basis. By comparison, the rates of other illicit substance use in the age-group are considerably lower but still of high concern given the health risks, overdose potential, and addictive potency of several specific substances. Most notably, many adolescents struggle with stimulant (0.7%), cocaine (0.2%), methamphetamine (0.2%), heroin (0.1%), and tranquilizer (0.4%) use.

Still the developmental trajectory of substance use patterns remains varied. The typical adolescent will start experimenting with substances when they are 13 years old (Tobler & Komro, 2010). Many adolescents who initially experiment with alcohol or substance use will not eventually proceed to develop a substance abuse disorder (Hawkins et al., 1992). What differentiates individuals who can experiment but avoid developing problems related to their usage from those who experiment and eventually develop a substance use disorder is not entirely clear. It is likely a myriad of individual and contextual factors play a role including the type of substance chosen, the individual's physiological and psychological reaction to consuming the substance, the contexts where the usage regularly occurs, and the presence or relative absence of both positive and negative consequences personally, socially, and scholastically/occupationally associated with using the substance (Newcomb and Bentler, 1989). For certain one of the strongest predictors of substance abuse disorders is the age of initial experimentation. Specifically, the earlier the age that the individual starts using substances the more likely he or she will eventually develop a substance abuse problem (Rowe, 2012). For this reason alone it is critical for prevention purposes for parents and other adults charged with the care of children to do all they can to prevent a youth's experimentation with substances as long as possible.

The prognosis, life course, and outcome for adolescents diagnosed with a substance abuse disorder is guarded for most and tragically quite poor for a sizable portion of these individuals. Adolescents diagnosed with a substance abuse disorder are more likely to engage in delinquent behaviors and high-risk sexual behaviors, have increased mortality rates due to accidents and injuries, are at greater risk for school dropout, experience higher rates of chronic unemployment or underemployment, and report generally higher levels of dissatisfaction with their lives (Newcomb & Bentler, 1989). The comorbidity rate is alarmingly high as well. Approximately 60% of adolescents diagnosed with a substance abuse disorder have a comorbid DSM mental health disorder (Armstrong & Costello, 2002). Conduct Disorder (CD) and Oppositional Defiant Disorder (ODD) are the most common comorbid diagnoses, but depression and other internalizing disorders remain quite common as well. Further, the relapse risk is quite high for many of these individuals. As much as two-thirds to even 80% of adolescents diagnosed with a substance abuse disorder will relapse within a 6-month period following a community-based or inpatient treatment experience (Brown et al., 2001). Adolescents appear to be more vulnerable to relapse in cases where they are intent upon enhancing a positive emotional state or in cases where they experience a conflicted interpersonal situation that induced a negative affective state (Ramo & Brown, 2008). In short, adolescents who reach the diagnostic threshold of a substance abuse disorder are at risk for a long-term, debilitating life experience even when treatment is available and utilized.

Common Conceptualizations/Etiological Overview

There are a wide range of biological and psychological factors that can predispose an adolescent to developing a substance abuse problem (Tarter, 2002). A combination of maturation, social and environmental factors, as well as individual-environmental interactions all play critical roles in the development of problematic substance use patterns. Tarter (2002) has proposed a compelling developmental model of adolescent substance abuse that attempts to encapsulate several of the most prominent predictors of substance abuse in this population. Earlier on in life the model emphasizes genetic and physiological vulnerabilities that increase risk. As the individual matures social contagion and social selection factors become more prominent influences that determine whether the individual will engage in problematic usage. The model adheres to an epigenetic principle whereby risks factors experienced earlier in life increase risk for exposure to other risk factors later in development and eventual symptom manifestation. While other models of adolescent substance abuse will be discussed later in this section, Tarter's conceptualization provides an important basis from which to embark on the exploration of risk factors.

On a more specific level adolescence, in and of itself, may be a risk factor for a variety of reasons. Most notably, the adolescent brain may be less sensitive to the effects of a psychoactive substance. This results in increased levels of the substance needing to be consumed to achieve the desired effects. Over time repeated excessive usage patterns can lead to both dependency needs and harmful neurochemical changes in brain composition that are associated with additional mental health concerns (Grieve et al., 1979). Further, hormonal changes during adolescence strain the individual's capacity to self-regulate emotion and can lead to moments of intense negative affect and/or emotional lability. For certain, negative affect, emotional lability, and moodiness are strong risk factors for the development of a substance abuse disorder (Chassin et al., 1993).

Adolescents also have a high propensity to engage in risk-taking behaviors (Bardo et al., 1996). Not surprisingly, high sensation and novelty-seeking behaviors are one of the strongest predictors of substance abuse problems. Spear (2000) has theorized brain maturation changes during adolescence largely underlie the high risk-taking behaviors observed during this stage of development. Most notably the prefrontal cortex has not fully matured at this stage of development and therefore self-regulation and executive functioning can be compromised and the individual can be vulnerable to poor decision-making. As Tarter (2002) writes the adolescent brain is at increased risk for making poor choices due to, "an incapacity to identify all behavioral options, failure to fully appreciate the consequences of all available options, inaccurate estimation of the importance of the behavioral and medical consequences associated with each option, inability to estimate the probability of the consequences pertinent to each option, and limitations in information integration and synthesis that is required for selection of the best option" (pg. 173). Thus, there are a multitude of neurodevelopmental reasons why adolescents are vulnerable to developing a substance abuse disorder.

Research suggests that temperament and the quality of the parent-child attachment relationship can also impact the individual's risk of developing a substance abuse disorder. Specifically, children with a difficult temperament are at increased risk for developing a substance abuse disorder because of the challenges they experience regulating their emotions and a tendency to experience intense negative affect (Tarter et al., 1999). Further, the emotional regulation difficulties associated with a difficult temperament may strain the parent-child bonding process, resulting in an insecure or disorganized attachment formation. Poor parent-child bonding, in turn, is also associated with increased risk of a substance abuse disorder developing (Brook et al., 1986). Parental investment and supervision of the child may be relatively less forthcoming or consistent in these cases. Child maltreatment becomes an increased possibility. In addition, certain parent behaviors such as poor monitoring, harsh discipline, and/or inconsistent discipline may occur (Kamon et al., 2006). Collectively, these risk factors can greatly increase the risk for the child at later stages of development associating with a cohort that may be engaged in a variety of delinquent behaviors including substance use.

A child's cognitive abilities and school experience also seem to predict future substance use. Specifically, research suggests that cognitive limitations increase the likelihood of the individual experiencing executive functioning and decision-making deficits, increased aggression, and academic difficulties (Martin et al., 2000). School underachievement and/or failure can negatively impact both a child's self-esteem and/or abilities to make prosocial peer connections. This, in turn, can increase the risk for the child to disengage in school and/or pursue a cohort that engages in delinquent behaviors. Here, too, a picture emerges of how a single individual risk factor (i.e., cognitive limitations) can through a series of intermediary steps ultimately increase risk for a substance abuse disorder developing if proper supports are not in place.

As the youth continues to mature into adolescence, new influences seem to weigh more heavily upon whether the individual will engage in problematic substance use. Environmental and social factors, such as peer and media messages regarding the acceptability of substance use, can greatly influence an individual's decision to embark or refrain from experimenting with substance use. To gain acceptance in a particular peer group may require the adolescent to engage in some level of substance use. Not surprisingly, peer influences and pressure to engage in substance use also are among the strongest predictors of adolescent substance abuse (Hawkins et al., 1992). The implicit and explicit message the individual receives in these cases may minimize the risks associated with usage and, quite to the contrary, celebrate binging behaviors as normative and a sign of maturity. Social rejection and/or physical characteristics of the individual that sets him or her apart from the cohort may increase the risk of substance use as the individual struggles to find ways to fit in (Tarter, 2002). As one can clearly see, there are a wide range of individual risk factors and pathways toward maladaptive substance use during adolescence.

While, as previously stated, Tarter's (2002) epigenetic developmental model of adolescent substance abuse is a compelling framework to understand the phenomena, it is hardly the only way to conceptualize the disorder. Several early models of substance abuse viewed the issue as a matter of moral turpitude where the individual needed to re-examine his or her values and live a more pious life to improve. Over time this perspective has fallen out of favor. The Alcoholics Anonymous (AA) Disease Model reflects a biological understanding of the disorder and was developed in part as a reaction to the moral models in existence that appeared to blame the individual and assert that will power and values clarification were the keys to recovery. Other biological models view substance abuse disorders as primarily a specific form of an impulse control disorder or as a reward deficiency problem (e.g., Aharon et al., 2001).

There are several psychological models of substance abuse as well. For example, Khantzian (1997) argued that addictive behaviors occur in the context of the individual self-medicating when they experience uncomfortable emotional states. Similarly, Dodes (2002) believed unresolved intrapsychic conflicts rooted in earlier developmental stages were the source of problematic substance use. Cognitive-behavioral explanations of adolescent substance abuse highlight the importance of social learning and contingent reinforcement in the development of problematic usage patterns (Waldron & Turner, 2008). Specifically, adolescents who were exposed to adults and/or peers who consume alcohol to excess would learn to do the same through observation of these usage patterns in others. From a broader systems perspective, substance abuse disorders have also been explained as symptom of a society that has come to value behavioral excess (Orford, 2001).

Finally, Shaffer and colleagues (2004) have proposed a syndrome model of addiction that attempts to incorporate multiple perspectives into a coherent framework. The model recognizes that, at its basis, problematic substance use is rooted in a self-medication motivation where the individual is attempting to produce a desirable affective state. In addition, the model, "provides an integrative approach by including interactive biological, psychological, and social influences within a developmental process; in addition, the syndrome model identifies the unique and shared consequences of addiction that require a cocktail of synergistic treatment components" (Albanese & Shaffer, 2012). Thus, it encourages the use of multiple treatment strategies that are catered to the individual.

As one can see there are a multitude of risk factors that can increase the risk for substance abuse and several models of addiction that attempt to explain how a given individual may come to abuse substances. None of the models view substance abuse from an existential perspective or reference in more than passing detail existential concerns. After reviewing several more common treatment approaches, the author will offer an existential explanation of adolescent substance abuse.

Empirically Supported Treatments/Evidence-Based Practice Approaches

Given the costs and consequences of substance abuse and addiction, it is hardly surprising considerable research has been devoted to developing psychosocial treatments designed to treat this source of dysfunction. However, it is important to note at the outset that psychopharmacological treatments certainly can play an effective role in treating addiction and/or relapse prevention. Albanese and Shaffer (2012) have reviewed the variety of ways pharmacotherapy can be integrated with psychosocial treatments. Specifically, they state medications can serve as agonists (substitutes for the addictive agent), antagonists (these compete with the abused substance by blocking the effects of the substance), aversive agents (these cause violent negative reactions when the abused substance is used), and anticraving agents (these reduce cravings for the substance). Further, medications are commonly incorporated into a treatment protocol when comorbid psychiatric disorders (e.g., depression, anxiety) are present. Thus, the evidenced-based practices summarized below are psychosocial but may, in practice, be augmented by pharmacotherapy when implemented in a real-world setting.

There appear to be at least three "well–established" treatment modalities for treating adolescent substance abuse. Waldron and Turner (2008) conducted an extensive review of psychosocial treatments of adolescent substance abuse disorders that yielded several important findings in support of this view. Specifically, the researchers analyzed 17 studies conducted in outpatient settings where a total of 46 different intervention conditions were utilized with 2,307 adolescents. On the basis of their review they found that Functional Family Therapy (FFT) (Alexander &

Parsons, 1982), Multidimensional Family Therapy (MDFT) (Liddle, 2004), and Group Cognitive-Behavioral Therapy (CBT-G) (Waldron et al., 2007) were effective treatments. Each are briefly described here.

To begin, FFT is an integrative, family systems model that utilizes a combination of cognitive behavioral and multisystemic treatment approaches. Client and parent engagement is a major point of emphasis early in the treatment process. Relabeling strategies and noting the family's strong interconnections are specific techniques used to enhance rapport and motivation to change. As therapy progresses, FFT incorporates problem-solving and communication training to improve family interaction patterns pertaining to substance using behaviors. Therapists operating from this framework will also commonly work with extrafamilial systems such as school and juvenile justice agencies to coordinate care and improve outcome.

MDFT is a multidimensional family-based approach to treating substance abuse that shares many commonalities with FFT. It believes the causes and potential solutions to adolescent substance abuse are multifaceted and multidetermined. A client's motivation to change is not assumed by the therapist but can be positively influenced provided a strong therapeutic alliance is achieved and hope is instilled. The approach places a great emphasis on the person of the therapist. The therapist needs to serve as an advocate for both the adolescent and the parents, which requires a delicate balance of managing multiple alliances and often competing needs. MDFT also emphasizes the importance of a comprehensive family assessment prior to embarking on treatment where the individual, parents, family, and extrafamilial systems functioning are all formally evaluated. The treatment approach is flexible and catered to a specific family's needs and areas of deficiency. Both intrapersonal (a client's thinking and emotional reactions are analyzed) and extrapersonal communication patterns are common targets of intervention. The family unit is seen in various configurations with the parents and adolescent meeting altogether with the therapist at times and on other occasions separately depending on the particular treatment needs and areas of focus at a given time.

The third well-established approach to treating adolescent substance abuse is CBT-G. This intervention is based in learning theory where classical conditioning, operant conditioning, and modeling paradigms are thought to play roles in the develop and maintenance of problematic substance use behaviors. In a group format adolescents are provided information on how to detect stimulus cues that may trigger substance use and abuse. Further they are educated on the risks associated with substance use and are encouraged to identify the positive and negative consequences of usage and nonusage. There is a strong skill development component to the group intervention as well. Participants are taught how to communicate about craving experiences and seek social support, how to manage emotions that may trigger a desire to use (e.g., anger, depression), how to resist peer pressure, and how to formulate clear and achievable school and vocational goals that will improve their prognosis and reduce the risk for relapse. While family factors are not an explicitly stated focus of CBT-G, the model certainly considers this source of influence in the initiation and maintenance of problematic substance use. For example, parents who model substance use behaviors or who inconsistently reinforce and/or punish substance abuse behaviors would be considered as possible sources of influence in a functional analysis of the antecedents and consequences of substance use.

It is worth noting that Hogue and colleagues (2014) recently updated the Waldron and Turner (2008) research findings and found that the same three treatment modalities – FFT, MDFT, and CBT-G – remain well-established treatment for adolescent substance abuse. Beyond this basic replication finding, they offer cogent insights and recommendation on how researchers, clinicians, and policymakers can make these more labor-, cost-, and time-intensive interventions accessible to underserved populations. Finally, other researchers have noted several commonalities across various family-based treatments of adolescent substance abuse (Deas & Clark, 2009; Hogue & Dauber, 2013). In general, these approaches all view the substance abusing behavior as a problem that impacts the entire family as opposed to the individual alone. All approaches encourage how the adolescent's substance abusing behaviors impact the entire family system and how the family relates with extrafamilial systems. Further, all include a parent education and support component, promote and teach enhanced familial communication behaviors, and challenge dysfunctional family behavior patterns that help to maintain the problematic usage. Given the relatively strong research basis supporting a family-based approach to working with adolescents who are engaged in problematic substance use the author believes an EI intervention for treating this concern should incorporate parents and extrafamilial systems in the treatment process. Regardless of whether parents are actively attending sessions, ignoring the broader family system in both the initiation and maintenance of the behaviors of concern seems ill advised to say the least. Just as critically, parents and the extrafamilial systems remain a critical support system that can potentially enhance treatment outcome and reduce the risk for relapse. The remaining sections of this chapter explore adolescent substance abuse from an existential framework and provide an example of how EI can be utilized within a family-based treatment modality when working with an adolescent who presents with substance abusing behaviors.

EI Conceptualization

Like the other specific disorders reviewed in this book, Schneider (2008) conceptualizes substance abuse as stemming from maladaptive reactions to expansive dreads. He believes that the individual's choice of substance is not a haphazard occurrence. Rather it reflects the particular polarity of existence the individual dreads. More specifically, he believes individuals who abuse substances that have a primarily depressant effect (e.g., valium, alcohol) are engaged in a hyper-constrictive reaction to their dread of ultimate expansion. Their specific fears may vary, from concerns about asserting themselves, exerting autonomy, their potency, trusting others, life's complexities, standing out, etc. The individual escapes from their awareness of these overwhelming givens of our existence through the numbing and sedating effects of this type of narcotic. On the other hand, those individuals who struggle with the opposite polarity – the potential for ultimate constriction – will prefer stimulant substances such as cocaine and methamphetamine. The specific fears these individuals contend with include being vulnerable, feeling inadequate, limited, and/or rejected. They are drawn to the emboldening effects of stimulant substances that can at times provide a spectacular rush of power and agency, leaving the aforementioned fears behind in a distance wake. In simpler terms, the stimulants transform these individuals into false gods for a very brief window of time. Of course, there is a high price to pay for using these substances in this manner, as tolerance effects require more amounts of the substance to be consumed to achieve the desired "escape" or "rush," and the hangover, withdrawal, financial and social/occupational effects of repeated, escalating usage patterns can be tremendous.

Ballinger and colleagues (2008) have also offered an EI conceptualization of substance abuse and addiction. They emphasize the experience of being in treatment. A therapist approaching a client from an EI perspective essentially encourages their client to become more fully aware of what they are thinking and feeling in the present moment. They argue substance abusers suffer from a lack of self-awareness and willingness to tolerate the discomfort that is often associated with looking more deeply within oneself. Ballinger further maintains that substance abusers crave the predictable subjective experience associated with substance abuse. It provides the individual with the false illusion that he or she can control one's life or, as they more aptly put it, "[substance use] serves as a rigid and powerful chemical armor against an unappealing option - living life as it is" (pg. 181). Beyond engaging in substance abuse behaviors, many of these individuals, "construct a veil of distracting irritations and pleasures, or mental busywork, designed to protect us from awareness of our deepest existential concerns: death, isolation, responsibility, and how we are to find meaning in our lives" (pg. 180). While Ballinger concedes that some degree of diversion and mental distraction is adaptive and allows the individual to move forward unencumbered with existential dread, a life in which existential givens and fears are never contemplated remains fragile and constrained. One might assume that a mind-set so intent on avoidance and denial of existential concerns and unpleasant affect may avoid psychotherapy in perpetuity. Ballinger notes this tendency in substance abusers and states that it is only after a "boundary situation" has occurred that they will often seek treatment. A boundary situation is a term coined by Yalom (1980) and refers to a severe stressor that floods the individual with anxiety. Typically, in the case of a substance abuser, it is a brush with death and/or strong and repeated reminder by a physician that their chronic substance use patterns will shorten their life that finally causes the individual to seek treatment.

As previously mentioned, the author and a colleague have conceptualized adolescent substance abuse from an existential perspective where the problematic usage is viewed as a maladaptive reaction to Yalom's (1980) existential givens of human existence (Karavalaki & Shumaker, 2016). A brief summary of this effort is provided here. To begin, the interpretation first notes the complex relationship humans have with the existential given of freedom. While it can be wonderful to exercise one's autonomy and agency in a world devoid of external structure, it can simultaneously be overwhelming to have so many choices and the ability to potentially create a multitude of predicaments on a second-by-second basis during our conscious experience of life. One's freedom to choose goes hand-in-hand with assuming responsibility for our choices, actions, and consequences of those actions (Frankl, 1963). It is quite common for individuals who more deeply contemplate these matters of freedom, choice, and responsibility to feel anxiety and a sense of ambivalence at times about this fundamental condition of being. In some cases, the anxiety will be so intense, the dread of infinite expansiveness so overwhelming, that the individual will attempt to relinquish their freedom by living life inauthentically (Bauman & Waldo, 1998).

For certain, adolescence is a critical stage of life where the individual begins to confront this manner of concern. Adolescents both ask for and are expected to assume more autonomy and responsibility for their life choices and activities of daily living. At the same time, society does not view them as fully mature and retribution can be severe when they make poor choices or fail to conform with the expectations of the authority figures in their lives. Faced with pressure from above, uncertainty about how to proceed on a variety of fronts, and the overwhelming sense of responsibility for making the "right" choices, adolescents are particularly vulnerable to retreating from the burden of freedom through problematic substance use. To this end, To and colleagues (2007) have interviewed several adolescents who report that they abused substances in an effort to cope with the burden of freedom. Specifically, these adolescents state substance use can affirm their personal power in a world that can seem chaotic and unwieldy. Others maintain that substance use can help them at least temporarily escape the increasing weight of responsibility they experience in life. Unfortunately, chronic and intense substance abuse during adolescence quite often has the unintended effect of creating more chaos and responsibilities for the adolescent. Thus, the cure for a fear of overwhelming freedom and responsibility becomes a causal factor for more intense fears and struggles in this realm of existence.

A second existential given that adolescents contend with is isolation. This experience of aloneness can range in intensity according to one's context, state of being, and stage of development, but in certain moments and even over longer periods of time it can feel daunting, overwhelming, depressing, and/or numbing. Existential therapists believe it is possible through one's presence and empathic attunement to at least partially bridge the gap between themselves and their clients to achieve powerful moments of connection. But complete connection, complete understanding can never be achieved. Anxiety can emerge when the individual recognizes that their desire for connectedness can never fully be realized.

When viewed from an EI framework, adolescents who contemplate and struggle with feelings of isolation may fear the hyper-constrictive polarity of infinite smallness. Their sense of aloneness reinforces a sense of insignificance and ultimate invisibility. As this awareness and discomfort increases, adolescents may be vulnerable to committing allegiance to a group, cause, or belief system that provides at least the illusion of acceptance and connection. In these cases the adolescent's questions about his or her identity ("Who am I?") may have been solved on at least a temporary basis, but it remains to be seen whether the identity that is chosen is truly reflective of the individual's internal valuing process. As Hacker (1994) and others have noted, insecure and isolated adolescents remain very vulnerable to prematurely swearing allegiance to a group or cause. If the most attractive peer group that offers potential acceptance is engaged in substance abuse, one can obviously see the potential for substance abusing behaviors to emerge. Initially the chief motivation for consuming alcohol or using drugs may be obtaining the acceptance of one's peers. However, once the adolescent starts consuming substances on a more regular basis it is entirely possible that the substance itself comes to represent that which is primary and the object of the individual's emotional connection (Kemp & Butler, 2014).

Struggles with meaning and meaninglessness are a third existential given that can impact adolescent substance use behaviors. To live a meaningful life has been described as one where there is a "cognizance of order, coherence, and purpose in one's existence" (Reker & Wong, 1988). Existential theorists believe it is incumbent upon the individual to create meaning in their own lives. Many existentialists do not believe there is inherent meaning in the world or that an individual's life purpose is preordained (Yalom, 1980). When an adolescent achieves this realization of their own accord intense anxiety may surface. A world with no clear answers or path to meaning becomes a much scarier place. Frankl (1963) was particularly sensitive to this struggle and constructed Logotherapy in part to assist individuals who are struggling with this specific existential given. Drawing upon his own life experiences as a holocaust survivor, he strongly believed it was possible for individuals to overcome the despair and confusion that results from the realization that our existence has the potential to be meaningless. More recently, Damon and colleagues (2003) have demonstrated that questions of meaning are especially salient during adolescence. They and others have highlighted a strong connection between meaning and identity. That is, establishing a sense of meaning and intentionality goes a long way toward promoting a clear and stable self-identity.

Adolescents, like many adults, search for meaning in their intimate relationships, scholastic and occupational pursuits, leisure and creative activities, and the values and belief systems they adopt. However, many adolescents struggle to find meaning and/or validation in these pursuits. These individuals may be particularly vulnerable to resorting to problematic substance use (Frankl, 1963; Hacker, 1994). Kemp (2009) argues that substance use may be an attempt by the individual to acquire meaning vis-à-vis through the development of an identity. Alternatively, he also acknowledges that substance use may simply represent a brief respite and moment of ecstasy in a world perceived to be lacking in meaning. Thompson (2012) offers yet another interpretation where the psychophysiological effects of the substance are misinterpreted by the individual as representing a deeply meaningful life experience.

As the author previously demonstrated there is a small but compelling research basis to support the contention that adolescent substance abuse can be related to struggles with meaninglessness (Karavalaki & Shumaker, 2016). For example, Kinnier and colleagues (1994) found that adolescents who report less meaning in their lives are more likely to consumer higher levels of alcohol and illicit substances. Viewed from a different angle, Minehan and colleagues (2000) found that individuals who reported a higher level of purpose in their life were less likely to consume alcohol. Certainly, there is an abundance of research pertaining to adult substance abuse that shows a strong connection between meaninglessness and substance abuse (e.g., Martin et al., 2011).

The final existential given that may have a strong bearing on adolescent substance use behaviors is death and nonbeing. While from virtually the time consciousness develops individuals experience anxiety pertaining to nonbeing, adolescence represents a stage of development where one's eventual death is contemplated at a deeper level. This stage of life may also coincide with experiencing the first loss of someone close. Fantasies of youth and/or once cherished rituals and practices of childhood are abandoned and mourned as well. Many adolescents are prepared to compensate for these losses and, in fact, these experiences of loss will enrich their philosophy of life and sharpen their sense of purpose and direction. However, others will be overwhelmed by the intensity and scope of these losses or simply have difficulty reconciling the simple fact that they will eventually die themselves. Again, similar to the case of contemplating one's aloneness in the world, the subset of adolescents who fear death acutely are contending with the hyper-constrictive polarity of infinite smallness. It truly can get no smaller than nonexistence. In this scenario, problematic substance use develops out of a need to escape the omnipresent fear of nonbeing. In practice, as Schneider (2008) has noted, the escape can follow two routes. Alcohol and other substances that have a primarily depressant effect can serve a numbing, anesthetizing effect while stimulants such as cocaine or methylamphetamines may serve as a hyper-expansive compensatory response to the fear where the individual feels all-powerful and invulnerable.

Research seems to support the adolescent substance abuse as a reaction formation to the fear of death hypothesis. Specifically, Hirschberger and colleagues (2002) found that reminders of one's mortality increase adolescents' desire to engage in risk-taking behaviors, particularly drug use. Other researchers, relying more on case study analyses, note that substance abuse was motivated in part by a desire on the part of the adolescent to assert one's indestructibility and immortality (e.g., Hacker, 1994; Pelham, 1997). Of course, that which the adolescent fears – nonbeing – may be precisely that which they unintentionally ensure when their substance abusing behaviors result in overdose, accidents, or risk-taking behaviors that lead to death.

EI Case Example

Darren,[1] age 17 years, was referred by his attorney and parents in the fall of his senior year in high school after being charged with possession of alcohol. Approximately three weeks prior to his initial consultation he had been driving with three friends late at night on a weekend evening when he was pulled over by the local police for speeding. He denied he had been drinking and passed both a breathalyzer and field sobriety tests. However, two open containers of alcohol had been found in the back seat of his car. Neither Darren nor his friends assumed ownership of the alcohol when confronted by the officer. Privately, Darren later reported he had been the "designated driver" that evening and his friends had been consuming the alcohol. Facing a wall of silence the officer had chosen to charge Darren with possession. The car had been immediately impounded, Darren and his friends had been transported back to the police station in police cruisers where their parents picked them up, and Darren had lost his license. To make matters worse, within a week Darren had been kicked off the varsity football team for the final three games of the season due to a violation of the team's no-tolerance policy for alcohol and illicit substance use.

Following the incident the family sought legal counsel and began to vigorously defend against the charge. However, the experience of being detained and charged, loss of license, betrayal by his friends, forfeiture of the remainder of his final high school football season, and potentially compromised college application process had weighed heavily on Darren. Both his parents and attorney became quite concerned with his welfare when he expressed passive suicidal ideation (e.g., "My life is over", "I'd be better off dead") during a legal strategy meeting. These statements, in combination with several episodes of crying and a growing reluctance to attend school, were the impetus for the initial referral.

Darren and his parents arrived early for the initial consultation and greeted the author warmly but with uncertainty. Darren was an only child who had been a three-sport athlete and marginal student. He had received some interest from Division II and III lacrosse programs to play for them in college, but it was unlikely any of these schools would be offering him a scholarship. Darren's father, a formidable presence dressed in an expensive business suit who worked as an executive at a large investment firm, made it clear that neither him, his wife, or son had ever participated in counseling. He believed his son would only need to use the author's services for a brief period of time. Darren's mother, a striking presence who was a stay-at-home mother, also seemed pressured to confirm the family's strong mental health. She focused more on the injustices the family had experienced at the hands of the police, school, and her son's friends.

Darren carried himself with confidence and seemed relatively less anxious about the appointment, mimicking his father's strong handshake and piercing eye contact upon greeting the author and seamlessly easing himself comfortably into the office's reclining chair. He stood well over 6 feet tall and possessed an athletic build, choosing to wear his team's warm-up clothing into the session. When asked how he felt about attending the appointment he offered a dismissive chuckle and alluded to his attorney wanting him to attend but later acknowledged, "I've got a lot on my plate" and "I've been stressed lately." He also reported at other points in the session palpable anxiety about getting into and going away to college, a sense of directionless and uncertainty about what he wanted to do with his life, and a long-standing fear of death. This latter aspect of his being was conveyed when he discussed his suicidal ideation. Specifically, he offered that he would never kill himself because "Dying scares the crap out of me."

While Darren's previous comments indicative of suicidal ideation, his recent mood, and his stress levels and coping resources were a major focus of the initial session, the author also inquired about his substance use patterns. The author routinely asks about substance use behaviors during an initial family consultation in the presence of parents to assess familial communication and parent awareness about this aspect of the adolescent's life. The author, of course, revisits the topic later when meeting individually with the adolescent. Frequently the adolescent denies or greatly minimizes the extent of his or her usage patterns when in the parents' presence, but not always. Before Darren could answer the initial question on substance use, his father and mother spoke at length about their attitudes and practices regarding their son's alcohol and marijuana use. Specifically, his father stated, "Look. I'm a realist. I used to be a popular athlete like Darren and know what happens on the weekends. Don't get me wrong. We don't encourage it. But we just want Darren to be safe. We are really proud of him for being the designated driver. We've hosted parties and tell him not to let any of his friends leave if they have been drinking. So they'll sleep over. You know. These are good kids. Quite frankly, I don't see what is the big deal with having a beer or two."

Darren's mother essentially reiterated much of what her husband said, though she noted that she had a firm rule that her son was not allowed to smoke marijuana in the home. She seemed most concerned about the smell of marijuana but also referred to smoking in general as a disgusting habit and the illegality of the practice. During this discussion the family also pointed out the parents often consumed wine at meals and, within the past year, had been allowing Darren to share a glass with them. Though the author did not question them on this practice they offered a spontaneous defense of their decision, extolling the virtues of family tradition (i.e., alcohol was routinely consumed at family gatherings and on holidays) and preparing Darren to drink "responsibly" when he went off to college.

When Darren finally had an opportunity to answer the question about his substance using behaviors he appeared relatively comfortable acknowledging his alcohol and marijuana use in the presence of his parents. He reported that he started drinking alcohol and smoking marijuana in the summer between his freshman and sophomore year in high school. He described the usage during his sophomore and most of his junior year as opportunistic and mostly on weekends. He and his friends would attend upperclassmen parties where alcohol and marijuana were available, or they would pool money and find someone to purchase these substances for them, or they would simply raid the liquor cabinets at one of their homes when parents were out or at home but oblivious. Upon obtaining his license during his junior year he confirmed he and his parents formed an agreement where he could host "gatherings" where drinking and smoking would occur but with the understanding that nobody could leave intoxicated. In the scenarios where he was out with friends and became intoxicated, he knew he could call his parents for a ride and had done so on several occasions.

Citing the increased autonomy a license and car afforded him, pressure to get into college and figure out a direction in life, as well as the explicit approval of his parents to consume substances "responsibly," Darren acknowledged that his usage patterns had increased in recent months. He appeared less comfortable offering specific estimates of exactly how much or how frequently he drank and smoked, but a couple of his comments were quite concerning. Specifically, he acknowledged "passing out" on three occasions in the prior three months due to excessive alcohol use, he acknowledged smoking marijuana by himself prior to school on several occasions to help with boredom and stress, and he expressed the opinion that drinking 3–4 beers in a single sitting hardly constituted a significant amount of alcohol intake. Anything more than a six-pack of alcohol, an amount which he sheepishly acknowledged he consumed on more than a "few" occasions, was excessive in his mind. Again, this information was revealed in the presence of Darren's parents. Aside from a couple of occasions when his mother raised her eyebrows in apparent surprise upon learning the specific amounts of alcohol her son had consumed, the parents remained mostly subdued during this discussion.

After assessing Darren for safety utilizing a similar approach to that outlined in the preceding chapter on depression it seemed that Darren was low risk for engaging in a suicide attempt. This initial assessment was buttressed by several factors. While he acknowledged chronic stress and moments of uncertainty about his future, the more recent poignant moments of deep despair seemed isolated and reactive to a highly distressing incident as opposed to being a symptom of a longer-term, endogenous mood disorder. By all accounts Darren had never experienced significant mood or other psychological disturbances in the past. His mother conceded he was an "anxious little boy" but "he had largely grown out of that." Despite his recent setback his core self-concept seemed mostly positive. He demonstrated a combination of hope and uncertainty about the future. He possessed several positive attributes including advanced social skills, a keen wit, and physical attributes (e.g., size, athleticism, and physical attractiveness) that would likely make him sought out in social situations. His support system, while perhaps misguided in their assessment of his substance use behaviors, was heavily invested and very encouraging. Despite his initial comments that suggested he viewed the counseling as unnecessary, he seemed open and even relieved to engage in the process by the end of the first session. Thus, the author's initial prognosis was positive in respect to resolving the more acute despair and sadness he had felt and expressed in recent weeks since the incident. That said, a safety plan was put in place should suicidal ideation re-occur.

The author was quite concerned, however, about Darren's substance use behaviors, anxiety, and chronic stress. While under a high amount of stress related to his legal issues, Darren had reported increased irritability, sleeplessness, and self-doubt that had predated his police incident. As previously noted, he had reported smoking marijuana to relieve anxiety before school. He also later admitted to consuming alcohol to the point of intoxication to "forget about everything." Here is where normative existential anxiety concerns seemed to be taxing Darren's coping resources and impacting his substance use behaviors. Specifically, two existential givens – freedom and meaninglessness – seemed to weigh heavily upon Darren. He wanted to get into a good college but felt uncertain about his capacity to get into one that would meet his and his parents' standards and, on a deeper level, his ability to move away from home and "succeed." Further, he was even beginning to dare to question the meaning of his existence and the seemingly predetermined life script that had been assigned to him. This reflective process, while having the potential to lead to a life with increased intentionality and meaning, was deeply unsettling for Darren. Not to be overlooked, however, was Darren's decision to abstain from all alcohol and marijuana usage while his case was pending. His sleep problems, irritability, and debilitating moments of self-consciousness that verged on panic episodes had increased significantly since he had stopped using substances. Thus, it was possible that at least part of his increased distress was due to dependency needs.

Given this formulation, the author believed an EI family-based intervention for treating adolescent substance abuse was indicated. As previously outlined, an EI family-based intervention for adolescent substance abuse combines evidence-based practice with EI principles and generally includes the following components: (1) family participation in the initial meeting and a comprehensive assessment of substance use behaviors that may include an outside referral for diagnostic purposes; (2) individual and family work that incorporates the EI cornerstone treatment approaches of presence, invoking the actual, working with resistance, and rediscovering meaning and awe; (3) psychoeducation about substance abuse triggers, treatment options, course, and prognosis, as well as information about existential anxiety as it may relate to the substance using behaviors; (4) reframing, if indicated, of substance abusing behaviors as a symptom of existential and normative anxiety as opposed to a moral failure and correction of other cognitive distortions pertaining to usage; (5) a focus on improving family communication about substance use behaviors and encouragement of appropriate support and limit-setting by parents; (6) the development of cognitive and behavioral strategies for the adolescent to cope with triggers, cravings, and peer pressure to use substances; and (7) a focus on the adolescent's pursuit of meaning and the development of an identity that fosters a sense of intentionality that hopefully reduces reliance upon substance use (Karavalaki & Shumaker, 2016).

In Darren's case, the first part of the intervention consisted of the author openly sharing his concerns about Darren's substance use behaviors to him and his parents prior to the end of the initial consultation knowing full well that the family's openness and/or readiness to truly hear these concerns might be limited. After some initial resistance the family grudgingly agreed to arrange an outside diagnostic consultation with an expert in the field. Ultimately the consultant agreed that Darren's usage patterns met diagnostic criteria for both alcohol and cannabis abuse but felt that these concerns could be treated safely on an outpatient basis. The parents would continue to minimize Darren's usage throughout the course of treatment but agreed to stop hosting parties for their son where substances were used and to stop providing Darren wine with dinner. They also continued to support the author's work with their son despite their doubts about the accuracy of the author's substance use concerns. Darren seemed more open to the possibility that his substance use behaviors were more serious than he initially led on. In individual sessions he acknowledged that his "black outs" and loss of memory associated with binge episodes of drinking had frightened him and he came to see that relying upon marijuana as a coping mechanism to cope with the anxieties and stressors of everyday living was a concerning proposition. He also eventually shared the opinion that both of his parents were "functional alcoholics" who normalized his substance use as perhaps in part a means to justify their usage.

The increased openness Darren demonstrated over time to the possibility that his substance use patterns merited attention was perhaps due to his positive reaction to the EI components of the intervention. More specifically, in individual sessions Darren responded enthusiastically to the therapist's empathic presence, attempts to invoke the actual, and focus on what had meaning to him. He was fascinated with the concept of existential anxiety and concerns regarding meaninglessness, freedom, responsibility, death fears, and even one's fundamental aloneness all seemed to hold personal significance to him. Merely hearing another speak of these "unspeakable" sources of previously solitary consternation was greatly relieving to him. He confided that, despite his outwardly confident presentation, he doubted his capacity to succeed in life and wondered about what was truly important in this life. True to the spirit of an EI approach the therapist refrained from offering solutions or opinions regarding what might hold ultimate meaning for Darren while normalizing the struggle.

The specific substance abuse treatment component of the intervention included the main components of the CBT-G empirically supported approach outlined earlier in the chapter. This included a skill development component where Darren was taught how to detect triggers associated with craving, how to manage emotions that may trigger a desire to use (e.g., anxiety, anger, depression) utilizing relaxation techniques and creative/distracting substitute activities as outlets, how to resist peer pressure to use (through mostly role play activities and cognitive restructuring), and how to communicate with the therapist and his parents when he felt vulnerable to binging. Across the course of approximately 6 months and 20 sessions Darren eliminated his marijuana usage and curtailed his alcohol use dramatically. He was able to settle his legal difficulties and was accepted to a small liberal arts college that he believed would be a good fit for his personality and academic interests. He reconnected with his parents in more meaningful ways, playing tennis and golf with his father regularly and relying heavily on the counsel and support of his mother in seeing him through the college application and acceptance process. Therapy concluded at the time he graduated high school.

Note

1. The cases depicted in the book are composite representations of multiple client experiences where names, gender, and other potentially identifiable aspects of the case experience have been changed to protect client confidentiality.

References

Aharon, I., Etcoff, N., Ariely, D., Chabris, C. F., O'Connor, E., & Breiter, H. C. (2001). Beautiful faces have variable reward value: fMRI and behavioral evidence. *Neuron, 32*(3), 537–551.

Albanese, M. J., & Shaffer, H. J. (2012). Addiction: The genesis and evolution of an idea and its consequences. In H. J. Shaffer, D. A. LaPlante, S. E. Nelson (Eds.), *APA addiction syndrome handbook, Vol. 1: Foundations, influences, and expressions of addiction* (pp. 3–25). Washington, DC, US: American Psychological Association. doi:10.1037/13751-001

Alexander, J., & Parsons, B. V. (1982). *Functional family therapy.* Monterey, CA, US: Brooks/Cole Publishing Company. doi:10.1037/11621-000

Armstrong, T., & Costello, E. (2002). Community studies on adolescent substance use, abuse, dependence and psychiatric comorbidity. *Journal of Consulting and Clinical Psychology*, 70(6), 1224–1239.

Ballinger, B., Matano, R. A., & Amantea, A. C. (2008). A perspective on alcoholism: The case of Charles. In K. J. Schneider (Ed.), *Existential-integrative psychotherapy: Guideposts to the core of practice* (pp. 177–185). New York, NY, US: Routledge/Taylor & Francis Group.

Bardo, M. T., Donohew, R. L., & Harrington, N. G. (1996). Psychobiology of novelty seeking and drug seeking behavior. *Behavioural Brain Research, 77*(1–2), 23–43. doi:10.1016/0166-4328(95)00203-0

Bauman, S., & Waldo, M. (1998). Existential theory and mental health counseling: If it were a snake, it would have bitten! *Journal Of Mental Health Counseling*, *20*(1), 13–27.

Brook, J. S., Whiteman, M., Gordon, A. S., & Cohen, P. (1986). Some models and mechanisms for explaining the impact of maternal and adolescent characteristics on adolescent stage of drug use. *Developmental Psychology*, *22*(4), 460.

Brown, S. A., D'Amico, E. J., McCarthy, D. M., & Tapert, S. F. (2001). Four-year outcomes from adolescent alcohol and drug treatment. *Journal Of Studies On Alcohol*, *62*(3), 381–388. doi:10.15288/jsa.2001.62.381

Center for Behavioral Health Statistics and Quality. (2015). Behavioral health trends in the United States: Results from the 2014 National Survey on Drug

Use and Health (HHS Publication No. SMA 15-4927, NSDUH Series H-50). Retrieved from http://www.samhsa.gov/data/

Chassin, L., Pillow, D. R., Curran, P. J., Molina, B. G., & Barrera, M. J. (1993). Relation of parental alcoholism to early adolescent substance use: A test of three mediating mechanisms. *Journal Of Abnormal Psychology*, *102*(1), 3–19. doi:10.1037/0021-843X.102.1.3

Damon, W., Menon, J., & Bronk, K. C. (2003). The development of purpose during adolescence. *Applied Developmental Science*, *7*(3), 119–128. doi:10.1207/S1532480XADS0703_2

Deas, D., & Clark, A. (2009). Current state of treatment for alcohol and other drug use disorders in adolescents. *Alcohol Research & Health*, *32*(1), 76–82.

Dodes, L. M. (2002). *The heart of addiction*. New York, NY, US: HarperCollins Publishers.

Frankl, V. (1963). *Man's search for meaning: an introduction to logotherapy*. Oxford, England: Washington Square Press.

Grieve, S. J., Griffiths, P. J., & Littleton, J. M. (1979). Genetic influences on the rate of development of ethanol tolerance and the ethanol physical withdrawal syndrome in mice. *Drug And Alcohol Dependence*, *4*(1–2), 77–86. doi:10.1016/0376-8716(79)90042-5

Hacker, D. J. (1994). An existential view of adolescence. *The Journal Of Early Adolescence*, *14*(3), 300–327. doi:10.1177/0272431694014003001

Hawkins, J. D., Catalano, R. F., & Miller, J. Y. (1992). Risk and protective factors for alcohol and other drug problems in adolescence and early adulthood: Implications for substance abuse prevention. *Psychological Bulletin*, *112*(1), 64–105. doi:10.1037/0033-2909.112.1.64

Hirschberger, G., Florian, V., Mikulincer, M., Goldenberg, J. L., & Pyszczynski, T. (2002). Gender differences in the willingness to engage in risky behavior: A terror management perspective. *Death Studies*, *26*(2), 117–141. doi:10.1080/074811802753455244

Hogue, A., & Dauber, S. (2013). Assessing fidelity to evidence-based practices in usual care: The example of family therapy for adolescent behavior problems. *Evaluation And Program Planning*, *37*21–30. doi:10.1016/j.evalprogplan.2012.12.001

Hogue, A., Henderson, C. E., Ozechowski, T. J., & Robbins, M. S. (2014). Evidence base on outpatient behavioral treatments for adolescent substance use: Updates and recommendations 2007–2013. *Journal Of Clinical Child And Adolescent Psychology*, *43*(5), 695–720. doi:10.1080/15374416.2014.915550

Kamon, J. L., Stanger, C., Budney, A. J., & Dumenci, L. (2006). Relations between parent and adolescent problems among adolescents presenting for family-based marijuana abuse treatment. *Drug And Alcohol Dependence*, *85*(3), 244–254. doi:10.1016/j.drugalcdep.2006.05.015

Karavalaki, M., & Shumaker, D. (2016). An existential–integrative (EI) treatment of adolescent substance abuse. *The Humanistic Psychologist*, *44*(4), 381–399. doi:10.1037/hum0000036

Kemp, R., & Butler, A. (2014). Love, hate and the emergence of self in addiction recovery. *Existential Analysis*, *25*(2), 257–268.

Kemp, R. (2009). Relating to the other: Truth and untruth in addiction. *European Journal Of Psychotherapy And Counselling*, *11*(4), 355–368. doi:10.1080/13642530903444787

Khantzian, E. J. (1997). The self-medication hypothesis of substance use disorders: A reconsideration and recent applications. *Harvard Review Of Psychiatry*, *4*(5), 231–244. doi:10.3109/10673229709030550

Kinnier, R. T., Metha, A. T., Keim, J. S., & Okey, J. L. (1994). Depression, meaninglessness, and substance abuse in "normal" and hospitalized adolescents. *Journal Of Alcohol And Drug Education*, *39*(2), 101–111.

Liddle, H. A. (2004). Family-based therapies for adolescent alcohol and drug use: Research contributions and future research needs. *Addiction*, *99*(Suppl2), 76–92. doi:10.1111/j.1360-0443.2004.00856.x

Martin, C. S., Romig, C. J., & Kirisci, L. (2000). DSM-IV learning disorders in 10- to 12-year- old boys with and without a parental history of substance use disorders. *Prevention Science*, *1*(2), 107–113. doi:10.1023/A:1010042231697

Martin, R. A., MacKinnon, S., Johnson, J., & Rohsenow, D. J. (2011). Purpose in life predicts treatment outcome among adult cocaine abusers in treatment. *Journal Of Substance Abuse Treatment*, *40*(2), 183–188. doi:10.1016/j.jsat.2010.10.002

Minehan, J. A., Newcomb, M. D., & Galaif, E. R. (2000). Predictors of adolescent drug use: Cognitive abilities, coping strategies and purpose in life. *Journal Of Child & Adolescent Substance Abuse*, *10*(2), 33–52. doi:10.1300/J029v10n02_04

Newcomb, M. D., & Bentler, P. M. (1989). Substance use and abuse among children and teenagers. *American Psychologist*, *44*(2), 242–248. doi:10.1037/0003-066X.44.2.242

Orford, J. (2001). Addiction as excessive appetite. *Addiction*, *96*(1), 15–31. doi:10.1080/09652140120075233

Pelham, B. W. (1997). Human motivation has multiple roots. *Psychological Inquiry*, *8*(1), 44–47. doi:10.1207/s15327965pli0801_9

Ramo, D. E., & Brown, S. A. (2008). Classes of substance abuse relapse situations: A comparison of adolescents and adults. *Psychology Of Addictive Behaviors*, *22*(3), 372–379. doi:10.1037/0893-164X.22.3.372

Reker, G. T., & Wong, P. T. P. (1988). Aging as an individual process: Toward a theory of personal meaning. In J. E. Birren & V. L. Bengston (Eds.), Emergent theories of aging (pp. 214–246). New York, NY: Springer.

Rowe, C. L. (2012). Family therapy for drug abuse: Review and updates 2003–2010. *Journal Of Marital And Family Therapy, 38*(1), 59–81. doi:10.1111/j.1752-0606.2011.00280.x

Schneider, K. J. (2008). *Existential-integrative psychotherapy: Guideposts to the core of practice.* New York, NY, US: Routledge/Taylor & Francis Group.

Shaffer, H. J., LaPlante, D. A., LaBrie, R. A., Kidman, R. C., Donato, A. N., & Stanton, M. V. (2004). Toward a Syndrome Model of Addiction: Multiple Expressions, Common Etiology. *Harvard Review Of Psychiatry, 12*(6), 367–374. doi:10.1080/10673220490905705

Spear, L. P. (2000). The adolescent brain and age-related behavioral manifestations. *Neuroscience And Biobehavioral Reviews, 24*(4), 417–463. doi:10.1016/S0149-7634(00)00014-2

Tarter, R. E., Vanyukov, M., Giancola, P., Dawes, M., Blackson, T., Mezzich, A., & Clark, D. B. (1999). Etiology of early age onset substance use disorder: A maturational perspective. *Development And Psychopathology, 11*(4), 657–683. doi:10.1017/S0954579499002266

Tarter, R. E. (2002). Etiology of adolescent substance abuse: A developmental perspective. *The American Journal On Addictions, 11*(3), 171–191. doi:10.1080/10550490290087965

Thompson, G. (2012). A meaning-centered therapy for addictions. *International Journal Of Mental Health And Addiction, 10*(3), 428–440. doi:10.1007/s11469-011-9367-9

To, S., Ngai, S. S., Ngai, N., & Cheung, C. (2007). Young people's existential concerns and club drug abuse. *International Journal Of Adolescence And Youth, 13*(4), 327–341. doi:10.1080/02673843.2007.9747983

Tobler, A. L., & Komro, K. A. (2010). Trajectories or parental monitoring and communication and effects on drug use among urban young adolescents. *Journal Of Adolescent Health, 46*(6), 560–568. doi:10.1016/j.jadohealth.2009.12.008

Waldron, H. B., & Turner, C. W. (2008). Evidence-based psychosocial treatments for adolescent substance abuse. *Journal Of Clinical Child And Adolescent Psychology, 37*(1), 238–261. doi:10.1080/15374410701820133

Waldron, H. B., Kern-Jones, S., Turner, C. W., Peterson, T. R., & Ozechowski, T. J. (2007). Engaging resistant adolescents in drug abuse treatment. *Journal Of Substance Abuse Treatment, 32*(2), 133–142. doi:10.1016/j.jsat.2006.07.007

Yalom, I. D. (1980). *Existential psychotherapy.* New York, NY, US: Basic Books.

CHAPTER 8

EI Approaches to Treating Disruptive Behavior Disorders in Adolescents

Introduction

Adolescents who challenge authority, break rules, and/or demonstrate callous emotional traits are often among the most difficult to treat yet are at high risk for long-term maladjustment and could potentially benefit greatly from intensive therapeutic support. Often reluctant participants in therapy, they frequently attend only at the behest of desperate parents or as part of a court mandate. Resistance to treatment can take many forms, from refusal to attend, refusal to participate short of physically attending, minimization or blatant fabrication of their self-reported areas of concern, to even overt hostility and/or personal attacks on the therapist. The adversarial interpersonal stance can be disorienting and uncomfortable for therapists, leading to defensive reactions, unnecessary power struggles, negative counter transference issues, and ultimately unhelpful treatment responses. Even in cases where the adolescent displays minimal buy-in to the process, their problems in living can be so numerous and they can be engaged in so many high-risk behaviors (e.g., substance abuse, illegal activities, fighting) that the therapist can easily feel overwhelmed and ill-equipped to offer a clear pathway toward stability.

Unfortunately, there are certainly times where the therapist's stunned and sinking reaction to the depth of the adolescent's areas of concern reflects the reality of the situation. Often the families of these individuals seek treatment at a much later point in the adolescent's development when it is much harder to secure their cooperation and/or the complexity of the

D. Shumaker, *Existential-Integrative Approaches to Treating Adolescents*, DOI 10.1057/978-1-349-95211-3_8

mental health and adjustment concerns are so much greater. The caretakers, themselves, can be ambivalent about the need for treatment and model combative interpersonal stances that do not support the treatment process and goals. Regardless, whenever an adolescent who presents with symptoms consistent with a disruptive behavior disorder (DBD) enters the therapy room there is an opportunity for a skilled and patient therapist to positively intervene. Many might think that an existential therapeutic approach would have little to offer these clients, believing that a more structured and directive approach such as cognitive-behavior therapy (CBT) would be more conducive to promoting the development of prosocial skills, the anticipation and management of negative emotional responses, and the contemplation and pursuit of more rewarding life choices. While this logic is sound and there is a robust evidence basis supporting cognitive-behavioral and family systems approaches to working with adolescents diagnosed with DBDs, in certain cases an EI approach may augment the treatment and lead to better short- and long-term outcomes. In their own way, many adolescents who present with this type of mental health concern struggle with the existential givens of freedom, death, loneliness, and meaninglessness. More often than what one might assume the existential anxiety these adolescents experience in relation to ultimate concerns contributes at least partially to their disruptive behaviors and/or oppositional interpersonal stance. However, the internal struggles may never be revealed to a therapist due the adolescent's profound lack of trust in therapy and/or therapist behaviors that suggest a fundamental misunderstanding of the client's core being. This chapter explores specific cases where EI may be indicated in the treatment of DBDs during adolescence and specific ways in which it can be seamlessly integrated with evidence-based approaches. As previously indicated, adolescents who present with these concerns desperately need to be heard.

Clinical Description, Incidence, and Prevalence

The DSM-5 chapter on DBDs, referred to specifically as "Disruptive, Impulse Control, and Conduct Disorders," combines disorders from two prior chapters in the DSM-IV-TR ("Disorders Usually Diagnosed in Infancy, Childhood, or Adolescence" and "Impulse-Control Disorders Not Otherwise Specified"). The specific disorders included in this DSM-5 chapter are oppositional defiant disorder (ODD), conduct disorder (CD), antisocial personality disorder (APD), intermittent explosive disorder, pyromania, kleptomania, other specified disruptive, impulse-control, and conduct disorder, and unspecified disruptive, impulse-control, and conduct disorder. Attention deficit and hyperactivity disorder (ADHD) is no longer classified as a DBD but instead is listed in the DSM-5 chapter devoted to neurodevelopmental disorders. The main commonalities among these diagnoses are problems related to the regulation of emotions and/or behaviors that in some manner either violate the rights of others and/or create conflict between the individual and authority figures. They also are associated with the broader personality factors of increased disinhibition and negative emotionality. That said, the underlying causes for this pattern of relating with the world can be quite variable across the specific disorders. There are also significant differences across the disorders in the relative emphasis they place on the importance of emotional versus behavioral self-control (American Psychiatric Association, 2016).

The most common specific DBD diagnoses observed during adolescence are ODD and CD. These specific diagnoses are also the most common DBDs seen in the author's clinical practice. Thus, research and clinical observations pertaining to ODD and CD are this chapter's main focus. Regarding diagnosis, the DSM-5 diagnostic criteria for ODD has changed significantly from what was included in the DSM-IV-TR. While the main criteria of a pervasive pattern of anger, irritability, argumentative, and/or vindictive behavior over a six-month period remains, the specific symptoms are now grouped into three different categories: angry/irritable mood (three subcategories), argumentative/defiant behavior (four subcategories), and vindictiveness (one subcategory). An individual must have exhibited at least four of the subcategories over a six-month period with varying degrees of frequency depending upon the age of the child/adolescent. In addition, clinicians are now provided some guidance regarding the frequency in which the concerning behaviors should be observed in order to meet diagnostic threshold. Finally, a severity rating of ODD behaviors is now included (Gathright & Tyler, 2014).

The main DSM-5 diagnostic criterion for CD includes a repetitive and persistent pattern of behavior that violates the rights of others or societal norms where at least three specific rule-breaking or aggressive behaviors have occurred within a 12-month period. There are a total of 15 specific types of rule-breaking/aggressive behaviors classified under the following four categories: aggression to people and animals (seven subcategories), destruction of property (two subcategories), deceitfulness or theft (three subcategories), and serious violations of rules (three subcategories). There are provisions for childhood-, adolescent-, and unspecified-onset typologies as well. Further, there is a specifier option referred to as "With limited prosocial emotions" where the individual must have displayed at least two of the following traits over a 12-month period: lack of remorse or guilt, callous-lack of empathy, unconcerned about performance, shallow or deficient affect. Finally, the diagnostic criterion includes a severity specifier where mild, moderate, and severe presentations are listed as options.

Prevalence estimates for ODD and CD are similar. The average prevalence rate for ODD is 3.3% with the range of estimates falling between 1 and 11% (American Psychiatric Association, 2016; Canino et al., 2010). CD prevalence rates range from 2 to 10% with a median of 4% across studies (Costello et al., 2005). The diagnosis is more common in males for both disorders when the age of onset is prior to adolescence. However, a male predominance of ODD has not always been consistently demonstrated in samples of adolescents (Boylan et al., 2007). Both disorders demonstrate roughly equivalent prevalence rates across cultures and ethnic/racial groups (Canino et al., 2010). ODD often precedes CD (Rowe et al., 2010), yet a large proportion of children and adolescents diagnosed with ODD do not reach diagnostic criteria for a CD diagnosis later in life. Stringaris and Goodman (2009) suggest that the ODD symptoms of defiance, vindictiveness, and argumentativeness seem to most predict the development of CD while the anger and irritability symptoms are more likely to predict future mood disorders.

The age of onset for CD can occur as early as preschool (Moffitt & Scott, 2008), but more commonly children begin to demonstrate this pattern of behaviors later in childhood and in early adolescence. Most of the time CD symptoms remit when the individual reaches adulthood and a high proportion of individuals who are diagnosed with CD during adolescence go on to live productive and well-adjusted lives. However, when there is an early onset of CD the prognosis becomes much bleaker, and the risk for the future engagement in criminal behavior and development of substance abuse disorders is greatly increased (Burke et al., 2010). Similar to ODD, individuals diagnosed with CD are at increased risk for developing anxiety disorders, mood disorders, posttraumatic stress disorders, and psychotic disorders later in adulthood (Nock, 2003). A small but significant portion of individuals diagnosed with CD also eventually meet diagnostic criteria for APD later in life (American Psychiatric Association, 2016).

Common Conceptualizations/Etiological Overview

DBDs are among the most well-researched childhood disorders and this is reflected in the amount of attention devoted to identifying the etiology and developmental pathways that lead to onset. There are a wide range of risk factors for both ODD and CD, many of them common to each disorder. Tremblay (2010) has identified physical aggression and opposition-defiance as two of the most significant predictors of ODD and CD. This obviously makes conceptual sense since both of these behaviors feature very prominently in the diagnostic criteria (and even names) of these disorders. In the case of physical aggression, research indicates that the peak frequency of physical aggression occurs between the ages of 2 and 4 years (NICHD Early Child Care Research Network, 2004). However, most children will quickly reduce the frequency of their engagement in physical aggression when they reach elementary school. Only between 7 and 11% of elementary school children will develop Chronic Physical Aggression (CPA), which is simply defined as "a tendency to use physical aggression more frequently than the large majority of a birth cohort" (Tremblay, 2010, pg. 343). The seriousness of physically aggressive acts (i.e., types of aggression most likely to lead to physical harm and/or legal consequences for the perpetrator) generally seems to peak leading up to early adolescence and then decreases from mid-adolescence into adulthood. However, there is a small group of individuals who continue to engage in increasingly serious forms of aggression well into late adolescence. These individuals are at much higher risk for persisting problems related to violence and offending. Many likely engaged in more serious and persistent forms of aggression at a much earlier age.

The developmental trajectory for oppositional and defiant behaviors is similar to physical aggression where some degree of these behaviors is considered normative and only a few individuals go on to demonstrate clinically significant problems in the frequency and severity in which they engage in these behaviors (Tremblay, 2010). Thus, as any parent knows, children from an early age will normatively demonstrate some degree of anger, resentment, temper tantrums, refusals to comply, blaming behaviors, and vindictiveness. Like physical aggression, for most children tantrum behaviors seem to peak at age 2 years and then generally decrease over the course of an individual's youth. However, a small portion of individuals (7%) seem to continue to increase their oppositional patterns, particularly during the developmental window of ages 9–15 years old (Bongers et al., 2004). This can lead to chronic maladjustment and increase risk for a DBD diagnosis. Regardless of whether this manner of behavior increases or desists for a given individual, the point remains that engagement in oppositional and defiant behaviors early and often in an individual's lifespan is a robust predictor of DBDs later in youth.

There are multiple additional specific risk factors for the development of DBDs. Regarding genetic risk factors and a heritability component, family transmission research indicates a strong heritability for the development of DBDs (Hicks et al., 2004). In fact, Hicks and colleagues (2004) estimate the heritability index to be as high as 0.80 for children whose parents were diagnosed with either conduct disorder, an alcohol or drug dependence disorder, and/or engaged in antisocial behaviors. They speculate that the specific DBD disorder a child might be most vulnerable to developing could depend upon the specific types of emotional and behavioral concerns a parent demonstrated and/or other parental heritable traits such as personality factors, cognitive functioning, and even body size. Regarding specific biological risk factors, as previously alluded to it appears that temperament factors predict the development of DBDs. Specifically, in the case of ODD, negative emotionality and reactivity in infancy and toddlerhood predicts the disorder (American Psychiatric Association, 2016). Similar temperament traits seem to predict CD as well as lower than average intelligence (American Psychiatric Association, 2016). In addition, there are suggestions that reduced fear avoidance and autonomic arousal may also predict CD (Moffitt & Scott, 2008). Finally, children who display the early temperamental/personality trait of elevated interpersonal callousness (IC) (i.e., lack of guilt, deceitful and manipulative behaviors) are at increased risk for engaging in long-term delinquency (Byrd et al., 2012).

There a wide range of early childhood and familial risk factors associated with DBDs. Several maternal factors, including a mother's age when she gives birth to her first child, a premorbid history of engaging in antisocial behavior, a history of depression, and/or a history of low educational attainment all seem to increase risk for her offspring to develop a DBD (Tremblay 2010). Low family income, familial dysfunction, a lack of stimulation for the child, and a hostile-coercive parenting style are additional risk factors for the same (Tremblay, 2010). Thus, neglect, abuse, a lack of supervision, and chaotic living conditions with frequent changes in residences, caretakers, and disciplinary practices seem to create harsh environmental conditions where the development of a secure attachment and the modeling and teaching of critical life-skills and emotional/behavioral self-regulation strategies are sorely lacking. Spending one's youth living in these conditions can obviously be quite challenging. It is a testament to the human spirit and resiliency factors that so many *more* youth exposed to these challenges go on to live lives free from significant psychological and/or adjustment problems than those who do. Regarding community-level risk factors, research indicates that peer rejection, exposure to neighborhood violence, and developing an association with a delinquent peer group all increase the risk for developing a DBD (American Psychiatric Association, 2016). This, too, is hardly surprising since peer factors can play such a great influence during middle childhood and adolescence.

Shifting attention from consideration of DBD risk factors, there is also considerable data to suggest the presence of multiple developmental pathways among ODD, CD, APD, and ADHD. Of note, Loeber and colleagues have proposed the existence of three developmental pathways that explain the progression from relatively minor externalizing behaviors to more serious offending (for a review see Loeber & Burke, 2011). The pathways are as follows: (1) *authority conflict pathway:* starting before the age of 12 years these individuals demonstrate stubbornness and then disobedience and finally authority avoidance; (2) *covert pathway*: starting before the age of 15 years these individuals engage in minor acts of lying or deceitful behaviors, move on to property damage or vandalism, and may eventually graduate to more serious nonviolent offending (e.g., auto theft, burglary); and (3) *overt pathway:* this pathway starts with minor aggression such as bullying, graduates to physical fighting, and may ultimately lead to serious violence. In general, there is strong research support for conceptualizing and classifying youth DBDs in this manner. Loeber has also proposed a developmental sequence among DBDs and ADHD where an initial diagnosis of ODD and/or ADHD increases risk for CD and, over time, a small portion of individuals diagnosed with CD will develop APD. Again, while no single disorder is predictive of another, framing the various disorders in this manner can help clinicians and researchers better begin to understand how to predict and prevent the escalation of more persistent and aggressive forms of disruptive behaviors.

Empirically Supported Treatments/Evidence-Based Practice Approaches

Prior to discussing empirically supported and evidence-based approaches to treating adolescent DBDs, it is important to note that distinguishing normative from more serious forms of disruptive behavior can be challenging for even experienced clinicians. Recognizing this, McKinney and Morse (2012) have recently offered several best practice recommendations designed to assist clinicians who are faced with assessing the scope and severity of disruptive behaviors in children and adolescents. A brief summary of their effort is provided here. To begin, the authors recognize several methods for obtaining information should be utilized and several developmental areas of focus should be incorporated into an evaluation. Beyond conducting a basic diagnostic interview, they believe clinicians should utilize rating scales, observational assessments, intellectual and achievement assessments, and temperament and personality assessments. Specific attention should be paid to assessing the presence of callous-unemotional traits, behavioral disinhibition, executive functioning abilities, and social cognition of the individual. Under ideal circumstances, they recommend an evaluation consist of the following six steps: (1) obtain informed consent and conduct a diagnostic interview; (2) provide the child, parents, and teachers appropriate rating scales; (3) when meeting with the child build rapport, establish expectations for future testing, and further assess the child's understanding of his or her problems; (4) conduct individual personality, intellectual, and achievement testing with the child; (5) if a DBD is diagnosed further test and assess more specific areas of focus to clarify the diagnosis; and (6) complete a comprehensive assessment report and/or prepare to provide organized and coherent feedback to the child and parents that includes treatment recommendations. Following these general assessment steps can lead to a much more informed treatment selection process and avoid misdiagnosis.

Shifting focus from assessment to intervention, Eyberg and colleagues have conducted the most comprehensive and specific analyses of evidenced-based psychosocial treatments for adolescents with DBDs (Brestan & Eyberg, 1998; Eyberg et al., 2008). Their more recent analysis focused on the psychosocial treatment literature published between 1996 and 2007. In terms of methodology, they utilized the task force on promotion and dissemination of psychological procedures criteria for identifying both well-established and probably efficacious treatments

(Chambless & Hollon, 1998). The specific DBDs their analysis focused on were ODD and CD. ADHD interventions were not included in their analysis. Overall, they identified 1 well-established treatment and 15 probably efficacious treatments. While it is beyond the scope of this review to describe in detail all 16 of these interventions, several highlights pertaining to these findings are discussed.

To begin the single well-established treatment for DBD identified by Eyberg and colleagues (2008) is the Parent Management Training Oregon Model (PMTO) (Patterson et al., 1975). This intervention is a parent training program that teaches caretakers basic behavioral principles involved in caretaking and promoting positive behaviors in their children. It also encourages close supervision and assists parents in developing contingency management and behavioral modification programs designed to isolate and reduce maladaptive target behaviors in a child. However, it should be noted that the initial research was conducted with children between the ages of 3 and 12 years. Thus, the generalizability and applicability of this intervention with older adolescents is less understood. That said there are multiple reasons to suggest it can be effectively utilized with an adolescent population (Forgatch et al., 2016). Further, it seems important to contemplate why a parent training program, as opposed to an individual focused treatment modality, is currently the only intervention that meets criteria as a well-established treatment. While there can be many reasons for this finding, one likely possibility is that the initiation, perpetuation, and resolution of adolescent disruptive behaviors is highly contingent upon parenting/familial factors. Thus, as was the case in the treatment of adolescent substance abuse disorders, including parents and broader systems in any treatment of adolescent DBD's seems not only indicated but imperative.

With a broader systems perspective in mind, it is hardly surprising that multisystemic therapy (MST) (Henggeler & Lee, 2003) has been identified as one of the fifteen probably efficacious treatments for DBDs (Eyberg et al., 2008). MST has been extensively studied with adolescents who have engaged in serious antisocial and delinquent behaviors. As the intervention's name suggests, it is an intensive and multisystems approach to intervention that includes individual, family, and community-based components. The intervention specifically targets teenagers who are at high risk for requiring out-of-home placements due to aggressive, noncompliant, and/or delinquent behaviors with a chief goal being to keep the client in the home. CBT, parent training, family therapy, and pharmacological therapies are common components of the treatment package. Therapy occurs in the client's home. The typical course of treatment lasts between three to five months. However, during this time therapists are available to families at virtually all times and several contacts can occur over the course of a week. MST also emphasizes the importance of recognizing a family's strengths, increasing the adolescent's engagement in responsible behavior, fostering developmental appropriate competencies in both school and social settings, and assessing how problems are maintained within a family's current social environment. In this regard it reflects a general adherence to a cognitive-behavioral model of therapy. While it is a conceptually compelling and effective intervention, MST demands a lot of a therapist and is a costly intervention to implement. Thus its generalizability may be limited even though the authors of the approach make a compelling case for the resources that can be recouped through prevention.

Problem-solving skills training (PSST) (Kazdin, 2003) is another probably efficacious treatment that merits consideration here. Though the majority of studies conducted examining its efficacy have focused on children ranging from 7 to 13 years old, problem-solving and social skills deficits are commonly found in adolescents who meet the criteria for ODD or CDD. PSST teaches youth critical skills in identifying problems, developing multiple solutions, weighing decisions, and evaluating the impact of one's decisions. The information is imparted through in-session role-plays, behavioral modeling, corrective feedback, and homework assignments designed to test skill acquisition. This general approach, when utilized in combination with parent training where parents are taught how to promote and encourage their child's use of effective problem-solving skills, may be especially effective in reducing disruptive behaviors (Kazdin et al., 1987).

In summary, there are several potential modalities and areas of treatment focus that can remediate adolescent disruptive behaviors. Clinicians functioning in real-world settings with limited time and resources who also want to remain mindful of avoiding dual-role dilemmas may need to limit the scope of their intervention. One may not be able to do it *all,* a point that is unfortunately often lost on many researchers. So what is one to do? While there is no simple answer to the question of what single intervention represents the wisest use of a single therapist's attention and focus, some research attention has been devoted to this question. Specifically, in an attempt to delineate the most effective modality for preventing the escalation of adolescent DBDs, Dishion and Andrews (1995) compared a parent-training intervention with an adolescent-focused intervention in a sample of 119 families who included an adolescent engaged in disruptive behaviors. The parent intervention focused on the parents' use of noncoercive and effective parenting practices, while the adolescent focused intervention included self-regulation and social communication development. Overall, the researchers found evidence to support two general principles in working with adolescents who demonstrate disruptive behavioral concerns. First, they argue that interventions that have a strong parent and family focus are the most efficacious. Second, they believe that interventions that meet families in their home settings may also have the greatest relative impact. Working directly with the adolescent in an individual setting on social skills, social emotional regulation, and problem solving skills may be somewhat helpful in the shorter term. Adhering to these general principles would seem to be a prudent course of action.

EI Conceptualization

A review of the literature reveals that most existential theorists and therapists are silent when it comes to contemplating the roots of DBDs and their treatment. Schneider (2008) does not offer a specific opinion on where ODD and CD fall along the hyper-constrictive/hyper-expansive continuums of human existence. His conceptualization of other related diagnoses, however, provides important clues as to how DBDs might be conceptualized from an EI perspective. For example, in the case of disorders related to impulsivity (e.g., ADHD), he argues that the associated dread is of ultimate constriction. These individuals are thought to struggle in more regimented settings where certain routines are expected. Similarly, Schneider believes APD also reflects a dread of constriction where feelings of vulnerability, weakness, and/or victimization are avoided or negated through the adoption of a callous and aggressive interpersonal stance.

One might reasonably conclude, therefore, that ODD and CD are viewed in a similar manner from an EI perspective. Specifically, children and adolescents who struggle with deep-seated fears related to a dread of ultimate constriction may adopt an aggressive, oppositional, and/ornon-conformist interpersonal stance that represents a malignant over-compensation. As has been noted by Diamond (1996), acute inferiority feelings posited by Adler (1924) may be particularly salient for these youth and perhaps represent Individual Psychology's corollary to the existential threat of nonbeing. That these youth choose to assert their will, power, and being through defiance, aggression, and disregard for rules may be due to a combination of (a) the depth of their inferiority/nonbeing fears and (b) their exposure to the aforementioned genetic, temperamental, early attachment, parenting, familial, and other environmental risk factors for DBDs. One could further speculate that early childhood trauma, especially instances where the life of the child felt threatened, might further activate hyper-constrictive dreads that ultimately lead to aggressive and/or predatory interpersonal stances. In these cases, the adolescent has chosen to "fight" rather than to "flight" when under siege.

Of course, the range of motivations for aggressive, noncompliant, and/or illegal behaviors are multifold, and there are likely multiple case scenarios whereby a dread of ultimate expansion could account for these types of behaviors. For example, an adolescent who struggles with the ultimate anxiety of meaninglessness (chaos) may lash out or adopt a defiant attitude because, "Nothing matters anyway". This refrain, along with "I don't care!" and "Whatever!?!", have often been uttered by young clients the author has worked with who demonstrate an oppositional pattern of relating to the world. Often the youth is shouting these sentiments loudly and with passion. The amplified and animated tone allows one to hope that the care still exists, but the youth feels frustrated in their ability to be understood, affirmed, and/or to assert their will or agency.

Another hyper-expansive dread that could account for disruptive behaviors could be a struggle coming to terms with one's freedom and capacity to make an infinite array of life choices. The associated tension that comes with this fear is a concern with assuming responsibility for one's choices and actions. Again, while some adolescents who struggle with this existential concern seem to retreat within themselves and develop internalizing symptoms of depression and/or anxiety, there are others who seem more prone to compensating by adopting a negative attitude toward authority and/or by abdicating responsibility for making prosocial life choices altogether. In essence, they abandon the project of becoming responsible adults and resent/challenge those who tell them to behave as such. It is only through a close analysis of a client's self-narrative that one can truly begin to understand the causal mechanisms behind oppositional and aggressive behaviors. For there could be multiple pathways triggered at least in part by existential concerns that could lead to disruptive behaviors.

Existential analyses of adult aggression, violence, and antisocial behavior seem to generally confirm this premise. Diamond's (1996) and May's (1969; 1972) study of these behavioral stances, in particular, offer important insights that have implications for the discussion here. To begin, Diamond (1996) identifies rage as a critical source of violent behavior in humans. As was proposed above, he argues this emotion is an, "instinctual, defensive reaction to severe stress or physical threat" in which one's fight or flight response is activated. Thus, the existential threat of nonbeing can be the source of rage. He further describes the emotion as a "daimonic passion, capable of blindly pushing us into violently destructive behavior" (pg. 14). However, he takes pains to note that rage is not an inherently destructive emotion that will universally lead to violence. Further, he agrees with May and Sartre that engaging in violence can be a life affirming experience for the perpetrator where a sense of power, vitality, risk, and freedom can occur.

Rage, however, is not the only emotion that Diamond (1996) believes can fuel aggressive and/or violent behaviors. Specifically, frustration, which he defines as "that exasperating feeling of being foiled, thwarted, blocked, or baffled in our best efforts to find satisfaction" can also lead to aggression and ultimately violence (pg. 25). Diamond agrees with Rank that frustration begins at birth when the infant is forced from a mother's womb and faces daily life struggles to fulfill his or her destiny. Like rage, however, he takes pains to note that feelings of frustration do not always lead to aggressive behaviors. Still, he certainly allows for the fact that some youth and adults cope with this emotion in maladaptive ways that can resemble a DBD presentation. May (1972), too, believes powerlessness is the root of much violence, likening violent acts to "the explosion of impotence" (pg. 53). In fact, he argues that individuals who fail to achieve a sense of self-affirmation will be most vulnerable to engaging in aggressive and even violent acts. In clinical practice, the author frequently conducts post hoc analyses of fighting behaviors with his clients only to learn that frequently the main source of the physical aggression was frustration related to having one's plans thwarted or an inability to be understood or accepted by another. Many of these youth struggle to put words to their emotional experience and become vulnerable to resorting to physical aggression because of the challenge verbally expressing their emotions. Significant gains can often be made in reducing these physically aggressive outbursts by helping the youth identify his or her core emotion of frustration related to a sense of powerlessness and then providing alternative ways to cope with the emotion and communicate one's needs.

Beyond existential struggles pertaining to the threats of nonbeing, powerlessness, and being thrown into a life not of one's choice, Diamond believes "our sense of alienation, aloneness, and isolation" can be an additional existential source of violence. May (1969) agrees, writing that, "loneliness and its stepchild, alienation, can become forms of demon possession" (pg. 162). At a later point in time he further argued that if a youth's, "need for love and care is unmet, he may well become destructively aggressive and spend his life wreaking revenge upon the world" (May, 1972, pg. 124). Thus, those individuals who crave but fail to establish intimate connections with others may develop feelings of rage that can ultimately lead to violence. For certain, while maladaptive and unsustainable, making contact with another through an aggressive and/or oppositional stance does momentarily bridge the gap that isolates the individual from another. This is obviously what is commonly referred to from a CBT perspective as the youth seeking negative attention. Normalizing the urge for connection and teaching social skills designed to promote the establishment of meaningful positive connections are the common treatment responses when this dynamic is observed. Thus, there may be multiple existential concerns that trigger aggressive, oppositional, and/or violent behavior in adults that similarly affect youth.

Yet, could it not still be that some individuals, youth included, who engage in violent, cruel, hostile, and/or sadistic behaviors are evil or are at least choosing to engage in evil behaviors? As discussed in Chapter 4, psychology has often avoided discussions of evil, perhaps because of the religious and theological implications associated with the term (Diamond, 1996). The term is also harder to define. Diamond (1996) has tried, defining human evil as, "those attitudes and behaviors that promote excessive interpersonal aggression, cruelty, hostility, disregard for the integrity of others, self-destructiveness, psychopathology, and human misery in general" (pg. 57). May (1969), in his discussion of the daimonic, makes a strong case that individuals who deny the existence of any natural power within them that has the potential to take over their existence will be vulnerable to engaging in evil acts. Specifically, to avoid succumbing to one's darker impulses one must, "identify with that which haunts you, not in order to fight it off, but to take it into yourself" (pg. 133). Thus, as previously discussed in Chapter 4, it is incumbent upon the individual to engage in a consistent dialogue with oneself and others about one's inner hauntings and uglier impulses to avoid being overcome by them. Yet, as May notes, there will always be an element of distortion and self-aggrandizement in this self-analysis for even otherwise high-functioning adults.

What can one, therefore, reasonably expect of a preteen or teenager? Put differently, exactly what percentage of youth are capable of perpetually engaging in a penetrating self-analysis designed to more effectively integrate one's shadow side and steer clear of acts of violence and evil? Are DBDs the behavioral expression of a youth who either refuses to engage in cogent self-reflection and/or does so ineffectively? There are obviously no easy answers to these questions. Clearly the absence of prosocial role models and empathically attuned support systems makes it much less likely that a youth will be able to own up to, analyze, and channel one's destructive and unsavory urges in prosocial ways. But May firmly believes that each individual still should be held responsible for his or willingness to at least *try* to look within and self-improve. Some youth seem more inclined to do this than others. A perpetual unwillingness to look within, a mood congruent emotional experience when engaging in destructive, hurtful, and/or violent acts, a consistent lack of interest in contemplating the impact of one's behavior on others, perhaps these are the factors that distinguish a more environmental/state-like explanation from a characterological explanation of evil acts. Perhaps these are also the types of presenting concerns a clinician observes when he or she wrestles with the concept of whether evil exists and can be treated.

Shifting focus from the concept of evil, May (1950) also believed firmly that anxiety is the root emotion that underlies most, if not all, major psychiatric disturbances. He posited a very close link between anxiety and repression. More specifically, he observed that individuals often experience anxiety when they repress certain normative daimonic urges, such as those related to sexuality, hostility, and aggression. Thus, as previously stated it was the individual's failure to successful attend to and integrate these urges into their personality – not the urges themselves – that could lead to anxiety and neurotic formations. In cases of more extreme forms of repression the individual could become vulnerable to psychosis and/or rage reactions. Beyond repression, however, anxiety can be the emotion that often underlies frustration. Recalling the aforementioned cases where youth engage in fighting behaviors when they feel powerless to control their destiny, there is clearly an anxiety component to the frustration. Returning full circle, the core existential givens that one is alone, one will die, and life may have no inherent meaning are all sources of normative anxiety that also have the potential to lead to maladjustment. Thus, while anxiety may not be the root cause of all DBDs, this emotion often plays a critical role.

EI Case Example

Greta was a 13-year-old female referred to counseling by her parents prior to the holidays.[1] She had recently been suspended from school where she attended the eighth-grade for telling her math teaching to "go f...himself" when he asked her to remove her feet from a vacant chair next to her desk. School administrators had "strongly" suggested she attend counseling as a condition of her return to the classroom. The parents had been contemplating enrolling her in counseling prior to the suggestion so there was no consternation or hesitation on their part in seeking services. The oppositional behavior directed toward the math teacher was not an isolated incident but rather a culmination of increasingly provocative and noncompliant school behaviors directed toward multiple teachers and fellow students. The chief concerns were disruptive and disengaged classroom behaviors (e.g., making inappropriate comments, refusing to do work, muttering insults under her breath directed toward the teachers and several students), low academic achievement (she was flunking three out of five subjects), and bullying behaviors. Regarding this latter concern, earlier in the fall Greta had been accused of bullying a seventh-grade female repeatedly on the bus. While she had alternatively denied and then minimized the extent of aggression, the seventh grader had initially accused her of threatening to "rip her face off" and shoving her before backing off these allegations with the understanding that Greta would have no more contact with her. In short, Greta was leaving quite a wake in her path throughout the fall of her eighth year in school.

Greta's oppositional and aggressive behaviors were not isolated to school. As previously mentioned, her parents had been considering seeking psychiatric help prior to her suspension. During the initial phone inquiry her mother described Greta as a "terror" in the home and then proceeded to sob while recounting a long history of family turmoil. While she conceded that her daughter had always been "willful" and "independent minded," she stated these personality tendencies began to take on a more malignant quality in the summer before Greta began seventh grade. The onset had been insidious and without obvious cause. In her mother's opinion, Greta simply grew more rebellious, disengaged, and unmotivated. In recent months she had been isolating herself in her bedroom and refusing to do basic chores. She routinely spoke disrespectfully to her parents and older siblings, with her mother tearfully reporting over the phone that, "I've been called every name in the book." She often refused to sit with the family at dinner and was left at home during family outings because she was so disagreeable when forced to attend the parents had essentially abandoned hope of including her in a meaningful way.

While her mother couldn't be sure because Greta refused to speak with her about aspects of her personal life, there was no evidence that Greta maintained any casual, let alone, close friendships. On weekends she would retreat to her room, read, listen to music, and/or play video games on her computer or a game console she had in her bedroom. It was hard for her mother to know exactly what her daughter did because Greta frequently locked her bedroom door. The only small leverage the parents felt they had was restricting her access to her computer, phone, and game console when she became too unruly. But they instituted this consequence inconsistently and sparingly, fearing the backlash that would come when Greta was deprived of these outlets. Her mother also noted that Greta had never participated in sports, in part because she suffered from a congenital condition that led her to have a noticeable limp and inability to run fast or maintain her balance at a level required for competitive sports. She recalled that Greta wore a bulky leg brace for much of her youth and had been quite sensitive about this vulnerability when younger.

In regard to family constellation, Greta was the youngest of four siblings, all girls. Her oldest sister was attending a prestigious college as a freshman while her remaining sisters were excelling academically and athletically in the twelfth and tenth grades at the local high school. Greta's mother commented repeatedly throughout the course of therapy that her older sisters were also physically attractive, referring to them often as "stunning" and "model material." By contrast, she noted that Greta refused to consistently attend to her personal hygiene and self-care, describing her as "dumpy" and "greasy." In short, Greta's older siblings were tough acts for a youngest child to follow. While initially supportive and patient, her older sisters had withdrawn from Greta in recent months and now communication was essentially nonexistent. Greta's father was a successful corporate attorney for a large law firm who was rarely at home and travelled frequently. He would ultimately only attend two counseling sessions. He expressed bewilderment and frustration toward his youngest daughter, frequently comparing her unfavorably with her older siblings.

While all family members were requested to attend the initial family consultation, Greta's mother stated this would simply be impossible as her husband was travelling and the two older siblings who lived at home had mandatory extracurricular activities. The author chose to still meet with Greta and her mother given the acuity of the concerns and in the spirit of meeting the family "where they are at." At the date and time the initial consultation was scheduled, however, Greta's mother appeared alone and distressed, stating that Greta was refusing to leave the car. She had apparently asked Greta to go for a ride with her under the pretense of attending a medical doctor's appointment, but when Greta realized the true nature of the appointment upon arriving at an office she did not recognize she refused to budge from her seat. To be clear the author had not advised Greta's mother to act in this somewhat deceitful manner, as there are rarely occasions when an adolescent will react positively to attending a counseling appointment in a state of surprise and betrayal. The author advised Greta's mother not to try and force Greta to enter the building against her will and suggested a combination of incentives for attending and consequences for refusing to attend the next appointment. The author also advised Greta's mother to link her daughter's resistance to attending to behavioral markers of positive change both at home and school.

The second attempt at an initial family consultation was slightly more successful in regard to Greta's participation. The good news was that Greta did attend. The not so good news was that, when the author went to greet her and her mother in the waiting area, she refused to look up from her phone and sighed "This is bulls... " when her mother encouraged her to do so. She then persisted in playing a video game on her phone and refused to leave her waiting area seat to follow the author and her mother into the room where the session would occur. The author, mindful of not getting into a power struggle, gently encouraged Greta to come into the therapy room "when you are ready" and left it to Greta and her mother to negotiate whether she would physically enter the therapy room. Several minutes later, after heated words were overheard between Greta and her mother in the waiting area, Greta stormed into the therapy room and crashed down into the couch, hissing "You happy now, bitch?" at her mother in the process. Her mother, upon hearing Greta's "bitch" comment, collapsed as if she had been shot into a chair and began sobbing silently in her seat. Greta seemed far from moved by her mother's display of emotion, sighing again in disgust before commenting, "Oh. So now you are going to try the guilt trip thing again." The author, a master of the obvious, thought it best to start by gently making the simple observation, "Hmm. I sense some tension here." Greta, who was wearing a hooded sweatshirt with the hood on in a way that hid much of her face, finally looked up from her phone and made eye contact through strands of her disheveled brown hair. She smirked upon hearing such an apparently moronic statement and then exclaimed, "No s…, Sherlock!". Therapy commenced from there.

Throughout the remainder of the initial consultation Greta barely spoke, initially refusing to answer even the most basic questions regarding her understanding of the purpose and nature of the appointment, her experiences at home and school, and her thoughts about attending. She did state the appointment was a "waste of time" and she was only attending in order to keep her phone and computer privileges. She also repeatedly muttered the word "bulls… " when her mother was recalling a laundry list of oppositional, aggressive, and noncompliant behaviors Greta had demonstrated in the home and at school. Further, she accused the author of being motivated solely by greed and mocked several of the questions posed to her. Such insults are hardly uncommon when the author works with adolescents who meet diagnostic criteria for a DBD. Still, it takes discipline and self-awareness to remain nondefensive and unemotional when one is serially being verbally eviscerated. Obviously therapists can set limits on what will be tolerated in terms of insults and provocations. The author tends to give clients a fair amount of latitude in terms of the amount and/or types of insults that are deemed acceptable, reframing them as a function of the adolescent's feelings of powerlessness, anxiety, and frustration.

Sensing Greta's staunch resistance and oppositional stance, the author incorporated two principles in working with her during that initial session. To begin, the author approached her from the Nonviolent Resistance (NVR) framework (Omer & Sappir, 2003), conceding the obvious point that he was powerless to make Greta participate in any meaningful way in therapy but remained hopeful and ready to work with Greta should she so choose. Secondly, the author remained mindful of Edgette's (2006) point that many adolescents who attend therapy not of their choosing will need to "save face" should they ultimately make the choice to participate in at least a minimally meaningful fashion. Thus, the author was careful not to push the point too aggressively that if she elected to continue to attend sessions and participate it would be because she was obviously finding some meaning and value to the sessions. Doing so would likely have put her in an unnecessary bind that could have scared her off from the process altogether. In practice, combining these principles resulted in the following exchange. Specifically, when Greta stated, "I'm only here because my parents made me," the author replied by stating, "Well, I understand you have your pressures and reasons at home for being here. I just want you to know that, from my end, there will never be any pressure for you to attend sessions, remain in the room, or answer my questions if you do not feel ready to do so. I certainly hope you will participate. But I realize I have no power to make you do so." This approach, previously outlined in Chapter 4, seemed to defuse a potential power struggle between the author and Greta, and she became noticeably more communicative thereafter.

Toward the end of the initial session the focus turned to defining the goals of therapy, the therapeutic modality, and the frequency of contact. The author, already suspecting strongly that there were individual and familial concerns contributing to Greta's DBD presentation, thought the optimal treatment package would approximate that of MST (Henggeler & Lee, 2003), consisting of individual sessions, family sessions, and outreach efforts directed to Greta's school and other extended familial supports. The inclusion of a broader support network in the treatment process is also a key component of an NVR intervention whereby relatives and other key influences in the adolescent's life are informed of the client's progress in order to increase accountability and motivation to behave in a prosocial manner. Cognitive-behavioral techniques, including contingency management and cognitive restructuring (Greta did seem to evidence a pretty strong hostile attribution bias), along with parent training appeared to be likely components of the intervention. Finally, the author suspected core existential concerns of loneliness, freedom, and responsibility, as well as frustration pertaining to her vulnerabilities/limitations and "throwness" into a life not of her choosing might all be future areas of focus should Greta eventually be open to opening up.

Ever mindful of avoiding a dual role of serving as both an individual and family therapist, the author initially recommended the family pursue the services of a separate family counselor as part of a multimodal treatment approach. Unfortunately, both Greta and her mother rejected the concept of pursuing a separate family therapist out of hand: Greta, saying she had only agreed to seeing the author once a week and would "die" before setting foot in a second therapist's office, and Greta's mother restating what she had said during the initial phone consultation that it would be "impossible" to get the rest of the family to attend. Therapists take different stances when confronted with reality of a pursuing a potentially suboptimal treatment approach when a family cannot and/or will not comply with a best practice recommendation. The author admittedly tends to adopt an attitude of "I will do the best I can with what I have to work with" provided there seems to be a reasonable chance of success while others may understandably say "I won't invest my time and/or a family's time embarking on a treatment course that I know is less than optimal." In this case, the author was encouraged by Greta's minimal buy-in toward the end of the initial consultation (she was participating even if it mostly involved insults directed toward the therapist and her mother) and thought it very likely that the fragile alliance could be shattered by insisting on the family pursuing an additional therapist. Further, Greta's mother's point regarding the simple lack of her husband and other daughters' availability seemed hard to dispute. In the end, therefore, all parties ultimately agreed to a plan where Greta would primarily participate in individual sessions with periodic participation by her mother (and father if available) to discuss progress and attempt to minimally improve family communication. Further, channeling the spirit of MST, whenever possible the therapist would conduct sessions in the family's home for the purposes of joining the family and assessing/intervening when problematic familial communication occurred. Ultimately, over the course of a year-long treatment the author conducted five in-home sessions that proved to be very powerful and effective. Real-world limitations (i.e., the family lived twenty minutes away from the author's office and finding a mutually agreeable to time devote two hours for an appointment was hard) made regular in-home sessions impossible. The author also took great pains to clarify the nature of confidentiality and communication among family members at the start of the multimodal treatment intervention to avoid alliance ruptures.

For the most part, however, therapy consisted of weekly individual sessions with Greta that occurred at the author's office. In her first individual session following the initial consultation with her mother, Greta was hardly effusive. She again entered the session with her cell phone and proceeded to play a video game. The therapist gently reinforced her presence in the room and, for a limited time, asked several open-ended questions designed to establish some rapport and communication. Greta continued to play her video game and was alternately entirely unresponsive to questions and/or minimally responsive with one word answers or "Don't know" responses. The author, mindful of not getting drawn into a power struggle but also believing setting some minimal conditions for the therapeutic hour would be essential, eventually confronted the issue of her continuing to focus on her phone and the video game. The intervention consisted of the author stating, "Greta, I see that you are really interested in the game on your phone. I am not trying to be a pain but I really get distracted and find I can't really connect with my clients when they are focused on their phones. So if you really need to be on your phone I will need for you to do it in the waiting area. I hope you will choose to stay and we can work together today. But I can't make that choice for you." Greta responded to the statement by tossing the phone onto the couch while muttering, "Jesus. Really?" The author thanked her profusely for complying with the request and the session proceeded from there.

Over the course of the next several sessions, despite her best efforts to continue to resist cooperating, Greta began to open-up more about her life and struggles. Again, the core EI treatment approaches consisting of the therapist's empathically attuned presence, efforts to invoke the actual, and various strategies designed to work with client resistance undoubtedly played critical roles in the thawing process. Greta grudgingly came to accept the idea floated by the therapist that the most efficient way for her to get what she wanted in life – which was more freedom and an end to therapy – was to "go with the flow" a bit and minimally participate in the process. She also seemed genuinely disarmed by the fact that the therapist continued to greet her with an eager smile each week despite her multiple insults and provocations during the initial meetings. The narrative she seemed to have written about what therapy was going to be like simply did not match the actual experience. Her therapist had not sided with her parents, condemned her, or told her what to do and not do. Rather, he empathized with her struggle of being the youngest child in a family of high achievers, complimented her on her strong will and courage to participate in counseling, and expressed excitement about the prospect of collaboratively finding ways for her to channel her will into an interpersonal stance that would get her more of what she wanted.

Over time (i.e., several months), Greta began to feel comfortable enough to shed more and more light on what was driving at least some of her oppositional behaviors. As suspected, she had certainly struggled with inferiority feelings due to both her physical condition and her sense of not measuring up to her siblings in regard to her intellectual abilities, social status, and physical attractiveness. She recounted numerous instances where her parents directly and indirectly compared her unfavorably to her siblings. Her self-concept had suffered. As evidence of this she struggled to identify a single aspect of herself she liked upon being asked to identify three positive self-qualities. At the core she felt weak, vulnerable, undesirable, and insignificant, certainly feelings consistent with the EI core dread of hyper-constriction. Certainly feelings that could lead to over-compensatory efforts to assert one's power through aggressive means.

Still there was a significant, hidden-in-plain-sight trauma that also fueled Greta's oppositional stance. While all parties acknowledged the transition from middle school to junior high school had been particularly painful for her, a key causal reason for this was overlooked by Greta's parents and school administrators. Greta had been a bullying victim for much of seventh grade. Specifically, three older girls who rode the bus to and from school with her noticed her limp and began to refer to her as "Peg" which was short for "Peg-leg." To add insult to injury these girls shared their cruel nickname with several older boys on the bus as well and, for a while, it seemed to Greta that the entire bus was making her the butt of their jokes. Greta had braved these insults stoically, never shedding a tear in these students' presence or giving any indication that it affected her. But she was understandably deeply, deeply hurt, confused, scared, and enraged by these cruel attacks upon her. Eventually, she stated that she had tried to seek help from her mother but her mother had been dismissive of her, minimizing the bullying and essentially telling her to ignore the insults. It was around this point in time that Greta began to adopt a nihilistic attitude about life and rebel against her tormentors and family. If the world was going to be cruel and attempt to crush her, she was going to be cruel back and reclaim some power. At one point in counseling, she summarized this transformation by stating,

> "You know. I just had had enough. I started firing back at those girls on the bus. Even threatened to stab one of them with my pencil once. Might have even done it if they kept coming after me. You know, I had been fantasizing about doing it. This got them off my back. I think they knew I meant business. They didn't even tell anyone because they knew they had been giving me s... all along. It was the best feeling in the world to finally fight back!"

Of all the techniques and approaches utilized in a nearly year-long intensive treatment protocol simply building up enough trust and safety in the therapeutic relationship to allow Greta to summon the courage to share her painful bullying story with an empathic other was perhaps the most powerful and effective. The author validated her experience, normalized her wide range of thoughts and emotions related to her bullying experiences on the bus and invalidating experiences at home, and cultivated a hero narrative in Greta in place of the villain narrative she had resigned herself to pursue. Greta had been painfully isolated and alone for nearly two years at the time she began counseling. This had made her less vulnerable to being hurt, of course, but it had come at a great expense of snuffing her hope, sense of creativity, and yearning to connect with others. While the positive connection she was able to make with a therapist who was patient with her and deeply committed to hearing her story was far from the only factor that resulted in her ultimately positive turnaround, it seemed to play a critical role in restoring some hope and confidence in her that better days were ahead. Through a combination of intense individual work, parent-training, and poignant family meetings where her parents grew to better appreciate Greta and her bullying experiences, a significant reduction in disruptive and oppositional behaviors were achieved over the course of therapy. Conceptualizing many of Greta's struggles from an EI framework and utilizing core EI treatment approaches most certainly contributed to the positive outcome.

Note

1. The cases depicted in the book are composite representations of multiple client experiences where names, gender, and other potentially identifiable aspects of the case experience have been changed to protect client confidentiality.

References

Adler, A. (1924). *The practice and theory of individual psychology.* Oxford, England: Harcourt, Brace.

American Psychiatric Association (2016). DSM-5 Psychiatry Online. http://dsm.psychiatryonline.org/doi/book/10.1176/appi.books.9781585624836.

Bongers, I. L., Koot, H. M., van der Ende, J., & Verhulst, F. C. (2004). Developmental trajectories of externalizing behaviors in childhood and adolescence. *Child Development, 75*(5), 1523–1537. doi:10.1111/j.1467-8624.2004.00755.x

Boylan, K., Vaillancourt, T., Boyle, M., & Szatmari, P. (2007). Comorbidity of internalizing disorders in children with oppositional defiant disorder. *European Child & Adolescent Psychiatry, 16*(8), 484–494. doi:10.1007/s00787-007-0624-1

Brestan, E. V., & Eyberg, S. M. (1998). Effective psychosocial treatments of conduct-disordered children and adolescents: 29 years, 82 studies, and 5,272 kids. *Journal Of Clinical Child Psychology, 27*(2), 180–189. doi:10.1207/s15374424jccp2702_5

Burke, J. D., Waldman, I., & Lahey, B. B. (2010). Predictive validity of childhood oppositional defiant disorder and conduct disorder: Implications for the DSM-V. *Journal Of Abnormal Psychology, 119*(4), 739–751. doi:10.1037/a0019708

Byrd, A. L., Loeber, R., & Pardini, D. A. (2012). Understanding desisting and persisting forms of delinquency: The unique contributions of disruptive behavior disorders and interpersonal callousness. *Journal Of Child Psychology And Psychiatry, 53*(4), 371–380. doi:10.1111/j.1469-7610.2011.02504.x

Canino, G., Polanczyk, G., Bauermeister, J. J., Rohde, L. A., & Frick, P. J. (2010). Does the prevalence of CD and ODD vary across cultures?. *Social Psychiatry And Psychiatric Epidemiology, 45*(7), 695–704. doi:10.1007/s00127-010-0242-y

Chambless, D. L., & Hollon, S. D. (1998). Defining empirically supported therapies. *Journal Of Consulting And Clinical Psychology, 66*(1), 7–18. doi:10.1037/0022-006X.66.1.7

Costello, E. J., Egger, H., & Angold, A. (2005). 10-Year Research Update Review: The Epidemiology of Child and Adolescent Psychiatric Disorders: I. Methods and Public Health Burden. *Journal Of The American Academy Of Child & Adolescent Psychiatry, 44*(10), 972–986. doi:10.1097/01.chi.0000172552.41596.6f

Diamond, S. A. (1996). *Anger, madness, and the daimonic: The psychological genesis of violence, evil, and creativity*. Albany, NY, US: State University of New York Press.

Dishion, T. J., & Andrews, D. W. (1995). Preventing escalation in problem behaviors with high- risk young adolescents: Immediate and 1-year outcomes. *Journal Of Consulting And Clinical Psychology, 63*(4), 538–548. doi:10.1037/0022-006X.63.4.538

Edgette, J. S. (2006). *Adolescent therapy that really works: Helping kids who never asked for help in the first place*. New York, NY, US: W W Norton & Co.

Eyberg, S. M., Nelson, M. M., & Boggs, S. R. (2008). Evidence-based psychosocial treatments for children and adolescents with disruptive behavior. *Journal Of Clinical Child And Adolescent Psychology, 37*(1), 215–237. doi:10.1080/15374410701820117

Forgatch, M. S., Rains, L. A., & Sigmarsdóttir, M. (2016). Early results from implementing PMTO: Full transfer on a grand scale. In M. J. Van Ryzin, K. L. Kumpfer, G. M. Fosco, M. T. Greenberg (Eds.), *Family- based prevention programs for children and adolescents: Theory, research, and large- scale dissemination* (pp. 113–133). New York, NY, US: Psychology Press.

Gathright, M. M. & Tyler, L. H. (2014). *Disruptive behaviors in children and adolescents.* Arkansas: Psychiatric Research Institute.

Henggeler, S. W., & Lee, T. (2003). Multisystemic treatment of serious clinical problems. In A. E. Kazdin, J. R. Weisz (Eds.), *Evidence-based psychotherapies for children and adolescents* (pp. 301–322). New York, NY, US: Guilford Press.

Hicks, B. M., Krueger, R. F., Lacono, W. G., McGue, M., & Patrick, C. J. (2004). Family transmission and heritability of externalizing disorders: A twin-family study. *Archives Of General Psychiatry, 61*(9), 922–928. doi:10.1001/archpsyc.61.9.922

Kazdin, A. E. (2003). Problem-solving skills training and parent management training for conduct disorder. In A. E. Kazdin, J. R. Weisz (Eds.), *Evidence-based psychotherapies for children and adolescents* (pp. 241–262). New York, NY, US: Guilford Press.

Kazdin, A. E., Esveldt-Dawson, K., French, N. H., & Unis, A. S. (1987). Effects of parent management training and problem-solving skills training combined in the treatment of antisocial child behavior. *Journal Of The American Academy Of Child & Adolescent Psychiatry, 26*(3), 416–424. doi:10.1097/00004583-198705000-00024

Loeber, R., & Burke, J. D. (2011). Developmental pathways in juvenile externalizing and internalizing problems. *Journal Of Research On Adolescence, 21*(1), 34–46. doi:10.1111/j.1532-7795.2010.00713.x

May, R. (1950). *The meaning of anxiety.* New York, NY, US: Ronald Press Company. doi:10.1037/10760-000

May, R. (1969). *Existential psychology.* New York, NY, US: Crown Publishing Group/Random House.

May, R. (1972). *Power and innocence: A search for the sources of violence.* Oxford, England: W. W. Norton.

McKinney, C., & Morse, M. (2012). Assessment of disruptive behavior disorders: Tools and recommendations. *Professional Psychology: Research And Practice, 43*(6), 641–649. doi:10.1037/a0027324

Moffitt, T. E., & Scott, S. (2008). Conduct disorders of childhood and adolescence. In M. Rutter, D. Bishop, D. Pine, S. Scott, J. Stevenson, E. Taylor, ... A. Thapar (Eds.), *Rutter's child and adolescent psychiatry* (pp. 543–564). New York: Wiley-Blackwell. doi:10.1002/9781444300895.ch35

NICHD Early Child Care Research Network. (2004). Type of child care and children's development at 54 months. *Early Childhood Research Quarterly, 19*(2), 203–230.

Nock, M. K. (2003). Progress review of the psychosocial treatment of child conduct problems. *Clinical Psychology: Science and Practice*, *10*(1), 1–28.

Omer, H. & Sappir, S. L. (2003). *Non-violent resistance: A new approach to violent and self-destructive children*. New York: Cambridge University Press.

Patterson, G.R., Reid, J.B., Jones, R.R. & Conger, R.E. (1975). *A social learning approach to family intervention, volume 1: Families with aggressive children*. Eugene, OR: Castalia Publishing Company.

Rowe, R., Costello, E. J., Angold, A., Copeland, W. E., & Maughan, B. (2010). Developmental pathways in oppositional defiant disorder and conduct disorder. *Journal Of Abnormal Psychology*, *119*(4), 726–738. doi:10.1037/a0020798

Schneider, K. J. (2008). *Existential-integrative psychotherapy: Guideposts to the core of practice*. New York, NY, US: Routledge/Taylor & Francis Group.

Stringaris, A., & Goodman, R. (2009). Longitudinal outcome of youth oppositionality: Irritable, headstrong, and hurtful behaviors have distinctive predictions. *Journal Of The American Academy Of Child & Adolescent Psychiatry*, *48*(4), 404–412. doi:10.1097/CHI.0b013e3181984f30

Tremblay, R. E. (2010). Developmental origins of disruptive behaviour problems: The original sin hypothesis, epigenetics and their consequences for prevention. *Journal Of Child Psychology And Psychiatry*, *51*(4), 341–367. doi:10.1111/j.1469-7610.2010.02211.x

CHAPTER 9

EI Approaches to Treating Trauma

Introduction

It seems fitting to close out this book with a chapter devoted to exploring how EI treatment approaches can be utilized with adolescents who have experienced trauma. Unfortunately, few if any individuals are entirely protected from trauma experiences during youth. As Rank (1924) noted in "The Trauma of Birth," from infancy one experiences an acute sense of vulnerability, need, and powerlessness, feelings that represent an accurate reflection of the state of one's affairs. While over time as one matures he or she develops an increasing sense of agency and power, for most a sense of personal inferiority and awareness of life's fragility lingers. Thus, there is a universality to the experience of fear for one's safety, the safety of loved ones, the senselessness and cruelty of life, and moments of horror and deep despair. For some the awareness is heightened when they are exposed to abuse, neglect, deprivation, and/or are witness to man-made or natural horrors. But, again, it would take a pretty idealistic existence for one to escape virtually all threat.

Schneider (2008) recognizes the universality of trauma experiences, featuring this aspect of human existence prominently in his conceptualization of existential anxiety and human psychopathology. As outlined in Chapter 1, he identifies three types of trauma – acute trauma, chronic trauma, and implicit trauma – as critical sources of influence that shape the way in which an individual comes to experience the universal hyper-constrictive and hyper-expansive polarities of the human condition.

D. Shumaker, *Existential-Integrative Approaches to Treating Adolescents*, DOI 10.1057/978-1-349-95211-3_9

Similarly, the model of existential anxiety proposed in this work identifies early trauma experiences as one of three major influences that impact the extent to which an adolescent may struggle with existential angst. While the ultimate anxiety pertaining to the hyper-constrictive dread of non-being is most often associated with trauma, certainly other ultimate anxieties can be activated as well when one experiences trauma. For example, a profound sense of life's meaninglessness can occur when one experiences and/or witnesses senseless atrocities. Can life truly hold meaning for a child who is abused or neglected by those who are supposed to care and protect? What sense can we reasonably expect a child to make of 911 or Hurricane Katrina? Thus, trauma experiences can activate many ultimate concerns associated with the human condition that can destabilize an adolescent's sense of the world at large and his or her place in it.

While trauma experiences can certainly trigger a DSM-5 PTSD presentation, it can be a risk factor for the development of anxiety, depressive, DBD, and substance abuse disorders as well as other adjustment concerns. Indeed, several of the case examples cited in this book featured premorbid trauma histories that appeared to play prominent roles in symptom development. Thus, it is important for clinicians who work with adolescents to remain open to the influence of trauma on the development and formation of virtually all presenting concerns. Further, while the DSM-5 maintains rigorous diagnostic standards for the type of environmental exposure that meets criteria for a trauma experience (i.e., indirect or direct exposure to death, threatened death, actual or threatened serious injury, or actual or threatened sexual violence), there are life experiences that may not meet this standard where one's sense of safety and vulnerability are activated. Cyber bullying, growing up in a home where one's parents are interlocked in a high-conflict divorce, and bearing witness to the death of a loved one even if it occurs under "natural" circumstances (e.g., loss of a grandparent to old age), can all be traumatic experiences for a youth that will potentially awaken dormant existential concerns. In these cases the youth may not feel in immediate fear for his or her safety or the safety of a loved one, but a threat is still perceived and weighs heavily. This chapter attempts to account for the influence of these types of traumas as well. For it is the author's contention that any life event that is experienced as a threat (including micro-aggressions), invalidates one's existence, and/or is experienced as the willful cruelty of another upon oneself has the potential to seriously damage a youth's psyche and activate the dreaded polarities of one's existence.

Clinical Description, Incidence, and Prevalence

There are several DSM-5 disorders associated with trauma experiences, including PTSD, acute stress disorder, adjustment disorders, and two disorders that are seen in childhood, reactive attachment disorder (RAD) and disinhibited social engagement disorder. All share the common feature of exposure to a traumatic or stressful event as a diagnostic component (American Psychiatric Association, 2017). The distress associated with exposure to a traumatic event can vary, with most individuals demonstrating a fear or anxiety-based reaction, while others may develop depressive, aggressive, and/or dissociative symptoms. The specific disorders vary in additional ways, including the typical age or timing of onset, the symptom pattern following trauma exposure, and the intensity and scope of maladjustment related to trauma exposure. The two disorders with a childhood onset, RAD, and disinhibited social engagement disorder, as well as PTSD will be explored in greater detail here.

RAD is characterized by a marked disturbance in a child's attachment relations. The individual rarely seeks out the protection, comfort, or support of a primary attachment figure and also rarely responds to the supportive efforts of a caretaker when distressed. These individuals also demonstrate a persistent and pervasive social and emotional disturbance. For example, they are often minimally responsive to others, demonstrate limited positive affect, or experience seemingly unprovoked episodes of irritability, sadness, or fear when engaged in nonthreatening interactions with caretakers. Finally, the child must have experienced "extreme" deficits of care such as chronic social and/or emotional neglect, repeated changes in caregivers that prevented the development of a secure attachment, and/or rearing in unusual settings that limited the opportunity for the child to form a selective attachment (e.g., an Eastern European orphanage). It is important to note that individuals diagnosed with RAD are believed to have the capacity to form selective attachments. They simply are not behaviorally inclined to do so given their histories of extreme deprivation. Presumably their earliest comfort seeking efforts went unheard and, later in life, they do not expect nor receive comfort when opportunities are offered. Of course, giving and receiving emotional support is a social skill that requires practice. So, while these individuals may retain the capacity to do so, their skill in doing so may be lacking.

The prevalence of RAD is unknown, but the disorder is assumed to be quite rare (American Psychiatric Association, 2017). It most commonly occurs in populations of children raised in foster care. However, Gleason and colleagues (2011) note that even in samples of youth who have been raised in foster care less than 10% of these children will meet diagnostic criteria for the disorder. The typical age of onset occurs anywhere between the ages of 9 months and 5 years old. The prognosis for these children appears highly dependent upon the quality of the caregiving following the discovery of the attachment deficits (Smyke et al., 2012). Little is known about gender or cultural differences in the prevalence rate, course, or symptom configuration of the disorder. In summary, while GAD seems rare and research is lacking, it is a disorder that provides compelling evidence that there can be devastating consequences when infants, toddlers, and young children are deprived of consistent and emotionally supportive attachment relationships. Youth in these cases have likely faced chronic and extreme fear of death, isolation, and abandonment from birth that results in a withdrawal from others rooted in a pervasive (yet well-placed) distrust in humanity. As these youth reach adolescence it is entirely possible that this interpersonal stance may come into conflict with environmental demands, leading to significant adjustment concerns and even existential angst as the individual is forced to confront whether trusting others and intimacy is a worthy life pursuit.

Disinhibited social engagement disorder is a more recently formulated diagnostic category that is similar in certain respects to RAD. The main difference is that, rather than a lack of emotional support seeking, the key diagnostic feature is a tendency to approach and interact with unfamiliar adults in an indiscriminate and socially inappropriate manner. Specifically, children in these cases will behave in an overly familiar manner with strangers in terms of both physical contact and verbal interactions. They are prone to wander off with unfamiliar adults and/or to fail and check-in with their primary caretakers even in unfamiliar settings. Like RAD, the second main diagnostic feature of disinhibited social engagement disorder is a history of severely deficient care that can include neglect, frequent caretaker changes, and/or a history of being raised in unusual settings. However, it is important to note that it is possible for the condition to occur when there are no obvious signs of an attachment disorder. The child, for example, can have a history of neglect, yet still seem to have a secure attachment to a caregiver while remaining vulnerable to approaching strangers in an overly familiar and socially inappropriate manner (Gleason et al., 2011).

Like RAD, disinhibited social engagement disorder appears to be very rare though precise prevalence estimates are unknown (American Psychiatric Association, 2017). Gleason et al., (2011) estimate as many as 20% of children raised in extreme deprivation settings may demonstrate this pattern of relating to strangers. In virtually all cases severe neglect occurs in the first months of life (Zeanah et al., 2005). Extreme attention-seeking behaviors often accompany the socially indiscriminate behaviors seen during toddler and preschool years (Tizard & Hodges, 1978). Upon reaching adolescence, many youth diagnosed with this disorder struggle to form meaningful and satisfactory peer relationships (Hodges & Tizard, 1989). Thus, the interpersonal deficits stemming from early neglect and deprivation can be long-standing and extremely debilitating. Conceptually it may be harder to understand the existential experience of adolescents diagnosed with this disorder. While outward signs of anxiety may be lacking, the indiscriminate pursuit of relationships coupled with difficulties forming closer connections to others suggest that loneliness and nonbeing concerns may also be activated in these individuals but the behavioral response is a hyper-expansive overcompensation as opposed to a hyper-constrictive retreat into oneself.

Shifting focus to the most well-known trauma-related disorder, PTSD consists of five major diagnostic criteria. In brief, these include the following: (1) exposure to actual or threatened death, serious injury, or sexual violence in at least one of four ways; (2) presence of at least one of five intrusive symptoms associated with the traumatic event; (3) persistent avoidance of stimuli associated with the intrusive event in at least one of two possible ways; (4) negative alterations in cognitions and mood associated with the traumatic event in at least two of seven possible ways; and (5) marked alterations in arousal and reactivity associated with the traumatic event in at least two of six possible ways. The intrusive re-experiencing events, avoidant behaviors, and cognitive/mood-related disturbances must also have been present for at least a month. The DSM-5 also includes specifiers for the presence of dissociative symptoms and slightly less rigorous diagnostic criteria for individuals ages 6 years and younger. Thus, PTSD is one of the more diagnostically complex disorders in the DMS-5.

The range of trauma inducing situations commonly associated with PTSD is quite broad, with exposure to war, threatened or actual physical or sexual assault, being kidnapped, terrorist attacks, torture, exposure to natural or man-made disasters, and severe motor accidents frequently cited (American Psychological Association, 2017). But certain restrictions exist.

For example, only certain medical events, such as waking up during surgery, qualify as potential trauma inducing situations. Witnessed events that are considered sufficiently traumatic encompass roughly the same categories as those experienced first-hand by the individual (e.g., seeing someone seriously injured or witnessing a death, observing a sexual assault). For a case of indirect exposure to be considered as the triggering event, the individual must have learned of a violent or accidental death or serious injury to a close relative or friend.

Kessler and colleagues (2005) estimate the projected lifetime risk for PTSD for individuals who reach age 75 years to be 8.7%. In the USA the 12-month prevalence rate is 3.5% (Kessler et al. 2005). Lower prevalence estimates are seen in European, Latin American, and African countries (Hinton & Lewis-Fernandez, 2011). The disorder is more common in females than males (Kessler et al., 2005). Survivors of rape, military veterans, first responder personnel, and those subject to internment are most likely to be diagnosed with PTSD (American Psychiatric Association, 2017). In regard to symptom course, the typical symptom onset is within three months of experiencing a trauma. But there are certainly cases where symptoms emerge several months and even years after a trauma occurred. There is also considerable variability in terms of symptom duration, with almost half of individuals diagnosed with the disorder experiencing a complete recovery within 3 months and others experiencing symptoms for over twelve months to upwards of 50 years (Bryant et al., 2011).

Exposure to trauma is common in youth with one estimate arguing that over two-thirds of youth will experience a traumatic event prior to the age of 16 years (Copeland et al., 2007). When this exposure leads to significant maladjustment the clinical expression of symptoms for children and adolescents diagnosed with PTSD can be different than that observed in adults. For example, young children are more likely to report a re-experiencing event as a generally bad dream without specific reference to a trauma. They may express their re-experiencing episodes and emotions pertaining to the trauma through symbolic play and story-telling. During adolescence, avoidant behaviors may take the form of reduced interest in trying new activities or pursuing intimate relationships. Many adolescents diagnosed with PTSD also will judge themselves extremely harshly. They will assume they are socially undesirable and lose hope for the future (American Psychiatric Association, 2017). PTSD in youth is frequently comorbid with anxiety, mood, psychotic, and substance abuse disorders (Reed et al., 2007). Further, these individuals are vulnerable to engaging in reckless and high-risk behaviors that place them at risk for injury (Pynoos et al., 2009). Finally, like all individuals diagnosed with PTSD, children and adolescents who meet diagnostic criteria for the disorder are at increased risk for suicidal ideation and attempts (Sareen et al., 2007). Thus, the disorder can have profound and even life-threating consequences of the individual. The occupational, social, personal, and medical costs associated with PTSD have been well documented (Kartha et al., 2008).

Clinical Conceptualizations/Etiological Overview

Kearney and colleagues (2010) have recently conducted a comprehensive review of risk factors associated with PTSD in youth. They first point out that the, "severity, frequency, duration, and proximity" of the threatening stimuli can be significant risk factors for the development of the disorder. Relatively more intense and direct exposure to the threatening stimuli as well as repeated trauma experiences (e.g., chronic sexual abuse) can obviously increase the likelihood of PTSD developing. It is incumbent, therefore, for clinicians to conduct a thorough assessment regarding the trauma exposure. This can be challenging, however, as clients can understandably be reluctant to recall aspects of the trauma experience and/or have difficulty remembering the same. Further, while it is imperative to obtain as complete a picture of the most recent trauma experience as possible, a client's previous trauma exposure and a history of significant stressful life events are other critical risk factors that merit consideration (Fletcher, 2003). A youth, for example, who has been previously traumatized may react more sensitively and adversely to a new trauma than one who has not.

Beyond specific aspects of the trauma and previous trauma exposure, a parental history of PTSD predicts childhood PTSD (Yehuda et al., 2008). Parental PTSD risk factors appear to be transmitted through genetics, behavior (e.g., parent empathic attunement and responsivity, parenting approaches), and learning (e.g., parent modeling of certain attitudes and behaviors commonly associated with the disorder). There are a multitude of potential genetic influences, including cortisol secretion, changes in the HPA axis, and even brain physiology. However, Kearney and colleagues (2010) note that it is difficult at this point to tell the extent to which these differences typically pre-date the trauma exposure as opposed to cases where they follow an individual's trauma exposure.

Certain cognitive vulnerabilities also appear to be risk factors for PTSD as well. Kearney and colleagues (2010) identify processing difficulties, disruptions in a youth's cognitive schema about one's relative safety in the world, negative self-evaluations about one's competence, and a tendency to engage in avoidant coping as predisposing cognitive risk factors. Further, children and adolescents who possess a negative attributional style and are vulnerable to feeling hopeless may be at greater risk for developing PTSD following trauma exposure (Evren et al., 2006). Elevated neuroticism, emotional dysregulation, and/or negative affect appear to be additional cognitive predisposing factors (Elwood et al., 2009). Finally, Kearney and colleagues note that adolescents who develop dysfunctional beliefs, fears pertaining to a lack of control, a pervasive and debilitating sense of weakness, and/or an elevated attentional bias toward perceiving threats will also be more vulnerable. Thus, as one can see, there are a myriad of cognitive risk factors for the development of the disorder.

Beyond the aforementioned heritability risk factor in the development of PTSD, there are a host of additional familial risk factors associated with the disorder. To begin, the most obvious source of familial influence is parental neglect and/or abuse. These highly destructive parental behaviors can be traumatic for the child and can serve a dual role as both a risk factor for PTSD and the actual trauma event. In addition, youth who are exposed to domestic violence, family disorder, low cohesiveness, divorce, and high conflict are at elevated risk for PTSD (Kearney et al., 2010). Several other concerning familial influences that are risk factors for a wide range of psychopathology are seen in adolescent PTSD, such as a lack of supervision, parental psychopathology in general, and parent inducement of guilt in a child (Friedman et al., 2008). Clearly a youth's family history and lived experience are critical components to account for when attempting to predict how an adolescent may react to a trauma.

As one can see, there are a multitude of genetic, individual, familial, and social risk factors for PTSD, suggesting the developmental process is complicated and multidetermined. Several integrative and transactional models of PTSD in youth have been developed that attempt to account for the complexity (e.g., Fletcher, 2003; van der Kolk, 2005; Weitzman, 2005). While it is beyond the scope of this brief review to consider all of these models in detail, van de Kolk (2005) has proposed an intriguing model that explains "Developmental Trauma Disorder" in youth that will be briefly reviewed here.

Developmental trauma disorder has been borne out of the study of maltreated youth (Kearney et al., 2010). van der Kolk (2005) and others (e.g., De Bellis et al., 2002; Koenen, 2006) have theorized that severe childhood maltreatment can negatively impact neuronal development through a variety of brain disruptions. When the brain is dysregulated in this manner they argue this leads to emotion processing and executive functioning difficulties that, in turn, lead to behavioral dysregulation. Over time, as the youth continues to experience multiple exposures to interpersonal stressors, this alters the youth's expectancies about life and can further dysregulate the individual's functioning across a variety of domains (e.g., affective, somatic, cognitive, and behavioral functioning). The altered life expectations can be wide-ranging and particularly devastating. van der Kolk (2005) cites a consistent negative self-attribution, a pervasive distrust of one's primary caretaker, a lack of faith in the ability of others to provide protection for oneself, and a sense that one will inevitability be victimized again in the future as examples of this process. A vicious cycle ensues where the youth's cognitive, emotional, and behavioral vulnerabilities increase risk for additional trauma exposure, which further strains the individual's limited coping capacities, leading to additional dysregulation and trauma exposure.

Empirically Supported Treatments/Evidence-Based Practice Approaches

Prior to discussing recent trends in the treatment of PTSD in youth, Kearney and colleagues (2010) note some important challenges associated with assessing the presence of PTSD symptoms in youth that are worth considering. To begin, they point out that symptom presentation for young children can be quite different than that observed in older children and adults. Specifically, they caution that young children who have been traumatized often do not display signs of withdrawal, avoidance, flashbacks, and fantasies that are commonly seen in older individuals. Therefore, they encourage clinicians to conduct a multimethod assessment in order to better ensure that important diagnostic clues are not being missed. Secondly, they state that many traditional assessment measures of PTSD do not factor in the multitude of contextual factors that could either enhance or reduce risk for symptom development. In particular, they identify, "prior learning experiences, resilience, family functioning, coping skills, culture, and ongoing trauma or proximity to an abuser," as areas commonly under-incorporated into traditional assessment measures. Thus, they encourage clinicians to be mindful of context when assessing for PTSD in youth.

A third shortcoming associated with traditional assessment measures of PTSD in youth is the relative lack of attention paid to ongoing stress, chronic maltreatment, and previous traumas as compared to the acute trauma that likely led to the referral (Kearney et al., 2010). Similar to the previous shortcomings, the remedy here is for clinicians to directly assess these areas as well as the possible presence of comorbid conditions such as anxiety and/or depression. Finally, Kearney and colleagues (2010) point out that maltreated youth may present differently than youth who have only experienced a single trauma. More specifically, it may be more difficult for them to trust the clinician. Therefore the clinician must pay close attention to not overlook potential trauma in these individuals due to an inability to establish rapport and/or a failure to create therapeutic conditions that promote disclosure of information.

With these helpful assessment recommendations in mind, focus shifts to discussing evidence-based approaches to treating PTSD in youth. Here Silverman and colleagues (2008) conducted an exhaustive review of evidence-based approaches to treating youth exposed to traumatic events covering the time-period from 1993 to 2007. They identified 21 studies that met minimal criteria for the review and classified them according to the Chambless et al., (2006) methodological standards that have been previously cited in earlier chapters. A single therapeutic approach, Trauma-Focused Cognitive-Behavioral Therapy (TF-CBT), was identified as a *well-established* treatment. Further, School-Based Group Cognitive-Behavioral Therapy (Stein et al., 2003) met the criteria as a *probably efficacious* intervention. The remaining approaches only met criteria as either a *possibly efficacious* or *experimental* treatment. TF-CBT and School-Based Cognitive-Behavioral Therapy will be reviewed in some detail here.

TF-CBT is a broad label that encompasses several cognitive-behavioral interventions with youth who have experienced trauma (Silverman et al., 2008). The interventions vary in regard to the participant ages, types of trauma experienced, specific treatment modalities used, and relative areas of treatment emphasis, but all operate essentially from a CBT framework. For example, in an early study Deblinger and Heflin (1996) investigated the efficacy of two forms of CBT in a sample of 100 youth between the ages of 7 and 13 years who had been sexually abused. Their intervention included several techniques common to CBT interventions, such as a psychoeducation component where participants were taught about health sexuality, child abuse, and safety. The intervention also included a behavioral component where the youth was supported in behavioral exposure tasks. In addition, there was a cognitive component designed to assist the individual in better managing thoughts about the abuse experience. When parents were included in the treatment process, this took the form of parent-training on behavioral management skills and psychoeducation regarding healthy sexuality, their child's body safety, and appropriate communication skills. The length of treatment was twelve weekly sessions lasting 45 minutes per session. The researchers found the intervention produced statistically and clinically significant improvements in trauma symptomatology as compared to control conditions.

More recently, Cohen and colleagues (2004) compared TF-CBT with client-centered therapy (CCT) in a sample of 229 youth between the ages of 8 and 14 years who had been sexually abused. While the treatment length remained twelve weeks, sessions were notably longer (90 minutes total including 45 minutes with the child and 45 minutes with a parent). The CCT approach consisted mostly of active listening, reflection, and a self-empowerment focus. The researchers found that participants in the TF-CBT condition achieved statistically significant better outcomes than those in the CCT condition across several child and parenting rating scales. Thus, TF-CBT has consistently demonstrated its efficacy across multiple studies and appears to be more effective than other common treatment approaches.

Shifting focus, the single approach that met criteria as a *probably efficacious* intervention in the Silverman et al. (2008) review was a School-Based Group Cognitive Behavioral Therapy (Stein et al., 2003). The efficacy of this approach was studied using a sample of 126 sixth-grade, multiethnic youth who had been exposed to community violence and were experiencing trauma reactions. The intervention consisted of 10 weekly group sessions comprised of 5–8 children per group lasting approximately a class period per session. The session format and content was very similar to TF-CBT. Specifically, students participated in psychoeducation, graded exposure tasks, cognitive skills training such as thought stopping, and social skills training during the group meetings. At the end of the intervention children who participated in the sessions demonstrated significant symptom reduction as compared to a waitlist control group.

In summary, it appears that CBT has established the most rigorous evidence base to support its use in the treatment of PTSD in youth. Its multimodal and multimethod approach seems to provide a solid basis from which a clinician can begin to treat such a complex phenomenon as youth PTSD. The key features, including psychoeducation about the disorder and healthier life alternatives, a cognitive component that can reduce intrusive thoughts and negative self-evaluations, and behavioral components designed to promote a sense of mastery during exposure to provocative stimuli and previously avoided situations, all appear to be very helpful aspects of the general intervention strategy. That being said, the final sections of this chapter will explore ways in which EI can hopefully be incorporated into a CBT treatment approach in a way that enhances outcome and further reduces vulnerability to future trauma exposure. This is an endeavor that has been endorsed by Corbett and Milton (2011) in a recent discussion of whether existential therapy can successfully treat trauma.

EI Conceptualization

As has been discussed in considerable detail in prior chapters, trauma experiences feature prominently in Schneider's (2008) account of various life occurrences that can activate an individual's expansive/constrictive polarities and a sense of dread. By way of review, he identifies acute traumas, chronic traumas, and implicit traumas as three environmental intrusions on the individual's sense of safety and security in the world. Acute traumas – defined as "the perception of an event as immediately contrary and shocking" (pg. 44) – most closely resemble the type of occurrence that is described in the DSM-5 as a traumatic event. Schneider cites the example of a child falling ill as this form of trauma, arguing that the experience of a loss of mobility for a child can not only be painful but also threaten the child's sense of "groundedness" in the world. The existential dreads associated with hyper-constriction where the child may fear "diminishment, minimization, imperceptibility, and perhaps even dissolution" (pg. 44) can be activated in this case. Whether long-term over compensation efforts (and psychopathology) develop are dependent upon the intensity of the child's fear and a felt sense of discrepancy that is experienced between how the child felt before the illness as compared to afterwards.

When a child experiences an acute trauma and engages in attempts to deny or minimize the event's effects through hyper-expansive efforts there is a risk that these efforts will be unsuccessful and a second trauma cycle will develop (Schneider, 2008). This secondary trauma experience, referred to as a chronic trauma, comprises ineffective, repeated efforts to counteract the effects of an acute trauma through hyper-constrictive attitudes and behaviors. In the example of the child who has fallen ill, a situation may occur where initial efforts to overcompensate through behaviors designed to demonstrate the child's strength, greatness, and invulnerability may not succeed in providing the child with the sense of security and affirmation that he or she seeks. Over time, as these efforts continue to fail in this regard, the child may begin to retreat from the world and reduce his or her profile in life in order to avoid future acute traumas. This retreat is likely also fueled by a growing sense of self-doubt about one's relative security and an overestimation of one's fragility. The response, while understandable, is ultimately unsatisfying in the sense that one can never be completely safe no matter how hard one tries to shrink and hide from the world. Further, the hyper-constrictive process is often associated with avoidant and withdrawal behaviors where the individual stops engaging in life-affirming pursuits.

Returning to the example of the ill child, perhaps that child decides to stop playing sports, greatly restricts his or her diet, or engages in compulsive behaviors designed to reduce the risk of infection in attempts to prevent recurrence of a future injury or illness. Though one can concede that these efforts may be partially effective in protecting the child, he or she is never fully protected and this increased security comes at the cost of a lot of potential fun and good tasting food. Also, in practice the author has observed many youth engage in hyper-constrictive and hyper-expansive overcompensation efforts in relatively close proximity in time. Thus, the same child who may on a given day react to a fear provoking situation in a more hyper-expansive manner will later react to a similar situation with a more hyper-constrictive approach. This would suggest both acute and chronic trauma formations are occurring simultaneously in the individual and that the working through process of reacting to a trauma is nonlinear.

Implicit traumas are the third scenario Schneider (2008) outlines that can activate the child's hyper-constrictive and hyper-expansive polarities. Defined as "indirect, vicariously transmitted traumas of caretakers and families" (pg. 45), implicit traumas occur indirectly and through modeling experiences. Schneider provides the example of a child witnessing a parent or relative overcompensate after being injured through adopting an overachievement approach to life. Over time the child may come to develop an overachieving orientation as well due to behavioral modeling. This stance is ultimately less fulfilling and can lead to maladjustment for both the parent and child. Here is where an implicit trauma has occurred. Schneider (2008) further notes that two minimal conditions must be met for an implicit trauma to potentially develop. First, the child must idolize the parent or relative who experienced the acute trauma and is engaging in the overcompensatory behaviors. Second, the child would need to demonstrate an inherent predisposition to engaging in the type of overcompensatory behaviors that the parent or relative is modeling. Thus, a historically shy and anxious child may be less likely to adopt an overachieving disposition even if a parent or relative that they looked up to modeled the behavior because it would be simply too uncomfortable. Hollis (2013), in *Hauntings: Dispelling the Ghosts Who Run Our Lives,* does a remarkable job of describing the essence of implicit traumas in much greater detail. Readers are advised to familiarize themselves with his insightful analysis of this process.

While Schneider (2008) clearly has much to say about how trauma is conceptualized from an EI framework, other prominent existential theorists and therapists have broached the topic as well. van Deurzen (2015), for example, has included a brief case study of her existential approach to working with an adult male who experienced trauma in her recent work *Paradox and Passion in Psychotherapy: An Existential Approach (2nd Ed.).* The client, named "Jerry," is described as a 32-year-old single male of dual nationality who seeks therapy for post-traumatic stress after experiencing life-threatening injuries sustained in a motorcycle accident. At the time of the referral, which is 9 months following the accident, he reports severe sleeping difficulties and near constant and acute anxiety and depressive symptoms. He also reports flashbacks, difficulty with memory and concentration, and an inability to work effectively. Thus, it clearly appears that the client meets DSM-5 diagnostic criteria for PTSD. van Deurzen proceeds to describe in masterful detail the existential approach she takes with the client to help him heal. While it is beyond the scope of this work to highlight all of the intervention strategies, a brief description of five important treatment components is mentioned here.

To begin, van Deurzen (2015) helps the client to recognize that the trauma experience has made him acutely aware of his vulnerability and relative weakness. In this discussion, she supportively but frankly notes his avoidant behaviors that are symptomatic of the fears that were activated by the accident, framing his behavior as stemming from a lack of courage. This is not done in a condemning way, rather her approach is, "one of approving his past coping strategy whilst exposing its current redundancy" (pg. 257). Second, she highlights the vicious cycle her client's avoidant behaviors have created. The client refuses to drive and becomes more dependent upon his mother for transportation which he resents. By merely raising his awareness of this cycle, she correctly believes that this will help him self-correct the process. Third, she works with her client to help him accept his own limitations without shame. Recognizing one's limitations is historically an area of emphasis in existential psychology and can paradoxically free the client to approach their life situation in a more productive and meaningful manner.

A fourth way van Deurzen (2015) approaches her client is through the encouragement of new meaning. As her client begins to heal and has achieved some symptom relief, she states that he begins to tackle "the work of relearning to exist" and ultimately makes several important life changes as a result of this deeper self-analysis of what has meaning for him. The final main component of the treatment process consists of a series of discussions that occurred at the termination phase of treatment where the client was encouraged to face guilt feelings stemming from the accident and to "get real" in terms of how he was approaching others in his life and lingering situations that he had perhaps been avoiding. Again, this reflects the general existential therapy approach of always encouraging clients to accept responsibility for their actions and to face harder and/or uncomfortable situations head-on. Clearly much can be learned about how trauma experiences can be tackled from an existential perspective in this case analysis.

Stolorow (2015) has proposed an existential perspective on emotional trauma that incorporates a phenomenological-contextual perspective. His discussion focuses extensively on the dynamics of developmental trauma and therefore is very relevant to clinicians who are considering working with adolescent trauma victims from an EI perspective. He argues that developmental trauma is rooted in, "a formative intersubjective context whose central feature is malattunement to painful affect – a breakdown of the child-caregiver interaffective system" (pg. 125). In essence, the child becomes overwhelmed and disorganized with painful affect when he or she does not have an adequate support system to help him or her through the pain. This leads Stolorow to declare that *pain itself is not pathology.* In the absence of adequate support, painful affect becomes crushing for the child and can lead the individual to believe that their unmet needs and yearnings are suggestive of a "loathsome defect" in themselves. Within this framework youth who endure developmental traumas also experience a "severe constriction and narrowing of the horizons of emotional experiencing" (Stolorow, 2015, pg. 126). These children will utilize repression to manage potentially uncomfortable and painful affect.

Stolorow (2015) draws close parallels between his account of emotional trauma from a phenomenological-contextual perspective and Heidegger's (1927) existential interpretation of anxiety. Specifically, he believes that Heidegger's description of anxiety, in which the everyday significance of the world collapses for the individual and a sense of uncanniness develops, very closely resembles emotional trauma. He writes, "trauma shatters the illusions of everyday life that evade and cover up the finitude, contingency, and embeddedness of our existence and the indefiniteness of its certain extinction" (pg. 131). In addition, he notes that emotional trauma experiences can fragment an individual's sense of time, as aspects of the trauma continuously intrude upon the individual's existence unexpectedly. This can lead to dissociation experiences where aspects of consciousness become splintered and fractured.

Given this conceptualization of developmental trauma, Stolorow (2015) utilizes a technique referred to as *emotional dwelling* to assist his clients with trauma histories in their recovery. He describes emotional dwelling as a hyper-intensive form of empathic listening where the therapist, "leans into the other's emotional pain and participates in it, perhaps with the aid of one's own analogous experiences of pain" (pg. 134). Echoing van Deurzen, Stolorow meets the client's pain "head-on" and avoids efforts to soothe, comfort, and/or reassure the client because these latter techniques will likely be experienced by the client as the therapist "shunning" or "turning away" from the trauma experience. This effort also closely resembles Schneider's (2008) core EI techniques of cultivating a sense of presence and invoking the actual. By meeting trauma victims and their unendurable pain head on, Stolorow (2015) maintains that clients' "shattered emotional worlds are enabled to shine with a kind of sacredness that calls forth an understanding and caring engagement within" (pg. 135). With repetition this deeply felt understanding can assist the client in transforming more unbearable states into relatively less painful and more identifiable emotional experiences.

EI Case Example

Erica,[1] a 15-year-old female attending the 10th grade, was referred to therapy by her father upon the recommendation of a school adjustment counselor. The school had been concerned about her multiple absences and several teachers had commented that she seemed "depressed," tired, and withdrawn in class. Erica's father, in the initial phone screen, acknowledged that he, too, had significant concerns about his oldest daughter. He stated that Erica's mother had died of a heroin overdose approximately two years earlier during the summer between Erica's 7th and 8th years in school. At the time of her death, Erica's mother had been living out of the home due to her heroin dependency. She had been growing increasingly despondent and hopeless at the prospect of reuniting with her four children just prior to her death. Though it was not officially ruled a suicide, many, including Erica's father, believed that the mother had intentionally overdosed. The family had been devastated by the loss but Erica had seemed to "bounce back" relatively quickly, assuming a much more active caretaking role of her two younger brothers, now ages 11 and 13 years, and her youngest sister, now age 9 years.

In recent months, however, Erica's father had noticed a similar withdrawal pattern that was being observed at school. Erica had chosen not to try out for the girl's varsity cross country team at her school despite excelling as a team member the previous year. She had cited the need to focus on her studies and remain available after school to help care for her youngest sister as reasons for foregoing the soccer season. Her father, while concerned about her decision, acknowledged that he had not pushed too hard for her to reconsider her choice since he was working approximately 50 hours per week in a labor position and drew comfort from knowing Erica was minding the home. But, more recently, even on the weekends when he was home, he stated Erica mostly slept and kept to herself in her bedroom. She had always been well liked by others and active socially, though she had never felt comfortable having friends over to the home due to her mother's chronic substance use problems. Instead, in the past she had often slept over her friends' homes. This, too, had faded. Finally, her father had noticed that Erica had been asking a lot more questions about her mother, specifically the circumstances of her mother's death and the extent of her mother's addiction problems. There was a morbid quality to Erica's questioning in the father's opinion that left him wondering if he was underestimating the degree to which his late spouse's death had affected Erica.

Erica's father had stated over the phone that she was open to the idea of counseling. The family was deeply religious and had sought the support of their pastor and church at the time of the mother's death. Counseling had been a taboo but the family had softened their stance somewhat after having some positive experiences with mental health professionals during Erica's mother's long battle with addiction. When Erica arrived with her father for the first session, she entered the room with a seemingly pained smile and tentative greeting. She was dressed casually in baggy sweat pants, a sweat shirt, and running shoes. She kept her brunette hair short and did not appear to wear make-up. Her eye contact was sparing and she spoke in a hushed tone. She conceded she was feeling "down" and isolated, but expressed uncertainty as to whether counseling could help. She admitted to feelings of nervousness about what would happen in counseling and what opinion the author would form of her. After receiving several assurances that she would not be judged and learning more about the counseling process rapport appeared to be quickly established. Erica was relieved that she would be in control of how sessions progressed and ultimately expressed a preference to spend the remainder of the initial session meeting individually with her father out of the room. Her father, a hulking man of few words, also seemed relieved. In his case the relief seemed to stem from being released to go read magazines in the waiting area. As it turned out, this would be the first and last time he would set foot in the therapists' office for the duration of the ten-month treatment.

The initial focus of individual work was on rapport building and assessment of Erica's current functioning. With further probing she acknowledged that she had been feeling 'down' in recent weeks and sleep had been difficult. She denied previous self-harm behaviors or active suicidal ideation, plan, or attempt. However, she conceded that, following her mother's death, she had questioned the "meaning of it all" and had, in moments of despair, wondered if she would be better off dead. This latter revelation came out so casually that the author was amazed to learn he was the first person she had confided in about her suicidal ideation. Like many adolescents, however, it seemed that no one had ever thought to ask (or felt comfortable asking) her about her depressive thoughts or whether she had thought of suicide.

Erica further revealed in the initial session that she had been experiencing "flashbacks" of seeing her mother passed out on multiple occasions throughout her youth. Typically, her mother would be lying in "weird" positions on the family couch in the living room, but there were times where she found her mother on the kitchen or bathroom floors. These incidents had been intermittent but apparently occurring over a long window of Erica's young life. Her earliest memories of seeing her mother in a severely impaired state was around the time she was six or seven years old. The most frightening instance, however, had been the impetus to her father finally "kicking" her mother out of the home for good and child welfare services becoming involved. Erica, age 12 years old at the time, had come home from school to find her mother passed out in her parents' upstairs bathtub with drug paraphernalia strewn throughout the bathroom. What had been particularly terrifying about this occasion was that her mother had been dangerously close to sliding below the water-line in the bathtub and potentially drowning. Erica described in frightening detail the Herculean efforts on her part to get her mother out of the tub and summon both her father and emergency services. While initially relieved to learn that her mother was going to be "okay" and was getting treatment, Erica felt extreme guilt for having called 911. The family had apparently tried to keep her mother's addiction private in order to avoid potential child welfare services involvement. Erica had been instructed by her father to only call him if he found her mother in an impaired state. While he had never faulted her for calling emergency services in the bathroom instance, Erica's mother had not been so forgiving. Months after the incident in a bout of anger her mother had apparently told Erica that she (Erica) was the reason why the family "broke apart." Erica had been devastated. A short time later her mother was dead.

Further assessment revealed that Erica's trauma reaction met diagnostic criteria for PTSD. In addition to bearing witness to the near death of her mother in a drug overdose, she had been re-experiencing memories of the event in the form of both flashbacks and nightmares. She avoided her parent's bedroom and master bathroom where the incident had occurred even though scheduling needs in the morning would naturally dictate that she take her showers in that bathroom. Additional analyses indicated mood, cognitive, and arousal alterations that were consistent with the diagnosis as well. Of note, Erica's sleep was particularly disrupted as she feared experiencing nightmares of the event. She would stay awake as long as she could in the evenings, listening to music on her headphones or watching television. As a result she was chronically sleep deprived and this had certainly contributed to her multiple school absences and academic underachievement. However, sleep deprivation was not the only cause of her decline in school functioning. Erica acknowledged that life simply had "no meaning" at times for her and she felt both utterly alone and guilt-ridden. She couldn't help but wonder if she had somehow not called emergency services that last time her mother overdosed in the family home that her mother would still be alive. She no longer trusted herself and found even small decisions were difficult for her. She found it easier to retreat to her bedroom and withdraw, and held out little hope for a meaningful future. Finally, her mother's absence had had an incredible de-stabilizing effect upon Erica in terms of how she related to the world. She described feeling "out of sorts" and de-realization and depersonalization experiences that, while not of an intensity indicative of psychosis, certainly suggested a significant disturbance in Erica's subjective experience of herself. Thus, Erica was struggling with multiple core existential "givens" of her existence, including questions of meaning, isolation, condemnation, and death.

With this conceptualization in mind, the author integrated EI principles and techniques with the TF-CBT approach to treating PTSD. Specifically, the main treatment components included the following: (1) *psychoeducation:* the etiology, symptoms, and treatment of PTSD were explained to Erica in general terms followed by discussions of how her specific trauma-related symptomatology (nightmares, flashbacks, avoidance, hypervigilance, etc.) were consistent with the diagnosis; (2) *behavioral strategies:* though Erica did not engage in extensive avoidant behaviors over time she and the author collaborated on how she could increase her exposure to aspects of the home (e.g., her parents' bedroom and master bathroom) and other reminders of her mother (e.g., family photo albums) that she had been avoiding in order to help her feel more in control and at ease in her home and with her family members when they wanted to discuss her mother[2]; (3) *cognitive strategies:* these strategies focused on addressing Erica's underlying fear that she was potentially destined to succumb to addiction and an early death like her mother as well as the extensive guilt inducing beliefs she had developed surrounding the circumstances of her mother's death and overestimation of her responsibility for her mother's welfare; (4) *emotional dwelling/therapist presence/invoking the actual existential strategies:* here the author attempted to reflect as rich and deep an understanding as possible of the horror experiences Erica had experienced through the core counseling basic attending skills of reflection of feelings, paraphrasing, minimal encouragers, open-ended questioning, and limited self-disclosure regarding the author's emotional experience of listening to Erica; (5) *existential discussions pertaining to life's fragility and meaning:* two existential strategies utilized by van

Deurzen (2015) were incorporated into Erica's treatment – specifically the author and her discussed how Erica's mother's death had underscored life's fragility and activated core fear of death concerns in her and how it was also very normal to question the "meaning of it all" after experiencing such an event and that it was incumbent upon the individual to find new meanings in life; and (6) *subtle encouragement of hero metaphors in the therapy dialogue and creative pursuits for the client:* the author repeatedly noted Erica's courage in contending with her incredibly difficult family situation and worked with her to rekindle her interest in creative outlets that could continue to help her through her grief process and to find new meaning in life.

The outcome of these efforts seemed largely positive. Over a 10-month span of time the PTSD symptomatology and suicidal ideation essentially disappeared. Above all, it seemed Erica most appreciated the author's unflinching willingness to listen to her story and traumatic memories without judgment, without attempts to rescue, and without attempts to minimize. There were certainly other times in therapy when cognitive strategies were utilized that hopefully released Erica from at least some of the burden she felt regarding the circumstances of her mother's overdose, leaving the home, and death. But at no time did the author knowingly attempt to placate or divert attention from more uncomfortable discussions of her darkest memories and doubts. This allowed Erica the critical opportunity to work through several unresolved aspects of her life experience that had been haunting her. In addition to her PTSD re-experiencing symptomatology dissipating, Erica's sense of self grew more grounded and her mood improved. She ultimately chose not to pursue extracurricular sports the following year in school and continued to focus more on her family as opposed to friends. But this choice appeared to be made from a position of strength and a careful assessment of what had meaning to her, as opposed to an act of withdrawal borne out of a sense of despair and disillusion.

Notes

1. The cases depicted in the book are composite representations of multiple client experiences where names, gender, and other potentially identifiable aspects of the case experience have been changed to protect client confidentiality.
2. Similar exposure strategies were utilized to help Erica overcome her fear of going asleep and experiencing nightmares.

References

American Psychiatric Association (2017). DSM-5 Psychiatry Online. http://dsm.psychiatryonline.org/doi/book/10.1176/appi.books.9781585624836.

Bryant, R.A., Brooks, R., Silove, D., Creamer, M., O'Donnell, M., and McFarlane, A.C. (2011). Peritraumatic dissociation mediates the relationship between acute panic and chronic posttraumatic stress disorder. *Behaviour Research and Therapy*, *49*, 346–351.

Chambless, D. L., Crits-Christoph, P., Wampold, B. E., Norcross, J. C., Lambert, M. J., Bohart, A. C., &…Johannsen, B. E. (2006). What Should Be Validated?. In J. C. Norcross, L. E. Beutler, R. F. Levant, (Eds.), *Evidence-based practices in mental health: Debate and dialogue on the fundamental questions* (pp. 191–256). Washington, DC, US: American Psychological Association. doi:10.1037/11265-005

Cohen, J., Goodman, R. F., Brown, E. J., & Mannarino, A. (2004). Treatment of childhood traumatic grief: Contributing to a newly emerging condition in the wake of community trauma. *Harvard Review Of Psychiatry*, *12*(4), 213–216. doi:10.1080/10673220490509543

Copeland, W. E., Keeler, G., Angold, A., & Costello, E. J. (2007). Traumatic events and posttraumatic stress in childhood. *Archives Of General Psychiatry*, *64*(5), 577–584. doi:10.1001/archpsyc.64.5.577

Corbett, L., & Milton, M. (2011). Existential therapy: A useful approach to trauma?. *Counselling Psychology Review*, *26*(1), 62–74.

De Bellis, M. D., Keshavan, M. S., Shifflett, H., Iyengar, S., Beers, S. R., Hall, J., & Moritz, G. (2002). Brain structures in pediatric maltreatment-related posttraumatic stress disorder: A sociodemographically matched study. *Biological Psychiatry*, *52*(11), 1066–1078. doi:10.1016/S0006-3223(02)01459-2

Deblinger, E., & Heflin, A. H. (1996). *Treating sexually abused children and their nonoffending parents: A cognitive behavioral approach.* Thousand Oaks, CA, US: Sage Publications, Inc.

Elwood, L. S., Hahn, K. S., Olatunji, B. O., & Williams, N. L. (2009). Cognitive vulnerabilities to the development of PTSD: A review of four vulnerabilities and the proposal of an integrative vulnerability model. *Clinical Psychology Review*, *29*(1), 87–100. doi:10.1016/j.cpr.2008.10.002

Evren, C., Kural, S., & Cakmak, D. (2006). Clinical correlates of childhood abuse and neglect in substance dependents. *Addictive Behaviors*, *31*(3), 475–485. doi:10.1016/j.addbeh.2005.05.030

Fletcher, K. E. (2003). Childhood posttraumatic stress disorder. In E. J. Mash, R. A. Barkley, (Eds.), *Child psychopathology*, 2nd *ed.* (pp. 330–371). New York, NY, US: Guilford Press.

Friedman, A. H., Stevens, S. B., & Morris, T. L. (2008). Posttraumatic stress disorder. In M. Hersen, D. Reitman, (Eds.), *Handbook of psychological assessment, case conceptualization, and treatment, Vol 2: Children and adolescents* (pp. 264–291). Hoboken, NJ, US: John Wiley & Sons Inc.

Gleason, M. M., Fox, N. A., Drury, S., Smyke, A., Egger, H. L., Nelson, C. I., &... Zeanah, C. H. (2011). Validity of evidence-derived criteria for reactive attachment disorder: Indiscriminately social/disinhibited and emotionally withdrawn/inhibited types. *Journal Of The American Academy Of Child & Adolescent Psychiatry*, *50*(3), 216–231. doi:10.1016/j.jaac.2010.12.012

Heidegger, M. (1927). *Sein und Zeit*. Gesamtausgabe Volume 2. [trans. by John Macquarrie and Edward Robinson (London: SCM Press, 1962)]

Hinton, D. E., & Lewis-Fernández, R. (2011). The cross-cultural validity of posttraumatic stress disorder: Implications for DSM-5. *Depression And Anxiety*, *28*(9), 783–801. doi:10.1002/da.20753

Hodges, J., & Tizard, B. (1989). Social and family relationships of ex-institutional adolescents. *Child Psychology & Psychiatry & Allied Disciplines*, *30*(1), 77–97. doi:10.1111/j.1469-7610.1989.tb00770.x

Hollis, J. (2013). *Hauntings: dispelling the ghosts who run our lives*. Asheville, NC: Chiron Publications.

Kartha, A., Brower, V., Saitz, R., Samet, J. H., Keane, T. M., & Liebschutz, J. (2008). The impact of trauma exposure and post-traumatic stress disorder on healthcare utilization among primary care patients. *Medical Care*, *46*(4), 388–393. doi:10.1097/MLR.0b013e31815dc5d2

Kearney, C. A., Wechsler, A., Kaur, H., & Lemos-Miller, A. (2010). Posttraumatic stress disorder in maltreated youth: A review of contemporary research and thought. *Clinical Child And Family Psychology Review*, *13*(1), 46–76. doi:10.1007/s10567-009-0061-4

Kessler, R. C., Chiu, W. T., Demler, O., & Walters, E. E. (2005). Prevalence, Severity, and Comorbidity of 12-Month DSM-IV Disorders in the National Comorbidity Survey Replication. *Archives Of General Psychiatry*, *62*(6), 617–627. doi:10.1001/archpsyc.62.6.617

Koenen, K. C. (2006). Developmental Epidemiology of PTSD: Self-Regulation as a Central Mechanism. In R. Yehuda, (Ed.), *Psychobiology of posttraumatic stress disorders: A decade of progress, Vol. 1071* (pp. 255–266). Malden: Blackwell Publishing.

Pynoos, R. S., Steinberg, A. M., Layne, C. M., Briggs, E. C., Ostrowski, S. A., & Fairbank, J. A. (2009). DSM-V PTSD diagnostic criteria for children and adolescents: A developmental perspective and recommendations. *Journal Of Traumatic Stress*, *22*(5), 391–398. doi:10.1002/jts.20450

Rank, O. (1924). The Trauma of Birth in Its Importance for Psychoanalytic Therapy. *Psychoanalytic Review*, *11*241–245.

Reed, P. L., Anthony, J. C., & Breslau, N. (2007). Incidence of drug problems in young adults exposed to trauma and posttraumatic stress disorder: Do early life experiences and predispositions matter?. *Archives Of General Psychiatry, 64*(12), 1435–1442. doi:10.1001/archpsyc.64.12.1435

Sareen, J., Cox, B. J., Stein, M. B., Afifi, T. O., Fleet, C., & Asmundson, G. G. (2007). Physical and mental comorbidity, disability, and suicidal behavior associated with posttraumatic stress disorder in a large community sample. *Psychosomatic Medicine, 69*(3), 242–248. doi:10.1097/PSY.0b013e31803146d8

Schneider, K. J. (2008). *Existential-integrative psychotherapy: Guideposts to the core of practice*. New York, NY, US: Routledge/Taylor & Francis Group.

Silverman, W. K., Ortiz, C. D., Viswesvaran, C., Burns, B. J., Kolko, D. J., Putnam, F. W., & Amaya-Jackson, L. (2008). Evidence-based psychosocial treatments for children and adolescents exposed to traumatic events. *Journal Of Clinical Child And Adolescent Psychology, 37*(1), 156–183. doi:10.1080/15374410701818293

Smyke, A. T., Zeanah, C. H., Gleason, M. M., Drury, S. S., Fox, N. A., Nelson, C. A., & Guthrie, D. (2012). A randomized controlled trial comparing foster care and institutional care for children with signs of reactive attachment disorder. *The American Journal Of Psychiatry, 169*(5), 508–514. doi:10.1176/appi.ajp.2011.11050748

Stein, B. D., Jaycox, L. H., Kataoka, S. H., Wong, M., Tu, W., Elliott, M. N., & Fink, A. (2003). A Mental Health Intervention for Schoolchildren Exposed to Violence: A Randomized Controlled Trial. *JAMA: Journal Of The American Medical Association, 290*(5), 603–611. doi:10.1001/jama.290.5.603

Stolorow, R. D. (2015). A phenomenological-contextual, existential, and ethical perspective on emotional trauma. *Psychoanalytic Review, 102*(1), 123–138. doi:10.1521/prev.2015.102.1.123

Tizard, B., & Hodges, J. (1978). The effect of early institutional rearing on the development of eight year old children. *Child Psychology & Psychiatry & Allied Disciplines, 19*(2), 99–118. doi:10.1111/j.1469-7610.1978.tb00453.x

van der Kolk, B. A. (2005). Developmental Trauma Disorder: Toward a rational diagnosis for children with complex trauma histories. *Psychiatric Annals, 35*(5), 401–408.

van Deurzen, E. (2015). Structural existential analysis (SEA): A phenomenological method for therapeutic work. *Journal Of Contemporary Psychotherapy, 45*(1), 59–68. doi:10.1007/s10879-014-9282-z

Weitzman, J. (2005). Maltreatment and Trauma: Toward a Comprehensive Model of Abused Children from Developmental Psychology. *Child & Adolescent Social Work Journal, 22*(3–4), 321–341. doi:10.1007/s10560-005-0014-9

Yehuda, R., Bell, A., Bierer, L. M., & Schmeidler, J. (2008). Maternal, not paternal, PTSD is related to increased risk for PTSD in offspring of

Holocaust survivors. *Journal Of Psychiatric Research*, *42*(13), 1104–1111. doi:10.1016/j.jpsychires.2008.01.002

Zeanah, C. H., Smyke, A. T., Koga, S. F., & Carlson, E. (2005). Attachment in Institutionalized and Community Children in Romania. *Child Development*, *76*(5), 1015–1028. doi:10.1111/j.1467-8624.2005.00894.x

Index

D. Shumaker, *Existential-Integrative Approaches to Treating Adolescents*, DOI 10.1057/978-1-349-95211-3

GPSR Compliance
The European Union's (EU) General Product Safety Regulation (GPSR) is a set of rules that requires consumer products to be safe and our obligations to ensure this.

If you have any concerns about our products, you can contact us on

ProductSafety@springernature.com

In case Publisher is established outside the EU, the EU authorized representative is:

Springer Nature Customer Service Center GmbH
Europaplatz 3
69115 Heidelberg, Germany

www.ingramcontent.com/pod-product-compliance
Lightning Source LLC
Chambersburg PA
CBHW040028070126
37739CB00032B/388

9781349952106